SIXTY-FIVE PRESS INTERVIEWS WITH ROBERT G. INGERSOLL

SIXTY-FIVE PRESS INTERVIEWS WITH ROBERT G. INGERSOLL

WHAT THE GREAT AGNOSTIC TOLD NUMEROUS NEWSPAPER REPORTERS DURING A QUARTER–CENTURY OF PUBLIC APPEARANCES AS A FREETHINKER AND ENEMY OF SUPERSTITION

Introduction by Madalyn Murray O'Hair

Foreword by Richard M. Smith

American Atheist Press
Cranford, New Jersey

American Atheist Press
225 Cristiani St.
Cranford, New Jersey, 07016-3214
First edition © 1983 American Atheist Press
Second corrected edition © 2000 American Atheist Press
Printed in the United States of America

Library of Congress Cataloging-in-Publication Data

Ingersoll, Robert Green, 1833-1899
    Sixty-five press interviews with Robert G. Ingersoll : what
the great agnostic told numerous newspaper reporters during a
quarter-century of public appearances as a freethinker and enemy
of superstition / introduction by Madalyn Murray O'Hair ;
foreword by Richard M. Smith.—2nd corr. ed.
    p. cm.
    ISBN 1-57884-910-1
    1. Free thought. I. Title.

BL2720.A4I54 2000   00-028855
211'.7—dc21

FOREWORD

One of the limitations of every human being is the desire for catharsis, a feeling of satisfaction of having obtained or achieved whatever it was he or she set out to obtain or achieve. In the case of eating a meal or achieving orgasm, no one wants to interminably involve themselves in the process of meeting those needs without getting some satisfaction. Not only that, but most people would like to reach a state in which they wouldn't have to work or worry much about where their next meal or sexual encounter was going to come from. It's only natural.

With active Atheism it is no different. I suspect every avowed Atheist longs for the day when there would be no more religion, no more struggle against the forces of superstition. That day seems ever farther in the future; but visible successes have been achieved against other primitive conditions such as disease, illiteracy, overt racism, etc., so the Atheist cannot just give up and assume that religion will win the day. In the meantime, though, the Atheist wants to see or believe that some tangible progress is being made. Probably most tempting of all is the desire to think that religion will just give up and die of its own. Also, many Atheists desire to separate their Atheism from other problems of the world such as politics, economics, etc. After all, it is enough of a battle for anyone just to take on the hydra-headed monster of religion.

Thus, many Atheists come to the conclusion that they or other Atheists have done enough, that there is no more work to be done, or that there is no hope in trying to do more.

Many people still have not read Robert Ingersoll or even heard of him. This is a sad state of affairs, and if American Atheists did not think so, it would not be involved in preserving, distributing and marketing his works. On the other hand, many people who are a little familiar with Ingersoll quickly come to the conclusion – for any one of the reasons outlined above – that no more sublime and eloquent words on the subject could be uttered, so Ingersoll must have been right on everything he said and nothing more needs to be done. This is pointedly true of many scientists and especially of the editors of the most prestigious scientific magazines in the country. Ingersoll, himself, appeared to have the delusion that orthodox Christianity was

i

going to die in his lifetime, or shortly thereafter, and that he needed to do little more than speak out against religion. This is painfully and obviously not true. While Atheists slept in this country, religion has effectively regained its power.

So, before you absorb this volume and take Ingersoll completely to your heart, be advised that there were some things about which he was dead wrong.

In the interview with *The Mail and Express,* New York, November 3, 1887 on the subject of anarchists, he had this heartless thing to say:

> There is no place in this country for the Anarchist. The source of power here is the people, and to attack the political power is to attack the people. If the laws are oppressive, it is the fault of the oppressed. If the laws touch the poor and leave them without redress, it is the fault of the poor."

I don't think it is necessary to lecture any of you about how mistaken this is. Just reflect on what chance a poor person, or even an oppressed Atheist, has in this country of really influencing the law.

In an interview with *The Tribune,* Chicago, Illinois, November 1891, on the subject of "The Tendency of Modern Thought," he suggested this "improvement" for church services:

> Let him [the preacher] show the debt that modern civilization owes to these people [the Greek]. Let him, too, give their religions, their mythology – *a mythology that has sown the seed of beauty in every land.* Then let him take up Rome. Let him show what a *wonderful* and practical people they were... Probably the Romans were the greatest lawyers.

Ingersoll suffered here from a classic case of rose-colored glasses. Read the first few pages of *On the Nature of the Universe* by Lucretius to find out about the "beauty" of the Greek religion. It is also unspeakable to call the Romans – who killed millions of people, who practiced slavery, who held murderous gladiator games – "wonderful people"; and to label them as "the greatest lawyers" doesn't reflect too well on law itself.

Ingersoll sometimes compromised with truth in order to be "popular." He claimed he hadn't the slightest idea whether there was life after death. This was a fatuous claim then, and it is even more so now. And, as already noted, Ingersoll rested on his laurels and made no preparation for the future of Atheism.

Enjoy Ingersoll to catharsis, but learn from his mistakes as well as his achievements; and don't imagine your catharsis is permanent.

Richard M. Smith

TABLE OF CONTENTS

INTRODUCTION
by Madalyn Murray O'Hair

Ever since he existed, agnostics and humanists have attempted to claim Robert Green Ingersoll for their own. His progeny to the third generation have felt that it would be more admirable for Ingersoll to be included in these "dignified" positions. His letters have been withheld, his work has been retouched to enhance his reputation as "The Great Agnostic." Volumes have been written about his love, devotion, understanding, compassion, humility, and through that extravagant praise Ingersoll has become a "saint." All of the attributes of this "loving man" are then claimed for the agnostic or the humanist position (in a reverse application of the doctrine of imputation).

Atheists are made of more honest stuff. We see Ingersoll for what he was and accept him as that. He was far from being a saint. Except for the issue of abolition, into which he was indoctrinated by both of his parents, he was on the "wrong" side of every human issue. Most frequently his changes of mind, and of heart, came from the influence of those he loved. His turn from religion, for example, should more honestly be seen as the result of his marriage to a woman who had abandoned it and who taught him that he should abandon any pretense of religion also.

He was a ruthless attorney for the railroads at the height of their rule of the land. In this function he had to influence legislation, fight against the claims of the farmers, of widows and children in order to brutally consolidate the power of his clients. The railroad empires of the post Civil War era were notorious for their rapacious land deals. And Robert Ingersoll climbed over the best of them all to get to the top. He opposed Abraham Lincoln until after the country was at war; he defended the most corrupt politicians of the nation; he wheeled and dealed in maneuvers that would make Barry Goldwater look like a goody-two-shoes; he clamored for a high protective tariff and gold-backed money; he opposed suffrage for black males and even proposed that they be sent away to a separate state or country set up for them. Today he would probably be a Reaganite.

Ingersoll's most astute move was to marry into a family of wealth. Even in the railroad industry, he was certain to see that he moved ruthlessly up through the ranks until he became the president of the Peoria lines. He charged enormous sums for his speaking appearances, averaging from $400 to $7,000 a lecture (in the 1870s). In today's money this is the equivalent of – perhaps – up to $50,000 a lecture. He never permitted his family to live in less than a mansion of extraordinary dimensions for the times. He resigned his commission during the Civil War and simply returned home, rather than seeing it through. He refused to come to the help of the Haymarket martyrs. Because of his Puritanism he balked at legal assistance for Atheist fighters who were arrested under the Comstock laws and, indeed, saw only minor changes needed in those repressive censorship laws. He did not obtain adequate education for his own children, both of whom were female. When he could not obtain the presidential appointment he coveted, he withdrew from his political game. He was a superb egotist. And he engaged in more than one drunken public brawl.

All of which is to say that Robert G. Ingersoll was human down to the fingertips. He was a very rich and powerful man, with close political ties to greater power. As such, he could speak out as he desired. Yet he was extremely cautious for many years, and his speeches often were quite innocuous. He introduced his attacks on religion carefully over a period of years. At first they were attacks on the corruption of the orthodox faiths. Only as he became more powerful and more assured were the attacks more lashing. He chose his brother-in-law to be the publicist for his speakers, and both of them together relied on the most outstanding Atheist press in the nation to do the printing – Peter Eckler Press.

Notwithstanding all of the anomalies of his character, he was magnificent when he did get going on either religion or the church. And he characterized himself as an Atheist.

Of course, he became the most powerful orator that the United States ever had. He excelled the speaking ability of "golden voiced" William Jennings Bryan or, later, the evangelist who was to become legendary, Billy Sunday. His speeches could easily run to three hours, and most often he held the audience in the palm of his hand. At 210 pounds, 5′ 10″ in stature, he had a splendid figure, a commanding presence. His voice was of great range and compass, with fine intonations ranging from mezzo profundo, through staccato, to pianissimo. His open countenance gave him an expression of honesty and his entire thrust was one of firmness in his convictions. Most often he spoke to standing-room-only crowds of people. And, of course, he was widely covered in the media. One must remember that his politics were not alone right wing, but that the Republican party was in his debt for his championing of their presidential aspirants. The media was forced to damn him with faint praise.

Robert Ingersoll, characteristically, wrote of his birth: "That which has happened to all, happened to me. I was born, and this event, which has never for a moment ceased to influence my life, took place, according to an entry found in one Bible, on the 12th day of August in the year of grace 1833, according to another entry in another Bible, on the 11th of August in the same year. So you will see, that a contradiction was about the first thing I found in the Bible, and I have continued to find contradictions in the 'Sacred Volume' all my life."

His father was ordained as a Congregationalist minister in 1823. As Ingersoll later explained, "After having received a certificate to the effect that he understood the mysteries of orthodoxy, and was able to show that the infinite love of God was perfectly consistent with the damnation of the whole human race, he started in search of employment." He was, however, an abolitionist at the time that the churches of the United States were uniformly in support of our system of slavery. He would obtain a church only to lose it, wandering throughout Vermont, New York, Ohio, Wisconsin, Michigan, Indiana, Kentucky, Tennessee and Illinois, staying only long enough for his views to be well-known, providing only somewhat for his family. He married in 1821 to a woman who is by one author described as a revivalist, and by another as an Atheist suffering in the home of the Congregationalist minister. The wife died in 1835 after producing five children in the marriage: Ruth, John (who became a doctor), Mary Jane, Ebon, Clark and Robert. The latter was born August 11, 1833 in Dresden, New York. The father was to marry two times more, to try to operate a small grocery store and otherwise to try to support his family as he wandered from church to church. Robert did not receive an education. In the fall of 1851 his father, worried about this, enrolled him in a school run by a fundamentalist in the basement of the Congregationalist church. The entire education was completed in less than a year. Robert Ingersoll's first job thereafter was as assistant to the clerk of the county circuit court. But, shortly thereafter he was found teaching, for "boarding round" in a tiny log cabin school "with a stove" in Tennessee.

Finally, he returned to Marion, Illinois, where he and his brother Clark studied law for one month, in the law office of a U.S. congressman,

xi

and then applied for admission to the bar, *ex gratia*, which was obtained on December 20, 1854. Full admission was to come after two additional months of study. He was then 21 years of age. The brothers decided that they would move to a port city, and there Robert again obtained work in the land office and in the office of the clerk of the county and circuit courts. While there, Ingersoll spent a great part of his time in the offices of an attorney, a state senator, who was later to become a member of the constitutional convention of the state of Illinois. This man was a "rationalist," with an excellent library. Clark, immediately getting into politics, was soon elected to the Illinois state legislature.

Seeing that Peoria, Illinois seemed to be a bustling town, and having received six city lots (worth about $250) for payment of legal fees, they moved there in February 1858 and set up their office at 4 Adams Street, across from the Court House. The unmarried Robert G. Ingersoll slept in the office, while brother Clark obtained a home for himself and his wife. At Peoria, the river traffic was at its peak. Railroads were just beginning their lobbying, and Robert G. was hired to lobby for the railroads at the state legislature. And in his first political stance, during the time of the Lincoln-Douglas debates, one of which was held in Peoria, Robert Ingersoll sided with Douglas and against complete abolition. He was nominated for representative of the Democrats to Congress on August 2, 1862, and at that point was against slavery but for "popular sovereignty" (for keeping slavery out of Illinois and territories but allowing it in the South). Peoria had pledged itself to the Union, and when the Civil War began on April 12, 1861, Ingersoll agreed to help mobilization. Eventually, however, he expressed himself as against Lincoln's Emancipation Proclamation. But he did assist in mustering troops, himself joining the Union Army on September 16, 1861. The regiment he assisted in forming was to be called the 11th Illinois Cavalry Regiment; and because of his success in calling men to volunteer service, he was appointed a colonel, his official commission coming through in October 1861.

As a lobbyist for the railroads and with a brother very actively engaged in politics, he was meeting more and more persons in positions of power. A circuit rider, traveling to other counties for some of his cases, including those for the railroads, he was invited to the mansion home of the most wealthy family in Tazewell County, that of Benjamin Weld Parker. There, he met and wooed the daughter, whom he married on February 13, 1862, in a *religious* ceremony (even though Eva, influenced by her grandmother, was a "rationalist" also). Shortly after the marriage (March 26, 1862) Robert Ingersoll headed off to the war and was soon involved in the Battle of Shiloh in April 1862. The Union losses were 15,000 killed, wounded, captured or missing, and the Confederacy lost at least as many. He stayed on with his regiment until he, and a small group of others, were taken captive near Corinth, Tennessee. He was sent, with the group, to St. Louis, Missouri to be processed for exchange. His wife joined him there and on June 18, 1863, he resigned his commission and returned home. He was formally discharged on June 30, 1863, although the war was to continue for two more bloody years. He resigned, he wrote to his brother Clark, because he had "seen enough of death and horror." (Another author gives the letter as saying enough of "bloodshed and humiliation.") Safely home, he began to make speeches for the preservation of the Union, and he advocated that Negroes be sent to their own country. It was about this time that Ingersoll entered the Republican Party. Meanwhile, his brother, Clark, was appointed to fill out an unexpired term in Congress caused by the death of a congressman. Later, when he ran for that office Robert became his campaign manager and they both endorsed Lincoln. He was elected in 1864, and reelected in 1866 and again in 1868.

It was also in 1868 that Ingersoll became interested in the gubernatorial nomination in Illinois. Many delegates thought favorably of him, but his unorthodox religious opinions were worrisome to the politicians. He was therefore asked to make some pledge to remain silent concerning the subject of religion. This he refused to do, and consequently was not put forth as a likely candidate.

Influenced by his wife, Robert Ingersoll did not go to church, but in his writings at this point he was stating his belief in personal immortality. It was not until May 14, 1866, at the age of 33, that he gave his first iconoclastic speech, "Progress," in Peoria. Basically this spoke of his budding abhorrence of superstition and concluded with a plea for the continuation of progress in thought. Meanwhile, his two daughters had been born (Eva Robert in 1863 and Maud Robert in 1864). He was now the attorney for the Peoria and Rock Island Railroad, the Peoria, Decatur and Evansville Railroad, the Toledo, Peoria, Atlanta and Decatur Railroad, the Chicago and Alton Railroad, the Chicago and Northwestern Railroad, the Indianapolis and St. Louis Railroad, the Illinois Midland Railroad, and the Chicago, Burlington and Quincy Railroads. He was on the board of directors of the Peoria and Rock Island Railroad. He had a friend in the governor (Oglesby) who appointed him attorney general of Illinois (a two-year term) on February 27, 1867. His official posture then was against Negro suffrage in Illinois. During this entire period, stories of his drinking and brawling continued. He matured, intellectually, slowly, for he did not begin to fight for woman's suffrage until 1870 – by which time he was 37 years old and married for eight years. At this time he was on the board of directors of the Peoria, Atlanta and Decatur Railroad Co. and the Peoria and Springfield Railway Co. As his oratorical abilities grew, he began to make speeches on specific topics and one of the first of these was "Thomas Paine." Many of the subjects were "safe." But in 1872, his "The Gods" made its appearance, with its noble cry: "Give me the storm and tempest of thought and action, rather than the dead calm of ignorance and faith." Two years later the first volume of his lectures was available to all.

In 1876 he moved into the Cockle Mansion, which had taken two years and $50,000 just to build. Constructed of brick and stone, four stories high, steam heated, it was the most outstanding residence in Peoria. During this period he was assisting the Republicans in a disputed election, defending a revenue officer charged with illicit dealings in whiskey (the famous Munn trial) and was heavily involved in politicking. He was chosen to give the nominating speech for James G. Blaine (of railroad interests) at the Republican Convention of 1876 and left the convention spellbound by his oratory. The presentation, called "the Plumed Knight speech," however, failed to carry the day, and Rutherford B. Hayes was nominated and later elected to the presidency of the United States. After campaigning for Hayes, Ingersoll expected an ambassadorship – even traveling to D.C. in anticipation of the award. However, once in office Hayes ignored Ingersoll. One author opines that this was because of Hayes' religion.

Ingersoll knew where he excelled – and that was in oratory. He began, therefore, in 1877 to lecture. His lowest fee was $200, but generally he asked for amounts up to $2,400. This quickly escalated to the $400 to $7,000 range. At this time a few more antireligious lectures appeared in his repertoire, such as "Heretics and Heresies" with a theme of growth and progress; and "Ghosts," which was an unrelieved assault on religion. However, his most popular lectures were innocuous, "Liberty of Man, Woman, and Child" and "Defense of Thomas Paine." In 1878, he moved his family to Washington, to a four-story brownstone and brick mansion close to the White House on Lafayette Square. And now all he was doing was lecturing. Two pieces which were to become loved by the nonreligious now appeared: "Hell" and "Some Mistakes of Moses," the latter of which, appearing in 1879, was a satirical treatment of the flood, Israel, and the morality of the Old Testament. Later still, his "Orthodoxy" was a fierce indictment of conventional theology. For a short period of time he became involved with several Atheist organizations, the New York State Freethinker's Association, the Manhattan Liberal Club, the American Secular Union, but at the same time he was in close association with the Jewish Ethical Society and financially supporting the Hebrew Orphan's Asylum of San Francisco, California. In 1877 he accepted the office of vice president of the National Liberal League of Philadelphia, which had held its first convention in that city in July 1876. He actually attended the second convention in October 1877, but would not join in demands of that organization for the repeal of the Comstock laws. He felt that it was necessary only to amend the laws to waive persecution for those persons who had conscientious and honest opinions. At the time, E. H. Heywood and D. G. M. Bennett were under indictment for their publication and distribution of birth control information, and Ingersoll not alone refused to assist them with his talents, but resigned from Atheist organizations because of their backing of Heywood and Bennett.

He continued, however, in heavy correspondence with George Holyoake, the English Atheist who coined the word "secularist," and he knew Charles Bradlaugh, Charles Watt, and G. W. Foote – all of Atheist renown. But rift from the Atheist organizations in the U.S., in 1880 he stumped for James A. Garfield for president at the same time that he was fashioning his lectures on "The Gods" and "What Great Infidels Have Done for Mankind."

Despite his grandiose pretensions in "Liberty of Man, Woman and Child," he was the chief counsel for the defense in the U.S. "star routes" mail contracts (of railroad fame). In this case, a U.S. senator and the assistant postmaster general of the United States were indicted for attempting to defraud the U.S. government through certain contracts for transporting the mails over what were known as "star routes" controlled by the railroads. Ingersoll beat the rap for his influential clients. And his income in the period 1879-83 was estimated to be about $200,000 a year. Translate that into current dollars!

In 1885, Ingersoll moved his family to New York City, 101 Fifth Ave., another mansion which he leased for one year. There it was discovered that he had growths on his vocal cords, and these needed to be removed. Whether from remorse or to amend, he did pick up Charles B. Reynolds' blasphemy charge and attempted to defend him. It was one of the few cases he lost, with Reynolds being convicted and fined $25. But at the same time he was refusing to defend August Spies and Michael Schwab of the Haymarket frame-up. After a great deal of pressure, he did write a letter to Governor Oglesby to ask for a pardon, which was not given. With law and politics as two parts of one equal and inseparable interest, it is doubtful if he could have defended any anarchist, anywhere.

During the next years, in 1886 he moved again to a larger mansion at 89 Fifth Ave., and in 1888 to a still larger one at 400 Fifth Ave. And in 1889 Eva married into fabulous railroad wealth. Her husband purchased 40 acres of land overlooking the Hudson River at Dobbs Ferry and there built "Castle Walston," where Ingersoll spent a great deal of time. It was there that he met Mark Twain and later Walt Whitman. And in 1891 he wrote his famous "A Christmas Sermon." But the love of politics never left him, and in 1896 he was back in the presidential campaigns again. Ingersoll became increasingly radical in respect to religion as he grew older – indeed, he became ever more bold. But in November 1896 he had a slight cerebral hemorrhage and incurred angina pectoris. A combined family effort brought his weight down from 220 to 176 pounds, and the family moved again to a still larger mansion at 220 Madison Ave. When he recovered, he began to lecture again – his last one being delivered to the American Free Religious Association, another Atheist group, in Boston, on April 2, 1899, the subject being "What Is Religion?"

On the evening of July 20, 1899, he died, it is believed, from a heart attack. He was cremated and then the ashes were buried in Arlington National Cemetery. Immediately, his widow put his library up for sale.

For all he was, and for all he wasn't, Robert G. Ingersoll was one of the most effective spokesmen for Atheism in the United States; and in oratory for the same no one has been his equal. He was grand and eloquent, this hero of ours, with his clay feet. But we cannot make a "saint" of him, for he was a "sinner" also. Robert G. Ingersoll had such wealth that he could have financed an Atheist movement which would have been able to defeat the religious forces in our nation. Our job would not be so difficult today had Robert G. Ingersoll been more aware of the need for organization and strength of numbers. He was a towering giant, but a lone one. His words were music to the ear, especially his own ear. He substituted his desire for individual fame for the good of the cause of Atheism and its advancement. But with it all – he is ours. He could have done more; he could not have done less. Everyone must give of that which they are and Ingersoll gave as an orator and a poet in prose. We love him for it. We damn him for his shortsightedness, and we all wish that we could do as well.

THE BIBLE AND A FUTURE LIFE

Q. Colonel, are your views of religion based on the Bible?

A. I regard the Bible, especially the Old Testament, the same as I do most other ancient books, in which there is some truth, a great deal of error, considerable barbarism, and a most plentiful lack of good sense.

Q. Have you found any other work, sacred or profane, which you regard as more reliable?

A. I know of no book less so, in my judgment.

Q. You have studied the Bible attentively, have you not?

A. I have read the Bible. I have heard it talked about a good deal, and am sufficiently well acquainted with it to justify my own mind in utterly rejecting all claims made for its divine origin.

Q. What do you base your views upon?

A. On reason, observation, experience, upon the discoveries of science, upon observed facts and the analogies properly growing out of such facts. I have no confidence in anything pretending to be outside, or independent of, or in any manner above nature.

Q. According to your views, what disposition is made of man after death?

A. Upon that subject I know nothing. It is no more wonderful that man should live again than that he now lives; upon that question I know of no evidence. The doctrine of immortality rests upon human affection. We love, therefore we wish to live.

Q. Then you would not undertake to say what becomes of man after death?

A. If I told or pretended to know what becomes of man after death, I would be as dogmatic as are theologians upon this question. The difference between them and me is I am honest. I admit that I do not know.

Q. Judging by your criticism of mankind, Colonel, in your recent lecture, you have not found his condition very satisfactory.

A. Nature, outside of man, so far as I know, is neither cruel nor merciful. I am not satisfied with the present condition of the human race, nor with the condition of man during any period of which we have any knowledge. I believe, however, the condition of man is improved, and this improvement is due to his own

1

exertions. I do not make nature a being. I do not ascribe to nature intention.

Q. Is your theory, Colonel, the result of investigation of the subject?

A. No one can control his own opinion or his own belief. My belief was forced upon me by my surroundings. I am the product of all circumstances that have in any way touched me. I believe in this world. I have no confidence in any religion promising joys in another world at the expense of liberty and happiness in this. At the same time, I wish to give others all the rights I claim for myself.

Q. If I asked for proofs for your theory, what would you furnish?

A. The experience of every man who is honest with himself, every fact that has been discovered in nature. In addition to these, the utter and total failure of all religionists in all countries to produce one particle of evidence showing the existence of any supernatural power whatever, and the further fact that the people are not satisfied with their religion. They are continually asking for evidence. They are asking for it in every imaginable way. The sects are continually dividing. There is no real religious sincerity in the world. All religions are opponents of intellectual liberty. I believe in absolute mental freedom. Real religion with me is a thing not of the head, but of the heart; not a theory, not a creed, but a life.

Q. What punishment, then, is inflicted upon man for crimes and wrongs committed in this life?

A. There is no such thing as intellectual crime. No man can commit a mental crime. To become a crime it must go beyond thought.

Q. What punishment is there for physical crime?

A. Such punishment as is necessary to protect society and for the reformation of the criminal.

Q. If there is only punishment in this world, will not some escape punishment?

A. I admit that all do not seem to be punished as they deserve. I also admit that all do not seem to be rewarded as they deserve; and there is in this world, apparently, as great failures in matter of reward as in matter of punishment. If there is another life, a man will be happier there for acting according to his highest ideals in this. But I do not discern in nature any effort to do justice. — *The Post,* Washington, D.C., 1878.

MRS. VAN COTT, THE REVIVALIST

Q. I see, Colonel, that in an interview published this morning, Mrs. Van Cott [the revivalist], calls you "a poor barking dog." Do you know her personally?

A. I have never met or seen her.

Q. Do you know the reason she applied the epithet?

A. I suppose it to be the natural result of what is called vital piety; that is to say, universal love breeds individual hatred.

Q. Do you intend making any reply to what she says?

A. I have written her a note of which this is a copy:

Buffalo, Feb. 24th, 1878

Mrs. Van Cott:

My dear Madam: Were you constrained by the love of Christ to call a man who has never injured you "a poor barking dog"? Did you make this remark as a Christian, or as a lady? Did you say these words to illustrate in some faint degree the refining influence upon woman of the religion you preach?

What would you think of me if I should retort, using your language, changing only the sex of the last word?

I have the honor to remain,

Yours truly,
R. G. Ingersoll

Q. Well, what do you think of the religious revival system generally?

A. The fire that has to be blown all the time is a poor thing to get warm by. I regard these revivalists especially barbaric. I think they do no good, but much harm, they make innocent people think they are guilty, and very mean people think they are good.

Q. What is your opinion concerning women as conductors of these revivals?

A. I suppose those engaged in them think they are doing good. They are probably honest. I think, however, that neither men nor women should be engaged in frightening people into heaven. That is all I wish to say on the subject, as I do not think it worth talking about. — *The Express*, Buffalo, New York, February 1878.

3

THE PRE-MILLENNIAL CONFERENCE

Q. What do you think of the Pre-Millennial Conference that was held in New York City recently?

A. Well, I think that all who attended it were believers in the Bible, and anyone who believes in prophecies and looks to their fulfillment will go insane. A man that tries from Daniel's ram with three horns and five tails and his deformed goats to ascertain the date of the second immigration of Christ to this world is already insane. It all shows that the moment we leave the realm of fact and law we are adrift on the wide and shoreless sea of theological speculation.

Q. Do you think there will be a second coming?

A. No, not as long as the church is in power. Christ will never again visit this earth until the freethinkers have control. He will certainly never allow another church to get hold of him. The very persons who met in New York to fix the date of his coming would despise him and the feeling would probably be mutual. In his day Christ was an Infidel, and made himself unpopular by denouncing the church as it then existed. He called them liars, hypocrites, thieves, vipers, whited sepulchres, and fools. From the description given of the church in that day, I am afraid that should he come again, he would be provoked into using similar language. Of course, I admit there are many good people in the church, just as there were some good Pharisees who were opposed to the crucifixion. — *The Express,* Buffalo, New York, Nov. 4, 1878.

4

THE SUNDAY LAWS OF PITTSBURGH

The manager of the theater where Colonel Ingersoll lectured, was fined $50, which Colonel Ingersoll paid.

Q. Colonel, what do you think of the course the mayor has pursued toward you in attempting to stop your lecture?

A. I know very little except what I have seen in the morning paper. As a general rule, laws should be enforced or repealed; and so far as I am personally concerned, I shall not so much complain of the enforcing of the law against Sabbath breaking as of the fact that such a law exists. They were passed by superstition, and the enlightened people of today should repeal them. Ministers should not expect to fill their churches by shutting up other places. They can only increase their congregations by improving their sermons. They will have more hearers when they say more worth hearing. I have no idea that the mayor has any prejudice against me personally and if he only enforces the law, I shall have none against him. If my lectures were free, the ministers might have the right to object, but as I charge one dollar admission and they nothing, they ought certainly to be able to compete with me.

Q. Don't you think it is the duty of the mayor, as chief executive of the city laws, to enforce the ordinances and pay no attention to what the statutes say?

A. I suppose it to be the duty of the mayor to enforce the ordinance of the city and if the ordinance of the city covers the same ground as the law of the state, a conviction under the ordinance would be a bar to a prosecution under the state law.

Q. If the ordinance exempts scientific, literary, and historical lectures, as it is said it does, will not that exempt you?

A. Yes, all my lectures are historical; that is, I speak of many things that have happened. They are scientific because they are filled with facts, and they are literary, of course. I can conceive of no address that is neither historical nor scientific, except sermons. They fail to be historical because they treat of things that never happened and they are certainly not scientific, as they contain no facts.

Q. Suppose they arrest you; what will you do?

A. I will examine the law and if convicted will pay the fine, unless I think I can reverse the case by appeal. Of course, I would like to see all these foolish laws wiped from the statute books. I want the law so that everybody can do just as he pleases on Sunday, provided he does not interfere with the rights of others. I want the Christian, the Jew, the Deist, and the Atheist to be exactly equal before the law. I would fight for the right of the Christian to worship God in his own way just as quick as I would fight for the Atheist to enjoy music, flowers, and fields. I hope to see the time when even the poor people can hear the music of the finest operas on Sunday. One grand opera, with all its thrilling tones, will do more good in touching and elevating the world than 10,000 sermons on the agonies of hell.

Q. Have you ever been interfered with before in delivering Sunday lectures?

A. No, I postponed a lecture in Baltimore at the request of the owners of the theater because they were afraid some action might be taken. That is the only case. I have delivered lectures on Sunday in the principal cities of the United States, in New York, Boston, Buffalo, Chicago, San Francisco, Cincinnati, and many other places. I lectured here last winter; it was on Sunday and I heard nothing of its being contrary to law. I always supposed my lectures were good enough to be delivered on the most sacred days. — *The Leader,* Pittsburgh, Pennsylvania, Oct. 27, 1879.

IDEAS ON RELIGION

Q. I would like to know something of the history of your religious views.

A. I may say right here that the Christian idea that any God can make me his friend by killing mine is about as great a mistake as could be made. They seem to have the idea that just as soon as God kills all the people that a person loves, he will then begin to love the Lord. What drew my attention first to these questions was the doctrine of eternal punishment. This was so abhorrent to my mind that I began to hate the book in which it was taught. Then, in reading law, going back to find the origin of laws, I found one had to go but a little way before the legislator and priest united. This led me to study a good many of the religions of the world. At first I was greatly astonished to find most of them better than ours. I then studied our own system to the best of my ability, and found that people were palming off on children and on one another as the inspired word of God a book that upheld slavery, polygamy, and almost every other crime. Whether I am right or wrong, I became convinced that the Bible is not an inspired book; and then the only question for me to settle was as to whether I should say what I believed or not. This really was not the question in my mind, because, before even thinking of such a question, I expressed my belief, and I simply claim that right and expect to exercise it as long as I live. I may be damned for it in the next world, but it is a great source of pleasure to me in this.

Q. It is reported that you are the son of a Presbyterian minister.

A. Yes, I am the son of a New School Presbyterian minister.

Q. About what age were you when you began this investigation which led to your present convictions?

A. I cannot remember when I believed the Bible doctrine of eternal punishment. I have a dim recollection of hating Jehovah when I was exceedingly small.

Q. Then your present convictions began to form themselves while you were listening to the teachings of religion as taught by your father?

A. Yes, they did.

Q. Did you discuss the matter with him?

A. I did for many years, and before he died he utterly gave up the idea that this life is a period of probation. He utterly gave up the idea of eternal punishment, and before he died he had the happiness of believing that God was almost as good and generous as he was himself.

Q. I suppose this gossip about a change in your religious views arose or was created by the expression used at your brother's funeral, "In the night of death hope sees a star and listening love can hear the rustle of a wing."

A. I never willingly will destroy a solitary human hope. I have always said that I did not know whether man was or was not immortal, but years before my brother died, in a lecture entitled "The Ghosts," which has since been published, I used the following words: "The idea of immortality, that like a sea has ebbed and flowed in the human heart, with its countless waves of hope and fear, beating against the shores and rocks of time and fate, was not born of any book, nor of any creed, nor of any religion. It was born of human affection, and it will continue to ebb and flow beneath the mists and clouds of doubt and darkness as long as love kisses the lips of death. It is the rainbow – hope, shining upon the tears of grief."

Q. The great objection to your teaching urged by your enemies is that you constantly tear down, and never build up.

A. I have just published a little book entitled, *Some Mistakes of Moses*, in which I have endeavored to give most of the arguments I have urged against the Pentateuch in a lecture I delivered under that title. The motto on the title page is, "A destroyer of weeds, thistles, and thorns is a benefactor, whether he sows grain or not." I cannot for my life see why one should be charged with tearing down and not rebuilding simply because he exposes a sham, or detects a lie. I do not feel under any obligation to build something in the place of a detected falsehood. All I think I am under obligation to put in the place of a detected lie is the detection. Most religionists talk as if mistakes were valuable things and they did not wish to part with them without a consideration. Just how much they regard lies worth a dozen I do not know. If the price is reasonable, I am perfectly willing to give it, rather than to see them live and give their lives to the defense of delusions. I am firmly convinced that to be happy here will not in the least detract from our happiness in another world should we be so fortunate as to reach another world; and I cannot see the value of any philosophy that reaches beyond the intelligent happiness of the present. There may be a God who will make us happy in another world. If he does, it will be more than he has accomplished in this. I suppose that he will never have more than infinite power and never have less than infinite wisdom, and why people should expect that he should do better in another world than he has in this is something that I have never been able to explain. A being who has the power to prevent it and yet allows thousands and millions of his children to starve; who devours them with earthquakes; who allows whole nations to be enslaved, cannot in my judgment be implicitly depended on to do justice in another world.

Q. How do the clergy generally treat you?

A. Well, of course there are the same distinctions among clergymen as among other people. Some of them are quite respectable gentlemen, especially those with whom I am not acquainted. I think that since the loss of my brother nothing could exceed the heartlessness of the remarks made by the average clergyman. There have been some noble exceptions, to whom I feel not only thankful but grateful; but a large majority have taken this occasion to say most unfeeling and brutal things. I do not ask the clergy to forgive me, but I do request that they will so act that I will not have to forgive them. I have always insisted that those who love their enemies should at least tell the truth about their friends, but I suppose, after all, that religion must be supported by the same means as those by which it was founded. Of course, there are thousands of good ministers, men who are endeavoring to make the world better, and whose failure is no particular fault of their own. I have always been in doubt as to whether the clergy were a necessary or an unnecessary evil.

Q. I would like to have a positive expression of your views as to a future state.

A. Somebody asked Confucius about another world, and his reply was: "How should I know anything about another world when I know so little of this?" For my part, I know nothing of any other state of existence, either before or after this, and I have never become personally acquainted with anybody that did. There may be another life, and if there is, the best way to prepare for it is by making somebody happy in this. God certainly cannot afford to put a man in hell who has made a little heaven in this world. I

9

propose simply to take my chances with the rest of the folks, and prepare to go where the people I am best acquainted with will probably settle. I cannot afford to leave the great ship and sneak off to shore in some orthodox canoe. I hope there is another life, for I would like to see how things come out in this world when I am dead. There are some people I would like to see again, and hope there are some who would not object to seeing me; but if there is no other life I shall never know it. I do not remember a time when I did not exist; and if, when I die, that is the end, I shall not know it, because the last thing I shall know is that l am alive, and if nothing is left, nothing will be left to know that I am dead; so that so far as I am concerned I am immortal; that is to say, I cannot recollect when I did not exist, and there never will be a time when I shall remember that I do not exist. I would like to have several millions of dollars, and I may say that I have a lively hope that some day I may be rich, but to tell you the truth I have little evidence of it. Our hope of immortality does not come from any religion, but nearly all religions come from that hope. The Old Testament, instead of telling us that we are immortal, tells us how we lost immortality. You will recollect that if Adam and Eve could have gotten to the tree of life, they would have eaten of its fruit and would have lived forever; but for the purpose of preventing immortality God turned them out of the garden of Eden, and put certain angels with swords or sabers at the gate to keep them from getting back. The Old Testament proves – if anything, and I do not think it does – that there is no life after this; and the New Testament is not specific on the subject. There were a great many opportunities for the Savior and his apostles to tell us about another world, but they did not improve them to any great extent; and the only evidence, so far as I know, about another life is, first, that we have no evidence; and secondly, that we are rather sorry that we have not, and wish we had. That is my position.

Q. According to your observation of men, and your reading in relation to the men and women of the world and of the church, if there is another world divided according to orthodox principles between the orthodox and heterodox, which of the two that are known as heaven and hell would contain, in your judgment, the most good society?

A. Since hanging has got to be a means of grace, I would prefer hell. I had a thousand times rather associate with the pagan philosophers than with the inquisitors of the Middle Ages. I certainly should prefer the worst man in Greek or Roman history to John Calvin; and I can imagine no man in the world that I would not rather sit on the same bench with than the Puritan fathers and the founders of orthodox churches. I would trade off my harp any minute for a seat in the other country. All the poets will be in perdition, and the greatest thinkers, and, I should think, most of the women whose society would tend to increase the happiness of man; nearly all the painters, nearly all the sculptors, nearly all the writers of plays, nearly all the great actors, most of the best musicians, and nearly all the good fellows – the persons who know stories, who can sing songs, or who will loan a friend a dollar. They will mostly all be in that country, and if I did not live there permanently, I certainly would want it so I could spend my winter months there. But, after all, what I really want to do is to destroy the idea of eternal punishment. That doctrine subverts all ideas of justice. That doctrine fills hell with honest men, and heaven with intellectual and moral paupers. That doctrine allows people to sin on a credit. That doctrine allows the basest to be eternally happy and the most honorable to suffer eternal pain. I think of all doctrines it is the most infinitely infamous and would disgrace the lowest savage; and any man who believes it, and has imagination enough to understand it, has the heart of a serpent and the conscience of a hyena.

Q. Your objective point is to destroy the doctrine of hell, is it?

A. Yes, because the destruction of that doctrine will do away with all cant and all pretense. It will do away with all religious bigotry and persecution. It will allow every man to think and to express his thoughts. It will do away with bigotry in all its slimy and offensive forms. — *Chicago Times*, Nov. 14, 1879.

RELIGION AND THOMAS PAINE

Q. Is there anything new about religion since you were last here?

A. Since I was here I have spoken in a great many cities, and tomorrow I am going to do some missionary work at Milwaukee. Many who have come to scoff have remained to pray, and I think that my labors are being greatly blessed, and all attacks on me so far have been overruled for good. I happened to come in contact with a revival of religion, and I believe what they call an "outpouring" at Detroit, under the leadership of a gentleman by the name of Pentecost. He denounced me as God's greatest enemy. I had always supposed that the devil occupied that exalted position, but it seems that I have, in some way, fallen heir to his shoes. Mr. Pentecost also denounced all businessmen who would allow any advertisements or lithographs of mine to hang in their places of business, and several of the gentlemen thus appealed to took the advertisements away. The result of all this was that I had the largest house that ever attended a lecture in Detroit. Feeling that ingratitude is a crime, I publicly returned thanks to the clergy for the pains they had taken to give me an audience. And I may say, in this connection, that if the ministers do God as little good as they do me harm, they had better let both of us alone. I regard them as good but exceedingly mistaken men. They do not come much in contact with the world and get most of their views by talking with the women and children of their congregations. They are not permitted to mingle freely with society. They cannot attend plays nor hear operas. I believe some of them have ventured to minstrel shows and menageries, where they confine themselves strictly to the animal part of the entertainment. But, as a rule, they have few opportunities of ascertaining what the real public opinion is. They read religious papers, edited by gentlemen who know as little about the world as themselves, and the result of all this is that they are rather behind the times. They are good men, and would like to do right if they only knew it, but they are a little behind the times. There is an old story told of a fellow who had a post office in a small town in North Carolina, and being the only man in town who could read, a few people used to gather in the post office on Sunday, and he would read to them a weekly paper that was published in Washington. He commenced always at the top of the first column and read right straight through, articles, advertisements, and all, and whenever they got a little tired of reading he would make a mark of red ochre and commence at that place the next Sunday. The result was that the papers came a great deal faster than he read them, and it was about 1817 when they struck the War of 1812. The moment they got to that, every one of them jumped up and offered to volunteer. All of which shows that they were patriotic people, but a little slow, and somewhat behind the times.

Q. How were you pleased with the Paine meeting here, and its results?

A. I was gratified to see so many people willing at last to do justice to a great and maligned man. Of course, I do not claim that Paine was perfect. All I claim is that he was a patriot and a political philosopher; that he was a revolutionist and an agitator; that he was infinitely full of suggestive thought, and that he did more than any man to convince the people of America not only that they ought to separate from Great Britain, but that they ought to found a representative government. He has been despised simply because he did not believe the Bible. I wish to do what I can to rescue his name from theological defamation. I think the day has come when Thomas Paine will be remembered with Washington, Franklin, and Jefferson, and that the American people will wonder that their fathers could have been guilty of such base ingratitude. — *Chicago Times*, Feb. 8, 1880.

REPLY TO CHICAGO CRITICS

Q. Have you read the replies of the clergy to your recent lecture in this city on "What Must We Do to Be Saved?" and if so what do you think of them?

A. I think they dodge the point. The real point is this: If salvation by faith is the real doctrine of Christianity, I asked on Sunday before last, and I still ask, why didn't Matthew tell it? I still insist that Mark should have remembered it, and I shall always believe that Luke ought, at least, to have noticed it. I was endeavoring to show that modern Christianity has for its basis an interpolation. I think I showed it. The only Gospel on the orthodox side is that of John, and that was certainly not written, or did not appear in its present form, until long after the others were written.

I know well that the Catholic Church claimed during the Dark Ages, and still claims, that references had been made to the Gospels by persons living in the 1st, 2nd, and 3rd centuries; but I believe such manuscripts were manufactured by the Catholic Church. For many years in Europe there was not one person in 20,000 who could read and write. During that time the church had in its keeping the literature of our world. They interpolated as they pleased. They created. They destroyed. In other words, they did whatever in their opinion was necessary to substantiate the faith.

The gentlemen who saw fit to reply did not answer the question, and I again call on the clergy to explain to the people why, if salvation depends on belief on the Lord Jesus Christ, Matthew didn't mention it. Someone has said that Christ didn't make known this doctrine of salvation by belief or faith until after his resurrection. Certainly none of the Gospels were written until after his resurrection; and if he made that doctrine known after his resurrection, and before his ascension, it should have been in Matthew, Mark, and Luke, as well as in John.

The replies of the clergy show that they have not investigated the subject; that they are not well acquainted with the New Testament. In other words, they have not read it except with the regulation theological bias.

14

There is one thing I wish to correct here. In an editorial in the *Tribune* it was stated that I had admitted that Christ was beyond and above Buddha, Zoroaster, Confucius, and others. I did not say so. Another point was made against me, and those who made it seemed to think it was a good one. In my lecture I asked why it was that the disciples of Christ wrote in Greek, whereas, in fact, they understood only Hebrew. It is now claimed that Greek was the language of Jerusalem at that time, that Hebrew had fallen into disuse; that no one understood it except the literati and the highly educated. If I fell into an error on this point it was because I relied on the New Testament. I find in the 21st chapter of the Acts an account of Paul having been mobbed in the city of Jerusalem; that he was protected by a chief captain and some soldiers; that, while on the stairs of the castle to which he was being taken, he obtained leave from the captain to speak unto the people. In the 40th verse of that chapter I find the following:

> And when he had given him license, Paul stood on the stairs and beckoned with the hand unto the people. And when there was made a great silence, he spake unto them in the Hebrew tongue, saying...

And then follows the speech of Paul, wherein he gives an account of his conversion. It seems a little curious to me that Paul, for the purpose of quieting a mob, would speak to that mob in an unknown language. If I were mobbed in the city of Chicago, and wished to defend myself with an explanation, I certainly would not make that explanation in Choctaw, even if I understood that tongue. My present opinion is that I would speak in English; and the reason I would speak in English is because that language is generally understood in this city, and so I conclude from the account in the 21st chapter of the Acts that Hebrew was the language of Jerusalem at that time, or that Paul would not have addressed the mob in that tongue.

Q. Did you read Mr. Courtney's answer?

A. I read what Mr. Courtney read from others, and think some of his quotations good; and have no doubt that the authors will feel complimented by being quoted. There certainly is no need of my answering Dr. Courtney; sometime I may answer the French gentlemen from whom he quoted.

Q. But what about there being "belief" in Matthew?

A. Mr. Courtney says that certain people were cured of diseases on account of faith. Admitting that mumps, measles, and

15

whooping-cough could be cured in that way, there is not even a suggestion that salvation depended on a like faith. I think he can hardly afford to rely on the miracles of the New Testament to prove his doctrine. There is one instance in which a miracle was performed by Christ without his knowledge; and I hardly think that even Mr. Courtney would insist that any faith could have been great enough for that. The fact is, I believe that all these miracles were ascribed to Christ long after his death, and that Christ never, at any time or place, pretended to have any supernatural origin. He claimed simply to be a man; no less, no more. I do not believe Mr. Courtney is satisfied with his own reply.

Q. And now as to Professor Swing?

A. Mr. Swing has been out of the orthodox church so long that he seems to have forgotten the reasons for which he left it. I do not believe there is an orthodox minister in the city of Chicago who will agree with Mr. Swing that salvation by faith is no longer preached. Professor Swing seems to think it of no importance who wrote the gospel of Matthew. In this I agree with him. Judging from what he said there is hardly difference enough of opinion between us to justify a reply on his part. He, however, makes one mistake. I did not in the lecture say one word about tearing down churches. I have no objection to people building all the churches they wish. While I admit that it is a pretty sight to see children on a morning in June going through the fields to the country church, I still insist that the beauty of that sight does not answer the question how it is that Matthew forgot to say anything about salvation through Christ. Professor Swing is a man of poetic temperament, but this is not a poetic question.

Q. How did the card of Dr. Thomas strike you?

A. I think the reply of Dr. Thomas is in the best possible spirit. I regard him today as the best intellect in the Methodist denomination. He seems to have what is generally understood as a Christian spirit. He has always treated me with perfect fairness, and I should have said long ago many grateful things had I not feared I might hurt him with his own people. He seems to be by nature a perfectly fair man; and I know of no man in the United States for whom I have a profounder respect. Of course, I don't agree with Dr. Thomas. I think in many things he is mistaken. But I believe him to be perfectly sincere. There is one trouble about him – he is growing; and this fact will no doubt give great trouble to many of his brethren. Certain Methodist hazel-brush feel a little uneasy in the shadow of an oak. To see the difference between him and some others, all that is necessary is to read his reply, and then read the remarks made at the Methodist ministers' meeting on the Monday morning. Compared with Dr. Thomas, they are as puddles by the sea. There is the same difference that there is between sewers and rivers, cesspools and springs.

Q. What have you to say to the remarks of the Rev. Dr. Jewett before the Methodist ministers' meeting?

A. I think Dr. Jewett is extremely foolish. I did not say that I would commence suit against a minister for libel. I can hardly conceive of a proceeding that would be less liable to produce a dividend. The fact about it is that the Rev. Mr. Jewett seems to think anything true that he hears against me. Mr. Jewett is probably ashamed of what he said by this time. He must have known it to be entirely false. It seems to me by this time even the most bigoted should lose their confidence in falsehood. Of course, there are times when a falsehood well told bridges over quite a difficulty, but in the long run you had better tell the truth, even if you swim the creek. I am astonished that these ministers were willing to exhibit their wounds to the world. I supposed, of course, I would hit some, but I had no idea of wounding so many.

Q. Mr. Crafts stated that you were in the habit of swearing in company and before your family?

A. I often swear. In other words, I take the name of God in vain; that is to say, I take it without any practical thing resulting from it, and in that sense I think most ministers are guilty of the same thing. I heard an old story of a clergyman who rebuked a neighbor for swearing, to whom the neighbor replied, "You pray and I swear, but as a matter of fact neither of us means anything by it." As to the charge that I am in the habit of using indecent language in my family, no reply is needed. I am willing to leave that question to the people who know us both. Mr. Crafts says he was told this by a lady. This cannot by any possibility be true, for no lady will tell a falsehood. Besides, if this woman of whom he speaks was a lady, how did she happen to stay where obscene language was being used? No lady ever told Mr. Crafts any such thing. It may be that a lady did tell him that I used profane language. I admit that I have not always spoken of the devil in a respectful way; that I have sometimes referred to his residence when it was not a necessary part of the conversation, and that at

17

divers times I have used a good deal of the terminology of the theologian when the exact words of the scientist might have done as well. But if by swearing is meant the use of God's name in vain, there are few preachers who do not swear more than I do, if by "in vain" is meant without any practical result. I leave Mr. Crafts to cultivate the acquaintance of the unknown lady, knowing as I do, that after they have talked this matter over again they will find that both have been mistaken.

I sincerely regret that clergymen who really believe that an infinite God is on their side think it necessary to resort to such things to defeat one man. According to their idea, God is against me, and they ought to have confidence enough in his infinite wisdom and strength to suppose that he could dispose of one man, even if they failed to say a word against me. Had you not asked me I should have said nothing on these topics. Such charges cannot hurt me. I do not believe it possible for such men to injure me. No one believes what they say, and the testimony of such clergymen against an Infidel is no longer considered of value. I believe it was Goethe who said, "I always know that I am traveling when I hear the dogs bark."

Q. Are you going to make a formal reply to their sermons?

A. Not unless something better is done than has been. Of course, I don't know what another Sabbath may bring forth. I am waiting. But of one thing I feel perfectly assured; that no man in the United States, or in the world, can account for the fact, if we are to be saved only by faith in Christ, that Matthew forgot about it, that Luke said nothing about it, and that Mark never mentioned it except in two passages written by *another* person. Until that is answered, as one grave digger says to the other in *Hamlet,* I shall say, "Ay, tell me that and unyoke." In the meantime I wish to keep on the best terms with all parties concerned. I cannot see why my forgiving spirit fails to gain their sincere praise.

— *Chicago Tribune,* Sept. 30, 1880.

INGERSOLL AND BEECHER

The sensation created by the speech of the Rev. Henry Ward Beecher at the Academy of Music, in Brooklyn, when he uttered a brilliant eulogy on Col. Robert G. Ingersoll and publicly shook hands with him has not yet subsided. A portion of the religious world is thoroughly stirred up at what it considers a gross breach of orthodox propriety. This feeling is especially strong among the class of positivists who believe that

> *"An Atheist's laugh's a poor exchange*
> *For deity offended."*

Many believe that Mr. Beecher is at heart in full sympathy and accord with Ingersoll's teachings but has not courage enough to say so at the sacrifice of his pastoral position. The fact that these two men are the very head and front of their respective schools of thought makes the matter an important one. The denouncement of the doctrine of eternal punishment, followed by the scene at the Academy, has about it an aroma of suggestiveness that might work much harm without an explanation. Since Colonel Ingersoll's recent attack on the personnel *of the clergy through the* Shorter Catechism *the pulpit has been remarkably silent regarding the great Atheist. "Is the keen logic and broad humanity of Ingersoll converting the brain and heart of Christendom?" was recently asked. Did the hand that was stretched out to him on the stage of the Academy reach across the chasm which separates orthodoxy from infidelity?*

Desiring to answer the last question if possible, a Herald *reporter visited Mr. Beecher and Colonel Ingersoll to learn their opinion of each other. Neither Of the gentlemen was aware that the other was being interviewed.*

Q. What is your opinion of Mr. Beecher?

A. I regard him as the greatest man in any pulpit of the world. He treated me with a generosity that nothing can exceed. He rose grandly above the prejudices supposed to belong to his class, and acted as only a man could act without a chain on his brain and only kindness in his heart.

I told him that night that I congratulated the world that it had a minister with an intellectual horizon broad enough and a mental sky studded with stars of genius enough to hold all creeds in scorn that shocked the heart of man. I think that Mr. Beecher has liberalized the English-speaking people of the world.

I do not think he agrees with me. He holds to many things that I most passionately deny. But in common, we believe in the liberty of thought.

My principal objections to orthodox religion are two – slavery here and hell hereafter. I do not believe that Mr. Beecher on these points can disagree with me. The real difference between us is he says God, I say nature. The real agreement between us is – we both say – liberty.

Q. What is his forte?

A. He is of a wonderfully poetic temperament. In pursuing any course of thought his mind is like a stream flowing through the scenery of fairyland. The stream murmurs and laughs while the banks grow green and the vines blossom.

His brain is controlled by his heart. He thinks in pictures. With him logic means mental melody. The discordant is the absurd.

For years he has endeavored to hide the dungeon of orthodoxy with the ivy of imagination. Now and then he pulls for a moment the leafy curtain aside and is horrified to see the lizards, snakes, basilisks, and abnormal monsters of the orthodox age, and then he utters a great cry, the protest of a loving, throbbing heart.

He is a great thinker, a marvelous orator, and, in my judgment, greater and grander than any creed of any church.

Besides all this, he treated me like a king. Manhood is his forte, and I expect to live and die his friend.

RELIGION IN POLITICS

Q. How do you regard the religious question in politics?

A. Religion is a personal matter – a matter that each individual soul should be allowed to settle for itself. No man shod in the brogans of impudence should walk into the temple of another's soul. While every man should be governed by the highest possible considerations of the public weal, no one has the right to ask for legal assistance in the support of his particular sect. If Catholics oppose the public schools I would not oppose them because they are Catholics, but because I am in favor of the schools. I regard the public school as the intellectual bread of life. Personally I have no confidence in any religion that can be demonstrated only to children. I suspect all creeds that rely implicitly on mothers and nurses. That religion is the best that commends itself the strongest to men and women of education and genius. After all, the prejudices of infancy and the ignorance of the aged are a poor foundation for any system of morals or faith. I respect every honest man, and I think more of a liberal Catholic than of an illiberal Infidel. The religious question should be left out of politics. You might as well decide questions of art and music by a ward caucus as to govern the longings and dreams of the soul by law. I believe in letting the sun shine whether the weeds grow or not. I can never side with Protestants if they try to put Catholics down by law, and I expect to oppose both of them until religious intolerance is regarded as a crime.

Q. Is the religious movement of which you are the chief exponent spreading?

A. There are ten times as many freethinkers this year as there were last. Civilization is the child of freethought. The new world has drifted away from the rotting wharf of superstition. The politics of this country are being settled by the new ideas of individual liberty; and parties and churches that cannot accept the new truths must perish. I want it perfectly understood that I am not a politician. I believe in liberty and I want to see the time when every man, woman, and child will enjoy every human right.

— *The Evening Express,* New York, Nov. 19, 1880.

MIRACLES AND IMMORTALITY

Q. You have seen some accounts of the recent sermon of Dr. Tyng on "Miracles," I presume, and if so, what is your opinion of the sermon, and also what is your opinion of miracles?

A. From an orthodox standpoint I think the Rev. Dr. Tyng is right. If miracles were necessary 1,800 years ago, before scientific facts enough were known to overthrow hundreds of passages in the Bible, certainly they are necessary now. Dr. Tyng sees clearly that the old miracles are nearly worn out, and that some new ones are absolutely essential. He takes for granted that, if God would do a miracle to found his gospel, he certainly would do some more to preserve it, and that it is in need of preservation about now is evident. I am amazed that the religious world should laugh at him for believing in miracles. It seems to me just as reasonable that the deaf, dumb, blind, and lame should be cured at Lourdes as at Palestine. It certainly is no more wonderful that the law of nature should be broken now than that it was broken several thousand years ago. Dr. Tyng also has this advantage: the witnesses by whom he proves these miracles are alive. An unbeliever can have the opportunity of a cross-examination. Whereas, the miracles in the New Testament are substantiated only by the dead. It is just as reasonable to me that blind people receive their sight in France as that devils were made to vacate human bodies in the holy land.

For one I am exceedingly glad that Dr. Tyng has taken this position. It shows that he is a believer in a personal God, in a God who is attending a little to the affairs of this world, and in a God who did not exhaust his supplies in the apostolic age. It is refreshing to me to find in this scientific age a gentleman who still believes in miracles. My opinion is that all thorough religionists will have to take the ground and admit that a supernatural religion must be supernaturally preserved.

I have been asking for a miracle for several years, and have in a mild, gentle, and loving way taunted the church for not producing a little one. I have had the impudence to ask any number of them to join in a prayer asking anything they desire for the purpose of testing the efficiency of what is known as supplication. They answer me by calling my attention to the miracles recorded in the

22

New Testament. I insist, however, on a new miracle, and, personally, I would like to see one now. Certainly, the Infinite has not lost his power, and certainly the Infinite knows that thousands and hundreds of thousands, if the Bible is true, are now pouring over the precipice of unbelief into the gulf of hell. One little miracle would save thousands. One little miracle in Pittsburgh, well authenticated, would do more good than all the preaching ever heard in this sooty town. The Rev. Dr. Tyng clearly sees this, and he has been driven to the conclusion, first, that God can do miracles; second, that he ought to; third, that he has. In this he is perfectly logical. After a man believes the Bible; after he believes in the flood and in the story of Jonah, certainly he ought not to hesitate at a miracle of today. When I say I want a miracle, I mean by that I want a good one. All the miracles recorded in the New Testament could have been simulated. A fellow could have pretended to be dead, or blind, or dumb, or deaf. I want to see a good miracle. I want to see a man with one leg, and then I want to see the other leg grow out.

I would like to see a miracle like that performed in North Carolina. Two men were disputing about the relative merits of the salve they had for sale. One of the men, in order to demonstrate that his salve was better than any other, cut off a dog's tail and applied a little of the salve to the stump, and, in the presence of the spectators, a new tail grew out. But the other man, who also had salve for sale, took up the piece of tail that had been cast away, put a little salve at the end of that, and a new dog grew out, and the last heard of those parties they were quarreling as to who owned the second dog. Something like that is what I call a miracle.

Q. What do you believe about the immortality of the soul? Do you believe that the spirit lives as an individual after the body is dead?

A. I have said a great many times that it is no more wonderful that we should live again than that we do live. Sometimes I have thought it not quite so wonderful for the reason that we have a start. But on that subject I have not the slightest information. Whether man lives again or not I cannot pretend to say. There may be another world and there may not be. If there is another world we ought to make the best of it after arriving there. If there is not another world, we ought to make the best of this. And since nobody knows, all should be permitted to have their opinions, and my opinion is that nobody knows.

If we take the Old Testament for authority, man is not immortal. The Old Testament shows man how he lost immortality. According to Genesis, God prevented man from putting forth his

23

hand and eating of the tree of life. It is there stated, had he succeeded, man would have lived forever. God drove him from the garden, preventing him eating of this tree, and in consequence man
became mortal; so that if we go by the Old Testament we are compelled to give up immortality. The New Testament has but little on
the subject. In one place we are told to seek for immortality. If we
are already immortal, it is hard to see why we should go on seeking
for it. In another place we are told that they who are worthy to
obtain that world and the resurrection of the dead are not given in
marriage. From this one would infer that there would be some
unworthy to be raised from the dead. On the question of immortality, the Old Testament throws but little satisfactory light. I do not
deny immortality, nor would I endeavor to shake the belief of anybody in another life. What I am endeavoring to do is to put out the
fires of hell. If we cannot have heaven without hell, I am in favor of
abolishing heaven. I do not want to go to heaven if one soul is
doomed to agony. I would rather be annihilated.

My opinion of immortality is this:

First — I live, and that of itself is infinitely wonderful. Second —
There was a time when I was not, and after I was not, I was. Third
— Now that I am, I may be again; and it is no more wonderful that
I may be again, if I have been, than that I am, having once been
nothing. If the churches advocated immortality, if they advocated
eternal justice, if they said that man would be rewarded and punished according to deeds; if they admitted that sometime in eternity there would be an opportunity given to lift up souls, and that
throughout all the ages the angels of progress and virtue would
beckon the fallen upward; and that sometime, and no matter how
far away they might put off the time, all the children of men would
be reasonably happy, I never would say a solitary word against the
church, but just as long as they preach that the majority of
mankind will suffer eternal pain, just so long I shall oppose them;
that is to say, as long as I live.

Q. Do you believe in a God; and, if so, what kind of a God?

A. Let me, in the first place, lay a foundation for an answer.
First — Man gets all food for thought through the medium of the
senses. The effect of nature on the senses and through the senses
on the brain must be natural. All food for thought, then, is natural.
As a consequence of this, there can be no supernatural idea in the
human brain. Whatever idea there is must have been a natural
product. If, then, there is no supernatural idea in the human brain,
then there cannot be in the human brain an idea of the supernatural. If we can have no idea of the supernatural, and if the God of

24

whom you spoke is admitted to be supernatural, then, of course, I can have no idea of him, and I certainly can have no fixed belief on any subject about which I have no idea.

There may be a God for all I know. There may be thousands of them. But the idea of an infinite being outside and independent of nature is inconceivable. I do not know of any word that would explain my doctrine or my views on that subject. I suppose pantheism is as near as I could go. I believe in the eternity of matter and in the eternity of intelligence, but I do not believe in any being outside of nature. I do not believe in any personal deity. I do not believe in any aristocracy of the air. I know nothing about origin or destiny. Between these two horizons I live, whether I wish to or not, and must be satisfied with what I find between these two horizons. I have never heard any God described that I believe in. I have never heard any religion explained that I accept. To make something out of nothing cannot be more absurd than that an infinite intelligence made this world, and proceeded to fill it with crime and want and agony, and then, not satisfied with the evil he had wrought, made a hell in which to consummate the great mistake.

Q. Do you believe that the world and all that is in it came by chance?

A. I do not believe anything comes by chance. I regard the present as the necessary child of a necessary past. I believe matter is eternal; that it has eternally existed and eternally will exist. I believe that in all matter, in some way, there is what we call force; that one of the forms of force is intelligence. I believe that whatever is in the universe has existed from eternity and will forever exist.

Secondly I exclude from my philosophy all ideas of chance. Matter changes eternally its form, never its essence. You cannot conceive of anything being created. No one can conceive of anything existing without a cause or with a cause. Let me explain; a thing is not a cause until an effect has been produced; so that, after all, cause and effect are twins coming into life at precisely the same instant, born of the womb of an unknown mother. The universe is the only fact, and everything that ever has happened, is happening, or will happen, are but the different aspects of the one eternal fact.
— *The Dispatch*, Pittsburgh, Pennsylvania, Dec. 11, 1880.

MR. BEECHER AND MOSES

Q. Mr. Beecher is here. Have you seen him?

A. No, I did not meet Mr. Beecher. Neither did I hear him lecture. The fact is, that long ago I made up my mind that under no circumstances would I attend any lecture or other entertainment given at Lincoln Hall. First, because the hall has been denied me, and secondly, because I regard it as exceedingly unsafe. The hall is up several stories from the ground, and in case of the slightest panic, in my judgment, many lives would be lost. Had it not been for this, and for the fact that the persons owning it imagined that because they had control, the brick and mortar had some kind of holy and sacred quality, and that this holiness is of such a wonderful character that it would not be proper for a man in that hall to tell his honest thoughts, I would have heard him.

Q. Then I assume that you and Mr. Beecher have made up?

A. There is nothing to be made up so far as I know. Mr. Beecher has treated me well, and, I believe, a little too well for his own peace of mind. I have been informed that some members of Plymouth Church felt exceedingly hurt that their pastor should so far forget himself as to extend the right hand of fellowship to one who differs from him on what they consider essential points in theology. You see, I have denied with all my might, a great many times, the infamous doctrine of eternal punishment. I have also had the temerity to suggest that I did not believe that a being of infinite justice and mercy was the author of all that I find in the Old Testament. As, for instance, I have insisted that God never commanded anybody to butcher women or to cut the throats of prattling babes. These orthodox gentlemen have rushed to the rescue of Jehovah by insisting that he did all these horrible things. I have also maintained that God never sanctioned or upheld human slavery; that he never would make one child to own and beat another.

I have also expressed some doubts as to whether this same God ever established the institution of polygamy. I have insisted that that institution is simply infamous; that is destroys the idea of home; that it turns to ashes the most sacred words in our language, and leaves the world a kind of den in which crawl the serpents of selfishness and lust. I have been informed that after Mr. Beecher had treated me kindly a few members of his congregation objected, and really felt ashamed that he had so forgotten himself. After that, Mr. Beecher saw fit to give his ideas of the position I had taken. In this he was not exceedingly kind, nor was his justice conspicuous. But I cared nothing about that, not the least. As I have said before, whenever Mr. Beecher says a good thing I give him credit. Whenever he does an unfair or unjust thing I charge it to the account of his religion. I have insisted, and I still insist, that Mr. Beecher is far better than his creed. I do not believe that he believes in the doctrine of eternal punishment. Neither do I believe that he believes in the literal truth of the Scriptures. And, after all, if the Bible is not true, it is hardly worthwhile to insist on its inspiration. An inspired lie is no better than an uninspired one. If the Bible is true it does not need to be inspired. If it is not true, inspiration does not help it. So that after all it is simply a question of fact. Is it true? I believe Mr. Beecher stated that one of my grievous faults was that I picked out the bad things in the Bible. How an infinitely good and wise God came to put bad things in his book Mr. Beecher does not explain. I have insisted that the Bible is not inspired, and, in order to prove that, have pointed out such passages as I have deemed unworthy to have been written even by a civilized man or a savage. I certainly would not endeavor to prove that the Bible is uninspired by picking out its best passages. I admit that there are many good things in the Bible. The fact that there are good things in it does not prove its inspiration, because there are thousands of other books containing good things, and yet no one claims they are inspired. Shakespeare's works contain a thousand times more good things than the Bible; but no one claims he was an inspired man. It is also true that there are many bad things in Shakespeare – many passages which I wish he had never written. But I can excuse Shakespeare, because he did not rise absolutely above his time. That is to say, he was a man; that is to say, he was imperfect. If anybody claimed now that Shakespeare was actually inspired, that claim would be answered by pointing to certain weak or bad or vulgar passages in his works. But every Christian will say that it is a certain kind of blasphemy to impute vulgarity or weakness to God, as they are all obligated to defend the weak, the bad, and the vulgar, so long as they insist upon the inspiration of the Bible.

Now, I pursued the same course with the Bible that Mr. Beecher has pursued with me. Why did he want to pick out my bad things? Is it possible that he is a kind of vulture that sees only the carrion of another? After all, has he not pursued the same method with me that he blames me for pursuing in regard to the Bible? Of course, he must pursue that method. He could not object to me and then point out passages that were not objectionable. If he found fault he had to find faults in order to sustain his ground. That is exactly what I have done with the Scriptures, nothing more and nothing less. The reason I have thrown away the Bible is that in many places it is harsh, cruel, unjust, coarse, vulgar, atrocious, infamous. At the same time, I admit that it contains many passages of an excellent and splendid character – many good things, wise sayings, and many excellent and just laws.

But I would like to ask this: Suppose there were no passages in the Bible except those upholding slavery, polygamy, and wars of extermination; would anybody then claim that it was the word of God? I would like to ask if there is a Christian in the world who would not be overjoyed to find that every one of these passages was an interpolation? I would also like to ask Mr. Beecher if he would not be greatly gratified to find that after God had written the Bible the devil had got hold of it, and interpolated all the passages about slavery, polygamy, the slaughter of women and babes, and the doctrine of eternal punishment? Suppose, as a matter of fact, the devil did get hold of it; what part of the Bible would Mr. Beecher pick out as having been written by the devil? And if he picks out these passages, could not the devil answer him by saying, "You, Mr. Beecher, are like a vulture, a kind of buzzard, flying through the tainted air of inspiration, and pouncing down on the carrion. Why do you not fly like a dove, and why do you not have the innocent ignorance of the dove, so that you could light on a carcass and imagine that you were surrounded by the perfume of violets?" The fact is that good things in a book do not prove that it is inspired, but the presence of bad things does prove that it is not.

Q. What was the real difficulty between you and Moses, Colonel, a man who has been dead for thousands of years?

A. We never had any difficulty. I have always taken pains to say that Moses had nothing to do with the Pentateuch. Those books, in my judgment, were written several centuries after Moses had become dust in his unknown sepulcher. No doubt Moses was quite a man in his day, if he ever existed at all. Some people say that Moses is exactly the same as "law-giver"; that is to say, as legislature, that is to say as Congress. Imagine somebody in the future as regarding the Congress of the United States as one person! And then imagine that somebody endeavoring to prove that Congress was always consistent. But, whether Moses lived or not makes but little difference to me. I presume he filled the place and did the work that he was compelled to do, and although according to the account God had much to say to him with regard to the making of altars, tongs, snuffers, and candlesticks, there is much left for nature still to tell. Thinking of Moses as a man, admitting that he was above his fellows, that he was in his day and generation a leader, and, in a certain narrow sense, a patriot, that he was the founder of the Jewish people; that he found them barbarians and endeavored to control them by thunder and lightning, and found it necessary to pretend that he was in partnership with the power governing the universe; that he took advantage of their ignorance and fear, just as politicians do now, and as theologians always will, still, I see no evidence that the man Moses was any nearer to God than his descendants, who are still warring against the Philistines in every civilized part of the globe. Moses was a believer in slavery, in polygamy, in wars of extermination, in religious persecution and intolerance, and in almost everything that is now regarded with loathing, contempt, and scorn. The Jehovah of whom he speaks violated or commands the violation of at least nine of the Ten Commandments he gave. There is one thing, however, that can be said of Moses that cannot be said of any person who now insists that he was inspired, and that is, he was in advance of his time. — *Brooklyn Eagle,* Jan. 31, 1881.

HADES, DELAWARE, AND FREETHOUGHT

Q. Now that a lull has come in politics, I thought I would come and see what is going on in the religious world?

A. Well, from what little I learn, there has not been much going on during the last year. There are 526 Congregational churches in Massachusetts, and 200 of these churches have not received a new member for an entire year, and the others have scarcely held their own. In Illinois there are 483 Presbyterian churches, and they have now fewer members than they had in 1879, and of the 483, 183 have not received a single new member for 12 months. A report has been made, under the auspices of the pan-Presbyterian council, to the effect that there are in the whole world about 3,000,000 Presbyterians. This is about one-fifth of one percent of the inhabitants of the world. The probability is that of the 3,000,000 nominal Presbyterians, not more than 200,000 or 300,000 actually believe the doctrine, and of them, not more than 500 or 600 have any true conception of what the doctrine is. As the Presbyterian church has only been able to induce one-fifth of one percent of the people to even call themselves Presbyterians, about how long will it take, at this rate, to convert mankind? The fact is, there seems to be a general lull along the entire line, and just at present little is being done by the orthodox people to keep their fellow-citizens out of hell.

Q. Do you really think that the orthodox people now believe in the old doctrine of eternal punishment, and that they really think there is the kind of hell that our ancestors so carefully described?

A. I am afraid that the old idea is dying out, and that many Christians are slowly giving up the consolations naturally springing from the old belief. Another terrible blow to the infamy is the fact that in the revised New Testament the consoling word "hell" has been left out. I am informed that in the revised New Testament the word "Hades" has been substituted. As nobody knows exactly what "Hades" means, it will not be quite so easy to frighten people at revivals by threatening them with something that they don't clearly understand. After this, when the impassioned orator cries out that all the unconverted will be sent to

30

Hades, the poor sinners, instead of getting frightened, will begin to ask each other what and where that is. It will take many years of preaching to clothe that word in all the terrors and horrors, pains and penalties, and pangs of hell. Hades is a compromise. It is a concession to the philosophy of our day. It is a graceful acknowledgment to the growing spirit of investigation, that hell, after all, is a barbaric mistake. Hades is the death of revivals. It cannot be used in song. It won't rhyme with anything with the same force that hell does. It is altogether more shadowy than hot. It is not associated with brimstone and flame. It sounds somewhat indistinct, somewhat lonesome, a little desolate, but not altogether uncomfortable. For revival purposes, Hades is simply useless, and few conversions will be made in the old way under the revised Testament.

Q. Do you really think that the church is losing ground?

A. I am not, as you probably know, connected with any orthodox organization, and consequently have to rely on them for my information. If they can be believed, the church is certainly in an extremely bad condition. I find that the Rev. Dr. Cuyler, only a few days ago, speaking of the religious condition of Brooklyn – and Brooklyn, you know, has been called the city of churches – stated that the great mass of that Christian city was out of Christ, and that more professing Christians went to the theater than to the prayer meeting. This, certainly, from their standpoint, is a most terrible declaration. Brooklyn, you know, is one of the great religious centers of the world – a city in which nearly all the people are engaged either in delivering or in hearing sermons; a city filled with the editors of religious periodicals; a city of prayer and praise; and yet, while prayer meetings are free, the theaters, with the free list entirely suspended, catch more Christians than the churches; and this happens while all the pulpits thunder against the stage, and the stage remains silent as to the pulpit. At the same meeting in which the Rev. Dr. Cuyler made his astounding statements, the Rev. Mr. Pentecost was the bearer of the happy news that four out of five persons living in the city of Brooklyn were going down to hell with no God and with no hope. If he had read the revised Testament he would have said "Hades," and the effect of the statement would have been entirely lost. If four-fifths of the people of that great city are destined to eternal pain, certainly we cannot depend on churches for the salvation of the world. At the meeting of the Brooklyn pastors they were in doubt as to whether they should depend on further meetings, or on a day of fasting and prayer for the purpose of converting the city.

In my judgment, it would be much better to devise ways and means to keep a good many people from fasting in Brooklyn. If they had more meat, they could get along with less meeting. If fasting would save a city, there are always plenty of hungry folks even in that Christian town. The real trouble with the church of today is that it is behind the intelligence of the people. Its doctrines no longer satisfy the brains of the 19th century; and if the church proposes to hold its power, it must lose its superstitions. The day of revivals is gone. Only the ignorant and unthinking can hereafter be impressed by hearing the orthodox creed. Fear has in it no reformatory power, and the more despicable and contemptible the doctrine of eternal misery will become. The tendency of the age is toward intellectual liberty, toward personal investigation. Authority is no longer taken for truth. People are beginning to find that all the great and good are not dead – that some good people are alive, and that the demonstrations of today are fully equal to the mistaken theories of the past.

Q. How are you getting along with Delaware?

A. First rate. You know I have been wondering where Comegys came from, and at last I have made the discovery. I was told the other day by a gentleman from Delaware that many years ago Colonel Hazelitt died; that Colonel Hazelitt was an old Revolutionary officer, and that when they were digging his grave they dug up Comegys. Back of that no one knows anything of his history. The only thing they know about him certainly is, that he has never changed one of his views since he was found, and that he never will. I am inclined to think, however, that he lives in a community congenial to him. For instance, I saw in a paper the other day that within a radius of 30 miles around Georgetown, Delaware, there are about 200 orphan and friendless children, These children, it seems, were indentured to Delaware farmers by the managers of orphan asylums and other public institutions in and about Philadelphia. It is stated in the paper that:

> Many of these farmers are rough taskmasters, and if a boy fails to perform the work of an adult, he is almost certain to be cruelly treated, half-starved, and in the coldest weather wretchedly clad. If he does the work, his life is not likely to be much happier, for as a rule he will receive more kicks than candy. The result in either case is almost certain to be wrecked constitutions, dwarfed bodies, rounded

32

shoulders, and limbs crippled or rendered useless by frost or rheumatism. The principal diet of these boys is cornpone. A few days ago, Constable W. H. Johnston went to the house of Reuben Taylor, and on entering the sitting room his attention was attracted by the moans of its only occupant, a little colored boy, who was lying on the hearth in front of the fireplace. The boy's head was covered with ashes from the fire, and he did not pay the slightest attention to the visitor, until Johnston asked what made him cry. Then the little fellow sat up and drawing an old rag off his foot said, 'Look there.' The sight that met Johnston's eye was horrible beyond description. The poor boy's feet were so horribly frozen that the flesh had dropped off the toes until the bones protruded. The flesh on the sides, bottoms and tops of his feet was swollen until the skin cracked in many places, and the inflamed flesh was sloughing off in great flakes. The frostbitten flesh extended to his knees, the joints of which were terribly inflamed. The right one had already begun suppurating. This poor little black boy, covered with nothing but a cotton shirt, drilling pants, a pair of nearly worn out brogans and a battered old hat, on the morning of December 30th, the coldest day of the season, when the mercury was 17 degrees below zero, in the face of a driving snow storm, was sent half a mile from home to protect his master's unshucked corn from the depredations of marauding cows and crows. He remained standing around in the snow until 4 o'clock, then he drove the cows home, received a piece of cold corn pone, and was sent out in the snow again to chop stove wood till dark. Having no bed, he slept that night in front of the fireplace, with his frozen feet buried in the ashes. Dr. C. H. Richards found it necessary to cut off the boy's feet as far back as the ankle and the instep."

This was but one case in several. Personally, I have no doubt that Mr. Reuben Taylor entirely agrees with Chief Justice Comegys on the great question of blasphemy, and probably nothing would so gratify Mr. Reuben Taylor as to see some man in a Delaware jail for the crime of having expressed an honest thought. No wonder that in the state of Delaware the Christ of intellectual liberty has been crucified between the pillory and the whipping post. Of course, I know that there are thousands of most excellent people in that state – people who believe in intellectual liberty, and who only need a little help – and I am doing what I can in that direction – to repeal the laws that now disgrace the statute book of that little commonwealth. I have seen many people from that state lately who really wish that Colonel Hazelitt had never died.

Q. What has the press generally said with regard to the action of Judge Comegys? Do they, so far as you know, justify his charge?

A. A great many papers having articles on the subject have been sent to me. A few of the religious papers seem to think that the judge did the best he knew, and there is one secular paper called the *Evening News,* published at Chester, Pennsylvania, that thinks "that the rebuke from so high a source of authority will have a most excellent effect, and will check religious blasphemers from parading their immoral creeds before the people." The editor of this paper should at once emigrate to the state of Delaware, where he properly belongs. He is either a native of Delaware, or most of his subscribers are citizens of that country; or, it may be that he is a lineal descendant of some Hessian who deserted during the Revolutionary War. Most of the newspapers in the United States are advocates of mental freedom. Probably nothing on earth has been so potent for good as an untrammeled, fearless press. Among the papers of importance there is not a solitary exception. No leading journal in the United States can be found on the side of intellectual slavery. Of course, a few rural sheets edited by gentlemen, as Mr. Greeley would say, "whom God in his inscrutable wisdom had allowed to exist," may be found on the other side, and may be small enough, weak enough and mean enough to pander to the lowest and basest prejudices of their most ignorant subscribers. These editors disgrace their profession and exert about the same influence on the heads as on the pockets of their subscribers – that is to say, they get little and give less.

Q. Do you not think after all, the people who are in favor of having you arrested for blasphemy are acting in accordance with the real spirit of the Old and New Testament?

A. Of course, they act in exact accordance with many of the commands in the Old Testament, and in accordance with several passages in the New. At the same time, it may be said that they violate passages in both. If the Old Testament is true, and if it is the inspired word of God, of course, an Infidel ought not to be allowed to live; and if the New Testament is true, an unbeliever should not be permitted to speak. There are many passages, though, in the New Testament that should protect even an Infidel. Among them this: "Do unto others as ye would that others should do unto you." But that is a passage that has probably had as little effect on the church as any other in the Bible. So far as I am concerned, I am willing to adopt that passage, and I am willing to extend to every other human being every right that I claim for myself. If the churches would act on this principle, if they would say every soul, every mind, may think and investigate for itself;

and around all, and over all shall be thrown the sacred shield of liberty, I should be on their side.

Q. How do you stand with the clergymen, and what is their opinion of you and of your views?

A. Most of them envy me; envy my independence; envy my success; think that I ought to starve; that the people should not hear me; say that I do what I do for money, for popularity; that I am actuated by hatred of all that is good and tender and holy in human nature; think that I wish to tear down the churches, destroy all morality and goodness, and usher in the reign of crime and chaos. They know that shepherds are unnecessary in the absence of wolves, and it is to their interest to convince their sheep that they, the sheep, need protection. This they are willing to give them for half the wool. No doubt, most of these ministers are honest and are doing what they consider their duty. Be this as it may, they feel the power slipping from their hands. They know that they are not held in the estimation they once were. They know that the idea is slowly growing that they are not absolutely necessary for the protection of society. They know that the intellectual world cares little for what they say, and that the great tide of human progress flows on careless of their help or hindrance. So long as they insist on the inspiration of the Bible, they are compelled to take the ground that slavery was once a divine institution; they are forced to defend cruelties that would shock the heart of a savage, and besides, they are bound to teach the eternal horror of everlasting punishment.

They poison the minds of children; they deform the brain and pollute the imagination by teaching the frightful and infamous dogma of endless misery. Even the laws of Delaware shock the enlightened public of today. In that state they simply fine and imprison a man for expressing his honest thoughts; and yet, if the churches are right, God will damn a man forever for the same offense. The brain and heart of our time cannot be satisfied with the ancient creeds. The Bible must be revised again. Most of the creeds must be blotted out. Humanity must take the place of theology. Intellectual liberty must stand in every pulpit. There must be freedom in all the pews, and every human soul must have the right to express its honest thought. — *Brooklyn Eagle*, Mar. 19, 1881.

A REPLY TO THE REV. MR. LANSING

Rev. Isaac J. Lansing of Meriden, Connecticut, recently denounced Col. Robert G. Ingersoll from the pulpit of the Meriden Methodist church, and had the Opera House closed against him. This led a Union reporter to show Colonel Ingersoll what Mr. Lansing had said and to interrogate him with the following result.

Q. Did you favor the sending of obscene matter through the mails as alleged by the Rev. Mr. Lansing?

A. Of course not, and no honest man ever thought that I did. This charge is too malicious and silly to be answered. Mr. Lansing knows better. He has made this charge many times and he will make it again.

Q. Is it a fact that there are thousands of clergymen in the country whom you would fear to meet in fair debate?

A. No; the fact is I would like to meet them all in one. The pulpit is not burdened with genius. There are a few great men engaged in preaching but they are not orthodox. I cannot conceive that a freethinker has anything to fear from the pulpit, except misrepresentation. Of course, there are thousands of ministers too small to discuss with – ministers who stand for nothing in the church – and with such clergymen I cannot afford to discuss anything. If the Presbyterians, or the Congregationalists, or the Methodists would select some man and endorse him as their champion, I would like to meet him in debate. Such a man I will pay to discuss with me. I will give him most excellent wages, and pay all the expenses of the discussion besides. There is but one safe course for ministers – they must assert. They must declare. They must swear to it and stick to it, but they must not try to reason.

Q. You have never seen Rev. Mr. Lansing. To the people of Meriden and thereabouts he is well-known. Judging from what has been told you of his utterances and actions, what kind of a man would you take him to be?

A. I would take him to be a Christian. He talks like one, and he acts like one. If Christianity is right, Lansing is right. If salvation depends on belief, and if unbelievers are to be eternally damned, then an Infidel has no right to speak. He should not be allowed to murder the souls of his fellow men. Lansing does the best he knows how. He thinks that God hates an unbeliever, and he tries to act like God. Lansing knows that he must have the right to slander a man whom God is to eternally damn.

Q. Mr. Lansing speaks of you as a wolf coming with fangs sharpened by $300 a night to tear the lambs of his flock. What do you say to that?

A. All I have to say is that I often get three times that amount, and sometimes much more. I guess his lambs can take care of themselves. I am not fond of mutton anyway. Such talk Mr. Lansing ought to be ashamed of. The idea that he is a shepherd – that he is on guard – is simply preposterous. He has few sheep in his congregation that know as little on the wolf question as he does. He ought to know that his sheep support him – his sheep protect him; and without the sheep poor Lansing would be devoured by the wolves himself.

Q. Shall you sue the Opera House management for breach of contract?

A. I guess not; but I may pay Lansing something for advertising my lecture. I suppose Mr. Wilcox (who controls the Opera House) did what he thought was right. I hear that he is a good man. He probably got a little frightened and began to think about the day of judgment. He could not help it, and I cannot help laughing at him.

Q. Those in Meriden who most strongly oppose you are radical Republicans. Is it not a fact that you possess the confidence and friendship of some of the most respected leaders of that party?

A. I think that all the respectable ones are friends of mine. I am a Republican because I believe in the liberty of the body, and I am an infidel because I believe in the liberty of the mind. There is no need of freeing cages. Let us free the birds. If Mr. Lansing knew me, he would be a great friend. He would probably annoy me by the frequency and length of his visits.

Q. During the recent presidential campaign did any clergymen denounce you for your teachings, that you are aware of?

A. Some did, but they would not if they had been running for office on the Republican ticket.

Q. What is most needed in our public men?

A. Hearts and brains.

Q. Would people be any more moral solely because of a disbelief in orthodox teaching and in the Bible as an inspired book, in your opinion?

A. Yes; if a man really believes that God once upheld slavery; that he commanded soldiers to kill women and babes; that he believed in polygamy; that he persecuted for opinion's sake; that he will punish forever, and that he hates an unbeliever, the effect in my judgment will be bad. It always has been bad. This belief built the dungeons of the Inquisition. This belief made the Puritan murder the Quaker, and this belief has raised the devil with Mr. Lansing.

Q. Do you believe there will ever be a millennium, and if so how will it come about?

A. It will probably start in Meriden, as I have been informed that Lansing is going to leave. — *The Sunday Union,* New Haven, Connecticut, April 10, 1881.

BEACONFIELD, LENT AND REVIVALS

Q. What have you to say about the attack of Dr. Buckley on you and your lecture?

A. I never heard of Dr. Buckley until after I had lectured in Brooklyn. He seems to think that it was extremely ill bred in me to deliver a lecture on the *Liberty of Man, Woman, and Child* during Lent. Lent is just as good as any other part of the year, and no part can be too good to do good. It was not a part of my object to hurt the feelings of the Episcopalians and Catholics. If they think that there is some subtle relation between hunger and heaven, or that faith depends on, or is strengthened by famine, or that veal, during Lent, is the enemy of virtue, or that beef breeds blasphemy, while fish feeds faith – of course, all this is nothing to me. They have a right to say that vice depends on victuals, sanctity on soup, religion on rice, and chastity on cheese; but they have no right to say that a lecture on liberty is an insult to them because they are hungry. I suppose that Lent was instituted in memory of the Savior's fast. At one time it was supposed that only a divine being could live forty days without food. This supposition has been overthrown.

It has been demonstrated by Dr. Tanner to be utterly without foundation. What possible good did it do the world for Christ to go without food for forty days? Why should we follow such an example? As a rule, hungry people are cross, contrary, obstinate, peevish, and unpleasant. A good dinner puts a man at peace with all the world – makes him generous, good natured, and happy. He feels like kissing his wife and children. The future looks bright. He wants to help the needy. The good in him predominates, and he wonders that any man was ever stingy or cruel. Your good cook is a civilizer, and without good food, well prepared, intellectual progress is simply impossible. Most of the orthodox creeds were born of bad cooking. Bad food produced dyspepsia, and dyspepsia produced Calvinism, and Calvinism is the cancer of Christianity. Oatmeal is responsible for the worst features of Scottish Presbyterianism. Half-cooked beans account for the religion of the Puritans. Lent is a mistake, fasting is a blunder, and bad cooking is a crime.

Q. It is stated that you went to Brooklyn while Beecher and Talmage were holding revivals, and that you did so for the purpose of breaking them up. How is this?

A. I had not the slightest idea of interfering with the revivals. They amounted to nothing. They were not alive enough to be killed. Surely one lecture could not destroy two revivals. Still, I think that if all the persons engaged in the revivals had spent the same length of time in cleaning the streets, the good result would have been more apparent. The truth is that the old way of converting people will have to be abandoned. The Americans are getting hard to scare, and a revival without the "scare" is scarcely worth holding. Such maniacs as Hammond and the "boy preacher" fill asylums and terrify children. After saying what he has about hell, Mr. Beecher ought to know that he is not the man to conduct a revival. A revival sermon with hell left out – with the brimstone gone – with the worm that never dies, dead, and the devil absent – is the broadest farce. Mr. Talmage believes in the ancient way. With him hell is a burning reality. He can hear the shrieks and groans. He is of that order of mind that rejoices in these things. If he could only convince others, he would be a great revivalist. He cannot terrify, he astonishes. He is the clown of the horrible – one of Jehovah's jesters. I am not responsible for the revival failure in Brooklyn. I wish I were. I would have the happiness of knowing that I had been instrumental in preserving the sanity of my fellow men.

Q. How do you account for these attacks?

A. It was not so much what I said that excited the wrath of the reverend gentlemen as the fact that I had a great house. They contrasted their failure with my success. The fact is the people are getting tired of the old ideas. They are beginning to think for themselves. Eternal punishment seems to them like eternal revenge. They see that Christ could not atone for the sins of others; that belief ought not to be rewarded and honest doubt punished forever; that good deeds are better than bad creeds, and that liberty is the rightful heritage of every soul.

Q. Were you an admirer of Lord Beaconsfield?

A. In some respects. He was on our side during the war, and gave it as his opinion that the Union would be preserved. Mr. Gladstone congratulated Jefferson Davis on having founded a new nation. I shall never forget Beaconsfield for his kindness, nor Gladstone for his malice. Beaconsfield was an intellectual gymnast, a political athlete, one of the most adroit men in the world.

40

In spite of the prejudices of 1,800 years, he rose to the highest position that can be occupied by a citizen. During his administration England again became a Continental power and played her game of European chess. I have never regarded Beaconsfield as a man controlled by principles, or by his heart. He was strictly a politician. He always acted as though he thought the clubs were looking at him. He knew all the arts belonging to his trade. He would have succeeded anywhere, if by "succeeding" is meant the attainment of position and power. But after all, such men are splendid failures. They give themselves and others a great deal of trouble – they wear the tinsel crown of temporary success and then fade from public view. They astonish the pit, they gain the applause of the galleries, but when the curtain falls there is nothing left to benefit mankind. Beaconsfield held convictions somewhat in contempt. He had the imagination of the East united with the ambition of an Englishman. With him, to succeed was to have done right.

Q. What do you think of him as an author?

A. Most of his characters are like himself – puppets moved by the string of self-interest. The men are adroit, the women mostly heartless. They catch each other with false bait. They have great worldly wisdom. Their virtue and vice are mechanical. They have hearts like clocks filled with wheels and springs. The author winds them up. In his novels Disraeli allows us to enter the green-room of his heart. We see the ropes, the pulleys and the old masks. In all things, in politics and in literature, he was cold, cunning, accurate, able, and successful. His books will, in a little while, follow their author to their grave. After all, the good will live the longest. — *Brooklyn Eagle,* April 24, 1881.

ANSWERING THE NEW YORK MINISTERS

Ever since Colonel Ingersoll began the delivery of his lecture called The Great Infidels, *the ministers of the country have made him the subject of special attack. One week ago last Sunday the majority of the leading ministers in New York made replies to Ingersoll's latest lecture. What he has to say to these replies will be found in a report of an interview with Colonel Ingersoll. No man is harder to pin down for a long talk than the Colonel. He is so beset with visitors and eager office seekers anxious for his help that he can hardly find five minutes unoccupied during an entire day. Through the shelter of a private room and the guardianship of a stout colored servant, the Colonel was able to escape the crowd of seekers after his personal charity long enough to give him time to answer some of the ministerial arguments advanced against him in New York.*

Q. Have you seen the attacks made on you by certain ministers of New York, published in the *Herald* last Sunday?

A. Yes, I read, or heard read, what was in Monday's *Herald*. I do not know that you could call them attacks. They are substantially a repetition of what the pulpit has been saying for a great many years, and what the pulpit will say just so long as men are paid for suppressing a truth and for defending superstition. One of these gentlemen tells the lambs of his flock that 3,000 men and a few women – probably with quite an emphasis on the word "few" – gave $1 each to hear their maker cursed and their Savior ridiculed. Probably nothing is so hard for the average preacher to bear as the fact that people are not only willing to hear the other side, but absolutely anxious to pay for it. The dollar that these people paid hurt their feelings vastly more than what was said after they were in. Of course, it is a frightful commentary on the average intellect of the pulpit that a minister cannot get so large an audience when he preaches for nothing, as an Infidel can draw at a dollar a head. If I depended on a contribution box, or on passing a saucer that would come back to the stage enriched with a few 5¢ pieces, eight or ten dimes, and a lonesome quarter, these

42

gentlemen would, in all probability, imagine infidelity was not to be feared.

The churches were all open on that Sunday, and all could go who desired. Yet they were not full, and the pews were nearly as empty of people as the pulpit of ideas. The truth is the story is growing old, the ideas somewhat moss-covered, and everything has a wrinkled and withered appearance. This gentleman says that these people went to hear their maker cursed and their Savior ridiculed. Is it possible that in a city where so many steeples pierce the air, and hundreds of sermons are preached every Sunday, there are 3,000 men, and a few women, so anxious to hear "their maker cursed and their Savior ridiculed" that they are willing to pay a dollar each? The gentleman knew that nobody cursed anybody's maker. He knew that the statement was utterly false and without the slightest foundation. He also knew that nobody had ridiculed the Savior of anybody, but, on the contrary, that I had paid a greater tribute to the character of Jesus Christ than any minister in New York has the capacity to do. Certainly it is not cursing the maker of anybody to say that the God described in the Old Testament is not the real God. Certainly it is not cursing God to declare that the real God never sanctioned slavery or polygamy, or commanded wars of extermination, or told a husband to separate from his wife if she differed with him in religion. The people who say these things of God – if there is any God at all – do what little there is in their power, unwittingly of course, to destroy his reputation. But I have done something to rescue the reputation of the deity from the slanders of the pulpit. If there is any God, I expect to find myself credited on the heavenly books for my defense of him. I did say that our civilization is due not to piety, but to infidelity. I did say that every great reformer had been denounced as an Infidel in his day and generation. I did say that Christ was an Infidel, and that he was treated in his day much as the orthodox preachers treat an honest man now. I did say that he was tried for blasphemy and crucified by bigots. I did say that he hated and despised the church of his time, and that he denounced the most pious people of Jerusalem as thieves and vipers. And I suggest that should he come again he might have occasion to repeat the remarks that he then made. At the same time I admitted that there are thousands and thousands of Christians who are exceedingly good people. I never did pretend that the fact that a man was a Christian even tended to show that he was a bad man.

Neither have I ever insisted that the fact that a man is an Infidel even tends to show what, in other respects, his character is. But I always have said, and I always expect to say, that a Christian who does not believe in absolute intellectual liberty is a curse to mankind, and an Infidel who does believe in absolute intellectual liberty is a blessing to this world. We cannot expect all Infidels to be good, nor all Christians to be bad, and we might make some mistakes even if we selected these people ourselves. It is admitted by the Christians that Christ made a great mistake when he selected Judas. This was a mistake of over eight percent.

Chaplain Newman takes pains to compare some great Christians with some great Infidels. He compares Washington with Julian, and insists, I suppose, that Washington was a great Christian. Certainly he is not familiar with the history of Washington, or he never would claim that he was particularly distinguished in his day for what is generally known as vital piety. That he went through the ordinary forms of Christianity nobody disputes. That he listened to sermons without paying any particular attention to them, no one will deny. Julian, of course, was somewhat prejudiced against Christianity, but that he was one of the greatest men of antiquity no one acquainted with the history of Rome can honestly dispute. When he was made emperor he found at the palace hundreds of gentlemen who acted as barbers, hair-combers, and brushers for the emperor. He dismissed them all, remarking that he was able to wash himself. These dismissed office-holders started the story that he was dirty in his habits, and a minister of the 19th century was found silly enough to believe the story. Another thing that probably got him into disrepute in that day – he had no private chaplains. As a matter of fact, Julian was forced to pretend that he was a Christian in order to save his life. The Christians of that day were of such a loving character that any man who differed with them was forced to either fall a victim to their ferocity or seek safety in subterfuge. The real crime that Julian committed, and the only one that has burned itself into the very heart and conscience of the Christian world, is that he transferred the revenues of Christian churches to heathen priests. Whoever stands between a priest and his salary will find that he has committed the unpardonable sin commonly known as the sin against the Holy Ghost.

This gentleman also compares Luther with Voltaire. If he will read the life of Luther by Lord Brougham, he will find that in his ordinary conversation he was exceedingly low and vulgar, and that no respectable English publisher could be found who would soil paper with the translation. If he will take the pains to read an essay by Macaulay, he will find that twenty years after the death of Luther there were more Catholics than when he was born, and that twenty years after the death of Voltaire there were millions less than when he was born. If he will take just a few moments to think, he will find that the last victory of Protestantism was won in Holland; that there has never been one since, and will never be another. If he would really like to think, and enjoy for a few moments the luxury of having an idea, let him ponder for a little while over the instructive fact that languages having their root in the Latin have generally been spoken in Catholic countries; and that those languages having their root in the ancient German are now mostly spoken by people of Protestant proclivities. It may occur to him, after thinking of this a while, that there is something deeper in the question than he has as yet perceived. Luther's last victory, as I said before, was in Holland; but the victory of Voltaire goes on from day to day. Protestantism is not holding its own with Catholicism, even in the United States. I saw the other day the statistics, I believe, of the city of Chicago, showing that, while the city had increased 200 or 300 percent, Protestantism had lagged behind at the rate of 12 percent. I am willing, for one, to have the whole question depend on a comparison of the worth and work of Voltaire and Luther. It may be, too, that the gentleman forgot to tell us that Luther himself gave consent to a person high in office to have two wives, but prudently suggested to him that he had better keep it as still as possible. Luther was, also, a believer in a personal devil. He thought that deformed children had been begotten by an evil spirit. On one occasion he told a mother that, in his judgment, she had better drown her child; that he had no doubt the devil was its father. This same Luther made this observation: "Universal toleration is universal error, and universal error is universal hell." From this you will see that he was an exceedingly good man, but mistaken on many questions. So, too, he laughed at the Copernican system, and wanted to know if these fool astronomers could undo the work of God. He probably knew as little about science as the reverend gentleman does about history.

Q. Does he compare any other Infidels with Christians?

A. Oh, yes; he compares Lord Bacon with Diderot. I have never claimed that Diderot was a saint. I have simply insisted that he was a great man; that he was grand enough to say that "incredulity is the beginning of philosophy"; that he had sense enough to know that the God described by the Catholics and Protestants of his day was simply an impossible monster; and that he also had the brain to see that the little selfish heaven occupied by a few monks and nuns and idiots that they had fleeced, was hardly worth going to; in other words, that he was a man of common sense, greatly in advance of his time, and that he did what he could to increase the sum of human enjoyment to the end that there might be more happiness in this world.

The gentleman compares him with Lord Bacon, and yet, if he will read the trials of that day – I think in the year 1620, he will find that the Christian Lord Bacon, the pious Lord Bacon, was charged with receiving pay for his opinions, and, in some instances, pay from both sides; that the Christian Lord Bacon, at first on his honor as a Christian Lord, denied the whole business; that afterward the Christian Lord Bacon, on his honor as a Christian Lord, admitted the truth of the whole business, and that, therefore, the Christian Lord Bacon was convicted and sentenced to pay a fine of 40,000 pounds, and rendered infamous and incapable of holding office. Now, understand me, I do not think Bacon took bribes because he was a Christian, because there have been many Christian judges perfectly honest; but, if the statement of the reverend gentleman of New York is true, his being a Christian did not prevent his taking bribes. And right here allow me to thank the gentleman with all my heart for having spoken of Lord Bacon in this connection. I have always admired the genius of Bacon, and have always thought of his fall with an aching heart, and would not now have spoken of his crime had not his character been flung in my face by a gentleman who asks his God to kill me for having expressed my honest thought.

The same gentleman compares Newton with Spinoza. In the first place, there is no ground of parallel. Newton was a very great man and a justly celebrated mathematician. As a matter of fact, he is not celebrated for having discovered the law of gravitation. That was known for thousands of years before he was born; and if the reverend gentleman would read a little more he would find that Newton's discovery was not that there is such a law of gravitation, but that bodies attract each other "with a force proportional directly to the quantity of matter they contain, and inversely to the squares of their distances." I do not think he made the discoveries on account of his Christianity. Laplace was certainly in many respects as great a mathematician and astronomer, but he was not a Christian.

Descartes was certainly not much inferior to Newton as a mathematician, and thousands insist that he was his superior; yet he was not a Christian. Euclid, if I remember right, was not a Christian, and yet he had quite a turn for mathematics. As a matter of fact, Christianity got its idea of algebra from the Mohammedans, and, without algebra, astronomical knowledge of today would have been impossible. Christianity did not even invent figures. We got those from the Arabs. The very word "algebra" is Arabic. The decimal system, I believe, however, was due to a German, but whether he was a Christian or not, I do not know.

We find that the Chinese calculated eclipses long before Christ was born; and, exactness being the rule at that time, there is an account of two astronomers having been beheaded for failing to tell the coming of an eclipse to the minute; yet they were not Christians. There is another fact connected with Newton, and that is that he wrote a commentary on the book of Revelation. The probability is that a sillier commentary was never written. It was so perfectly absurd and laughable that someone – I believe it was Voltaire – said that while Newton had excited the envy of the intellectual world by his mathematical accomplishments, it had gotten even with him the moment his commentaries were published. Spinoza was not a mathematician, particularly. He was a metaphysician, an honest thinker, whose influence is felt and will be felt so long as these great questions have the slightest interest for the human brain.

He also compares Chalmers with Hume. Chalmers gained his notoriety from preaching what are known as the astronomical sermons, and, I suppose, was quite a preacher in his day.

But Hume was a thinker, and his works will live for ages after Mr. Chalmers' sermons will have been forgotten. Mr. Chalmers has never been prominent enough to have been well known by many people. He may have been an exceedingly good man, and derived, during his life, great consolation from a belief in the damnation of infants.

Mr. Newman also compares Wesley with Thomas Paine. When Thomas Paine was in favor of human liberty, Wesley was against it. Thomas Paine wrote a pamphlet called *Common Sense*, urging the colonies to separate themselves from Great Britain. Wesley wrote a treatise on the other side. He was the enemy of human liberty; and if his advice could have been followed we would have been the colonies of Great Britain still. We never would have had a president in need of a private chaplain. Mr. Wesley had not a scientific mind. He preached a sermon once on the cause and cure of earthquakes, taking the ground that earthquakes were caused by sins, and that the only way to stop them was to believe on the Lord Jesus Christ. He also laid down some excellent rules for rearing children, that is, from a Methodist standpoint. His rules amounted to about this:

> *First.* Never give them what they want.
> *Second.* Never give them what you intend to give them, at the time they want it.
> *Third.* Break their wills at the earliest possible moment.

Mr. Wesley made every family an inquisition, every father and mother inquisitors, and all the children helpless victims. One of his homes would give an exceedingly vivid idea of hell.

At the same time, Mr. Wesley was a believer in witches and wizards, and knew all about the devil. At his request God performed many miracles. On several occasions he cured his horse of lameness. On others, dissipated Mr. Wesley's headaches. Now and then he put off rain on account of a camp meeting, and at other times stopped the wind blowing at the special request of Mr. Wesley. I have no doubt that Mr. Wesley was honest in all this – just as honest as he was mistaken. And I also admit that he was the founder of a church that does extremely well in new countries, and that thousands of Methodists have been exceedingly good men. But I deny that he ever did anything for human liberty. While Mr. Wesley was fighting the devil and giving his experience with witches and wizards, Thomas Paine helped to found a free nation, helped to enrich the air with another flag. Wesley was right on one thing, though. He was opposed to slavery, and, I believe, called it the sum of all villainies. I have always been obliged to him for that. I do not think he said it because he was a Methodist; but Methodism, as he understood it, did not prevent his saying it, and Methodism as others understood it, did not prevent men from being slaveholders, did not prevent them from selling babes from mothers, and in the name of God beating the naked back of toil. I think, on the whole, Paine did more for the world than Mr. Wesley. The difference between an average Episcopalian is not worth quarreling about. But the difference between a man who believes in despotism and one who believes in liberty is almost infinite. Wesley changed Episcopalians into Methodists; Paine turned lickspittles into men. Let it be understood, once for all, that I have never claimed that Paine was perfect. I was glad that the reverend gentleman admitted that he was a patriot and the foe of tyrants: that he sympathized with the oppressed, and befriended the helpless; that he favored religious toleration, and that he weakened the power of the Catholic Church. I am glad that he made these admissions. Whenever it can be truthfully said of a man that he loved his country, hated tyranny, sympathized with the oppressed, and befriended the helpless, nothing more is necessary. If God can afford to damn such a man, such a man can afford to be damned. While Paine was the foe of tyrants, Christians were the tyrants. When he sympathized with the oppressed, the oppressed were the victims of Christians. Paine never founded an Inquisition; never tortured a human being; never hoped that anybody's tongue would be paralyzed, and was always opposed to private chaplains.

It might be well for the reverend gentleman to continue his comparisons, and find eminent Christians to put, for instance, along with Humboldt, the Shakespeare of science; somebody by the side of Darwin, as a naturalist; some gentleman in England to stand with Tyndall, or Huxley; some Christian German to stand with Haeckel and Helmholtz. Maybe he knows some Christian statesman that he would compare with Gambetta. I would advise him to continue his parallels.

Q. What have you to say of the Rev. Dr. Fulton?

A. The Rev. Dr. Fulton is a great friend of mine. I am extremely sorry to find that he still believes in a personal devil, and I greatly regret that he imagines that this devil has so much power that he can take possession of a human being and deprive God of their services. It is in sorrow and not in anger that I find that he still believes in this ancient superstition. I also regret that he imagines that I am leading young men to eternal ruin. It occurs to me that if there is an infinite God, he ought not to allow anybody to lead young men to eternal ruin. If anything I have said, or am going to say, has a tendency to lead young men to eternal ruin, I hope that if there is a God with the power to prevent me, he will use it. Dr. Fulton admits that in politics I am on the right side. I presume he makes this concession because he is a Republican. I am in favor of universal education, of absolute intellectual liberty. I am in favor, also, of equal rights to all. As I have said before we have spent millions and millions of dollars and rivers of blood to free the bodies of men; in other words, we have been freeing the cages. My proposition now is to give a little liberty to the birds. I am not willing to stop where a man can simply reap the fruit of his hand. I wish him, also, to enjoy the liberty of his brain. I am not against any truth in the New Testament. I did say that I objected to religion because it made enemies and not friends. The Rev. Dr. says that is one reason why he likes religion. Dr. Fulton tells me that the Bible is the gift of God to man. He also tells me that the Bible is true and that God is its author. If the Bible is true and God is its author, then God was in favor of slavery 4,000 years ago. He was also in favor of polygamy and religious intolerance. In other words, 4,000 years ago he occupied the exact position the devil is supposed to occupy now. If the Bible teaches anything it teaches man to enslave his brother, that is to say, if his brother is a heathen. The God of the Bible always hated heathens. Dr. Fulton also says that the Bible is the basis of all law. Yet, if the legislature of New York would reenact next winter the Mosaic code, the members might consider themselves lucky if they were not hung on their return home. Probably Dr. Fulton thinks that had it not been for the Ten Commandments, nobody would ever have thought that stealing was wrong. I have always had an idea that men objected to stealing because the industrious did not wish to support the idle; and I have a notion that there has always been a law against murder because a large majority of people have always objected to being murdered. If he will read his Old Testament with care, he will find that God violated most of his own commandments – all except that "Thou shalt worship no other God before me," and, maybe, the commandment against work on the Sabbath day. With these two exceptions I am satisfied that God himself violated all the rest. He told his chosen people to rob the Gentiles; that violated the commandment against stealing. He said himself that he had sent out lying spirits; that certainly was a violation of another commandment. He ordered soldiers to kill men, women, and babes; that was a violation of another. He also told them to divide the maidens among the soldiers; that was a substantial violation of another. One of the commandments was that you should not covet your neighbor's property. In that commandment you will find that a man's wife is put on an equality with his ox. Yet his chosen people were allowed not only to covet the property of the Gentiles, but to take it. If Dr. Fulton will read a little more, he will find that all the good laws in the Decalogue had been in force in Egypt a century before Moses was born. He will find that like laws and many better ones were in force in India and China, long before Moses knew what a bulrush was. If he will think a little while, he will find that one of the Ten Commandments, the one on the subject of graven images, was bad. The result of that was that Palestine never produced a painter, or a sculptor, and that no Jew became famous in art until long after the destruction of Jerusalem. A commandment that robs a people of painting and statuary is not a good one. The idea of the Bible being the basis of law is almost too silly to be seriously refuted. I admit that I did say that Shakespeare was the greatest man who ever lived; and Dr. Fulton says in regard to this statement, "What foolishness!" He then proceeds to insult his audience by telling them that while many of them have copies of Shakespeare's works in their houses, they have not read twenty pages of them. This fact may account for their attending his church and being satisfied with that sermon. I do not believe today that Shakespeare is more influential than the Bible, but what influence Shakespeare has, is for good. No man can read it without having his intellectual wealth increased. When you read it, it is not necessary to throw away your reason. Neither will you be damned if you do not understand it. It is a book that appeals to everything in the human brain. In that book can be found the wisdom of all ages. Long after the Bible has passed out of existence, the name of Shakespeare will lead the intellectual roster of the world. Dr. Fulton says there is not one word in the Bible that teaches that slavery or polygamy is right. He also states that I know it. If language has meaning – if words have sense, or the power to convey thought – what did God mean when he told the Israelites to buy of the heathen round about, and that the heathen should be their bondmen and bondmaids forever?

What did God mean when he said, if a man strike his servant so that he dies, he should not be punished, because his servant was his money? Passages like these can be quoted beyond the space that any paper is willing to give. Yet the Rev. Dr. Fulton denies that the Old Testament upholds slavery. I would like to ask him if the Old Testament is in favor of religious toleration? If God wrote the Old Testament and afterward came upon the earth as Jesus Christ, and taught a new religion, and the Jews crucified him, was this not in accordance with his own law, and was he not, after all, the victim of himself?

51

Q. What about the other ministers?

A. Well, I see in the *Herald* that some ten have said they would reply to me. I have selected the two, simply because they came first. I think they are about as poor as any; and you know it is natural to attack those who are the easiest answered. All these ministers are now acting as my agents, and are doing me all the good they can by saying all the bad things about me that they can think of. They imagine that their congregations have not grown, and they talk to them as though they were living in the 17th instead of the 19th century. The truth is the pews are beyond the pulpit, and the modern sheep are now protecting the shepherds.

Q. Have you noticed a great change in public sentiment in the last three or four years?

A. Yes, I think there are ten times as many Infidels today as there were ten years ago. I am amazed at the great change that has taken place in public opinion. The churches are not getting along well. There are hundreds and hundreds who have not had a new member in a year. The young men are not satisfied with the old ideas. They find that the church, after all, is opposed to learning; that it is the enemy of progress; that it says to every young man, "Go slow. Don't allow your knowledge to puff you up. Recollect that reason is a dangerous thing. You had better be a little ignorant here for the sake of being an angel hereafter, than quite a smart young man and get damned at last." The church warns them against Humboldt and Darwin, and tells them how much nobler it is to come from mud than from monkeys; that they were made from mud. Every college professor is afraid to tell what he thinks, and every student detects the cowardice. The result is that the young men have lost confidence in the creeds of the day and propose to do a little thinking for themselves. They still have a kind of tender pity for the old folks, and pretend to believe some things they do not, rather than hurt grandmother's feelings. In the presence of the preachers they talk about the weather and other harmless subjects for fear of bruising the spirit of their pastor. Every minister likes to consider himself as a brave shepherd leading the lambs through the green pastures and defending them at night from Infidel wolves. All this he does for a certain share of the wool. Others regard the church as a kind of social organization, as a good way to get into society. They wish to attend sociables, drink tea, and contribute for the conversion of the heathen. It is always so pleasant to think that there is somebody worse

52

than you are, whose reformation you can help pay for. I find, too, that the young women are getting tired of the old doctrines, and that everywhere, all over this country, the power of the pulpit wanes and weakens. I find in my lectures that the applause is just in proportion to the radicalism of the thought expressed. Our war was a great educator, when the whole people of the North rose up grandly in favor of human liberty. For many years the great question of human rights was discussed from every stump. Every paper was filled with splendid sentiments. An application of these doctrines – doctrines born in war – will forever do away with the bondage of superstition. When man has been free in body for a little time, he will become free in mind, and the man who says, "I have an equal right with other men to work and reap the reward of my labor," will say, "I have, also, an equal right to think and reap the reward of my thought."

In old times there was a great difference between a clergyman and a layman. The clergyman was educated; the peasant was ignorant. The tables have been turned. The thought of the world is with the laymen. They are the intellectual pioneers, the mental leaders, and the ministers are following on behind, predicting failure and disaster, sighing for the good old time, when their word ended discussion. There is another good thing, and that is the revision of the Bible. Hundreds of passages have been found to be interpolations, and future revisers will find hundreds more. The foundation crumbles. That book, called the basis of all law and civilization, has to be civilized itself. We have outgrown it. Our laws are better; our institutions grander; our objects and aims nobler and higher.

Q. Do many people write to you on this subject; and what spirit do they manifest?

A. Yes, I get a great many anonymous letters – some letters in which God is asked to strike me dead, others of an exceedingly insulting character, others almost idiotic, others exceedingly malicious, and others insane, others written in an exceedingly good spirit, winding up with the information that I must certainly be damned. Others express wonder that God allowed me to live at all, and that, having made the mistake, he does not instantly correct it by killing me. Others prophesy that I will yet be a minister of the gospel; but, as there has never been any softening of the brain in our family, I imagine that the prophecy will never be fulfilled. Lately, on opening a letter and seeing that it is on this subject, and without a signature, I throw it aside without reading. I have so often found them to be so grossly ignorant, insulting, and malicious, that as a rule I read them no more.

Q. Of the hundreds of people who call on you nearly every day to ask your help, do any of them ever discriminate against you on account of your infidelity?

A. No one who has asked a favor of me objects to my religion, or, rather, to my lack of it. A great many people do come to me for assistance of one kind or another. But I have never yet asked a man or woman whether they were religious or not, to what church they belonged, or any questions upon the subject. I think I have done favors for persons of most denominations. It never occurs to me whether they are Christians or Infidels. I do not care. Of course. I do not expect that Christians will treat me the same as though I belonged to their church. I have never expected it. In some instances I have been disappointed. I have some excellent friends who disagree with me entirely on the subject of religion. My real opinion is that secretly they like me because I am not a Christian, and those who do not like me envy me the liberty I enjoy. — *Chicago Times,* May 29, 1881.

GUITEAU AND HIS CRIME

Our "Royal Bob" was found by The Gazette, *in the gloaming of a delicious evening during the past week within the open portals of his friendly residence, dedicated by the gracious presence within to a simple and cordial hospitality, to the charms of friendship and the freedom of an abounding comradeship. With intellectual and untrammeled life, a generous, wise and genial host, whoever enters finds a welcome, seasoned with kindly wit and Attic humor, a poetic insight and a delicious frankness which renders an evening there a veritable symposium. The wayfarer who passes is charmed, and he who comes frequently goes always away with delighted memories.*

What matters it that we differ? Such as he and his wisdom make our common life the sweeter. An hour or two spent in the attractive parlors of the Ingersoll homestead, amid that rare group, lends a newer meaning to the idea of home and a more secure beauty to the fact of family life. During the past exciting three weeks Colonel Ingersoll has been a busy man. He holds no office. No position could lend him an additional crown and even recognition is no longer necessary. But it has been well that amid the first fierce fury of anger and excitement, and the subsequent more bitter if not as noble outpouring of faction's suspicions and innuendoes, that so manly a man, so sagacious a counselor, has been enabled to hold so positive a balance. Cabinet officers, legal functionaries, detectives, citizens – all have felt the wise, humane instincts, and the capacious brain of this marked man affecting and influencing for this fair equipoise and calmer judgment.

Conversing freely on the evening of this visit, Colonel Ingersoll, in the abundance of his pleasure at the White House news, submitted to be interviewed, and with the following result.

Q. By the way, Colonel, you knew Guiteau slightly, we believe. Are you aware that it has been attempted to show that some money loaned or given him by yourself was really what he purchased the pistol with?

A. I knew Guiteau slightly; I saw him for the first time a few days after the inauguration. He wanted a consulate, and asked me to give him a letter to Secretary Blaine. I refused, on the ground that I didn't know him. Afterwards he wanted me to lend him $25, and I declined. I never loaned him a dollar in the world. If I had, I should not feel that I was guilty of trying to kill the president. On the principle that one would hold the man guilty who had innocently loaned the money with which he bought the pistol, you might convict the tailor who made his clothes. If he had had no clothes he would not have gone to the depot naked, and the crime would not have been committed. It is hard enough for the man who did lend him the money to lose that, without losing his reputation besides. Nothing can exceed the utter absurdity of what has been said on this subject.

Q. How did Guiteau impress you and what have you remembered, Colonel, of his efforts to reply to your lectures?

A. I do not know that Guiteau impressed me in any way. He appeared like most other folks in search of a place or employment. I suppose he was in need. He talked about the same as other people, and claimed that I ought to help him because he was from Chicago. The second time he came to see me he said that he hoped I had no prejudice against him on account of what he had said about me. I told him that I never knew he had said anything against me. I suppose now that he referred to what he had said in his lectures. He went about the country replying to me. I have seen one or two of his lectures. He used about the same arguments that Mr. Black uses in his reply to my article in the *North American Review,* and denounced me in about the same terms. He is undoubtedly a man who firmly believes in the Old Testament, and has no doubt concerning the new. I understand that he puts in most of his time now reading the Bible and rebuking people who use profane language in his presence.

Q. You most certainly do not see any foundation for the accusations of preachers like Sunderland, Newman, and Power, *et al.,* that the teaching of a secular liberalism has had anything to do with the shaping of Guiteau's character or the actions of his vagabond life or the inciting to his murderous deeds?

A. I do not think that the sermon of Mr. Power was in good taste. It is utterly foolish to charge the "stalwarts" with committing or inciting the crime against the life of the president. Ministers, though, as a rule, know but little of public affairs, and they always account for the actions of people they do not like or agree with, by attributing to them the lowest and basest motives.

56

This is the fault of the pulpit – always has been, and probably always will be. The Rev. Dr. Newman of New York tells us that the crime of Guiteau shows three things: First, that ignorant men should not be allowed to vote; second, that foreigners should not be allowed to vote; and third, that there should not be so much religious liberty.

It turns out, first, that Guiteau is not an ignorant man; second, that he is not a foreigner; and third, that he is a Christian. Now, because an intelligent American Christian tries to murder the president, this person says we ought to do something with ignorant foreigners and Infidels. This is about the average pulpit logic. Of course, all the ministers hate to admit that Guiteau was a Christian; that he belonged to the Young Men's Christian Association, or at least was generally found in their rooms; that he was a follower of Moody and Sankey, and probably instrumental in the salvation of a great many souls. I do not blame them for wishing to get rid of this record. What I blame them for is that they are impudent enough to charge the crime of Guiteau upon infidelity. Infidels and Atheists have often killed tyrants. They have often committed crimes to increase the liberty of mankind; but the history of the world will not show an instance where an Infidel or an Atheist has assassinated any man in the interest of human slavery. Of course, I am exceedingly glad that Guiteau is not an Infidel. I am glad that he believes the Bible, glad that he has delivered lectures against what he calls infidelity, and glad that he has been working for years with the missionaries and evangelists of the United States. He is a man of small brain, badly balanced. He believes the Bible to be the word of God. He believes in the reality of heaven and hell. He believes in the miraculous. He is surrounded by the supernatural, and when a man throws away his reason of course no one can tell what he will do. He is liable to become a devotee or an assassin, a saint, or a murderer; he may die in a monastery or in a penitentiary.

Q. According to your view, then, the species of fanaticism taught in sectarian Christianity, by which Guiteau was led to assert that Garfield dead would be better off than living – being in paradise – is more responsible than office seeking or political factionalism for his deed?

A. Guiteau seemed to think that the killing of the president would only open the gates of paradise to him, and that, after all, under such circumstances, murder was hardly a crime. This same kind of reasoning is resorted to in the pulpit to account for death. Guiteau reasoned in this way, and probably convinced himself, judging from his own life, that this world was, after all, of little worth. We are apt to measure others by ourselves. Of course, I do not think that Christianity is responsible for this crime. Superstition may have been, in part – probably was. But no man believes in Christianity because he thinks it sanctions murder. At the same time, an absolute belief in the Bible sometimes produces the worst form of murder. Take that of Mr. Freeman, of Pocasset, who stabbed his little daughter to the heart in accordance with what he believed to be the command of God. This poor man imitated Abraham; and, for that matter, Jehovah himself. There have been in the history of Christianity thousands and thousands of such instances, and there will probably be many thousands more that have been and will be produced by throwing away our own reason and taking the word of someone else – often a word that we do not understand.

Q. What is your opinion as to the effect of praying for the recovery of the president, and have you any confidence that prayers are answered?

A. My opinion as to the value of prayer is well known. I take it that everyone who prays for the president shows at least his sympathy and good will. Personally, I have no objection to anybody's praying. Those who think that prayers are answered should pray. For all who honestly believe this, and who honestly implore their deity to watch over, protect, and save the life of the president, I have only the kindest feelings.

It may be that a few will pray to be seen of men; but I suppose that most people on a subject like this are honest. Personally, I have not the slightest idea of the existence of the supernatural. Prayer may affect the person who prays. It may put him in such a frame of mind that he can better bear disappointment than if he had not prayed; but I cannot believe that there is any being who hears and answers prayer.

When we remember the earthquakes that have devoured, the pestilences that have covered the earth with corpses, and all the crimes and agonies that have been inflicted on the good and weak by the bad and strong, it does not seem possible that anything can be accomplished by prayer. I do not wish to hurt the feelings of anyone, but I imagine that I have a right to my own opinion. If the president gets well it will be because the bullet did not strike an absolutely vital part; it will be because he has been well cared for; because he has had about him intelligent and skillful physicians, men who understood their profession. No doubt he has received great support from the universal expression of sympathy and kindness. The knowledge that fifty millions of people are his friends has given him nerve and hope. Some of the ministers, I see, think that God was actually present and deflected the ball. Another minister tells us that the president would have been assassinated in a church, but that God determined not to allow so frightful a crime to be committed in so sacred an edifice. All this sounds to me like perfect absurdity – simple noise. Yet, I presume that those who talk in this way are good people and believe what they say. Of course, they can give no reason why God did not deflect the ball when Lincoln was assassinated. The truth is the pulpit first endeavors to find out the facts, and then to make a theory to fit them. Whoever believes in a special providence must, of necessity, be illogical and absurd; because it is impossible to make any theological theory that some facts will not contradict.

Q. Won't you give us, then, Colonel, your analysis of this act, and the motives leading to it?

A. I think Guiteau wanted an office and was refused. He became importunate. He was, substantially, put out of the White House. He became malicious. He made up his mind to be revenged: This, in my judgment, is the diagnosis of his case. Since he has been in jail he has never said one word about having been put out of the White House; he is lawyer enough to know he must not furnish any ground for malice. He is a miserable, malicious, and worthless wretch, infinitely egotistical, imagines that he did a great deal toward the election of Garfield, and on being refused the house a serpent of malice coiled in his heart, and he determined to be revenged. That is all!

Q. Do you, in any way, see any reason or foundation for the severe and bitter criticisms made against the Stalwart leaders in connection with this crime. As you are well known to be a friend of the administration, while not unfriendly to Mr. Conkling and those acting with him, would you mind giving the public your opinion on this point?

A. Of course, I do not hold Arthur, Conkling, and Platt responsible for Guiteau's action. In the first excitement a thousand unreasonable things were said; and when passion has possession of the brain, suspicion is a welcome visitor.

I do not think that any friend of the administration really believes Conkling, Platt, and Arthur responsible in the slightest degree. Conkling wished to prevent the appointment of Robertson. The president stood by his friend. One thing brought on another. Mr. Conkling petulantly resigned and made the mistake of his life. There was a good deal of feeling, but, of course, no one dreamed that the wretch, Guiteau, was lying in wait for the president's life. In the first place, Guiteau was on the president's side, and was bitterly opposed to Conkling. Guiteau did what he did from malice and personal spite. I think the sermon preached last Sunday in the Campbellite church was unwise, ill advised, and calculated to make enemies instead of friends. Mr. Conkling has been beaten. He has paid for the mistake he made. If he can stand it, I can; and why should there be any malice on the subject? Exceedingly good men have made mistakes, and afterward corrected them.

Q. Is it not true, Colonel Ingersoll, that the lesson of this deed is to point the real and overwhelming need of re-knitting and harmonizing the factions?

A. There is hardly faction enough left for "knitting." The party is in harmony now. All that is necessary is to stop talking. The people of this country care little as to who holds any particular office. They wish to have the government administered in accordance with certain great principles, and they leave the fields, the shops, and the stores once in four years, for the purpose of attending to that business. In the meantime, politicians quarrel about offices. The people go on. They plow fields, they build homes, they open mines, they enrich the world, they cover our country with prosperity, and enjoy the aforesaid quarrels. But when the time comes, these gentlemen are forgotten.

Principles take the place of politicians, and the people settle these questions for themselves. — *Sunday Gazette,* Washington, D.C., July 24, 1881.

FUNERAL OF JOHN G. MILLS
AND IMMORTALITY

Q. Have you seen the recent clerical strictures on your doctrines?

A. There are always people kind enough to send me anything they have the slightest reason to think I do not care to read. They seem to be animated by a missionary spirit, and apparently want to be in a position when they see me in hell to exclaim: "You can't blame me. I sent you all the impudent articles I saw, and if you died unconverted it was no fault of mine."

Q. Did you notice that a Washington clergyman said that the very fact that you were allowed to speak at the funeral was in itself a sacrilege, and that you ought to have been stopped.

A. Yes, I saw some such story. Of course, the clergy regard marriages and funerals as the perquisites of the pulpit, and they resent any interference on the part of the pews. They look at these matters from a business point of view. They made the same cry against civil marriages. They denied that marriage was a contract, and insisted that it was a sacrament, and that it was hardly binding unless a priest had blessed it. They used to bury in consecrated ground, and had marks on the graves, so that Gabriel might know the ones to waken. The clergy wish to make themselves essential. They must christen the babe – this gives them possession of the cradle. They must perform the ceremony of marriage – this gives them possession of the family. They must pronounce the funeral discourse – this gives them possession of the dead. Formerly they denied baptism to the children of the unbeliever, marriage to him who denied the dogmas of the church, and burial to honest men. The church wishes to control the world, and wishes to sacrifice this world for the next. Of course, I am in favor of the utmost liberty upon all these questions. When a Presbyterian dies, let a follower of John Calvin console the living by setting forth the "Five Points." When a Catholic becomes clay, let a priest perform such ceremonies as his creed demands, and let him picture the delights of purgatory for the gratification of the living. And when one dies who does not believe in any religion, having expressed a wish that somebody say a few words above his remains, I see no reason why such a proceeding should be stopped, and, for my part, I see no sacrilege in it. Why should the reputations of the dead, and the feelings of those who live, be placed at the mercy of the ministers? A man dies not having been a Christian, and who, according to the Christian doctrine, is doomed to eternal fire. How would an honest Christian minister console the widow and the fatherless children? How would he dare to tell what he claims to be truth in the presence of the living? The truth is, the Christian minister in the presence of death abandons his Christianity. He dare not say above the coffin, "the soul that once inhabited this body is now in hell." He would be denounced as a brutal savage. Now and then a minister at a funeral has been brave enough and unmannerly enough to express his doctrine in all its hideousness of hate. I was told that in Chicago, many years ago, a young man, member of a volunteer fire company, was killed by the falling of a wall, and at the very moment the wall struck him he was uttering a curse. He was a brave and splendid man. An orthodox minister said above his coffin, in the presence of his mother and mourning friends, that he saw no hope for the soul of that young man. The mother, who was also orthodox, refused to have her boy buried with such a sermon – stopped the funeral, took the corpse home, engaged a Universalist preacher, and, on the next day having heard this man say that there was no place in the wide universe of God without hope, and that her son would finally stand among the redeemed, this mother laid her son away, put flowers on his grave, and was satisfied.

Q. What have you to say to the charge that you are preaching the doctrine of despair and hopelessness, when they have the comforting assurance of the Christian religion to offer?

A. All I have to say is this: If the Christian religion is true, as commonly preached – and when I speak of Christianity, I speak of the orthodox Christianity of the day – if that be true, those whom I have loved the best are now in torment. Those to whom I am most deeply indebted are now suffering the vengeance of God. If this religion be true, the future is of no value to me. I care nothing about heaven, unless the ones I love and have loved are there. I know nothing about the angels. I might not like them, and they might not like me. I would rather meet there the ones who have loved me here – the ones who would have died for me, and for whom I would have died; and if we are to be eternally divided – not because we differed about friendship or love or candor, or the nobility of human action, but because we differed in belief about the atonement or baptism or the inspiration of the Scriptures – and if some of us are to be in heaven, and some in hell, then, for my part I prefer eternal sleep. To me the doctrine of annihilation is infinitely more consoling than the probable separation preached by the orthodox clergy of our time. Of course, even if there be a God, I like persons that I know better than I can like him – we have more in common – I know more about them; and how is it possible for me to love the infinite and unknown better than the ones I know? Why not have the courage to say that if there be a God, all I know about him I know by knowing myself and my friends – by knowing others? And, after all, is not a noble man, is not a pure woman, the finest revelation we have of God – if there be one? Of what use is it to be false to ourselves? What moral quality is there in theological pretense? Why should a man say that he loves God better than he does his wife or his children or his brother or his sister or his warm, true friend? Several ministers have objected to what I said about my friend Mr. Mills, on the ground that it was not calculated to console the living. Mr. Mills was not a Christian. He denied the inspiration of the Scriptures. He believed that restitution was the best repentance, and that, after all, sin is a mistake. He was not a believer in total depravity, or in the atonement. He denied these things. He was an unbeliever. Now, let me ask, what consolation could a Christian minister have given to his family? He could have said to the widow and the orphans, to the brother and the sister: "Your husband, your father, your brother, is now in hell; dry your tears; weep not for him, but try and save yourselves. He has been damned as a warning to you, care no more for him, why should you weep over the grave of a man whom God thinks fit only to be eternally tormented? Why should you love the memory of one whom God hates?" The minister could have said: "He had an opportunity – he did not take it. The lifeboat was lowered – he would not get in – he has been drowned, and the waves of God's wrath will sweep over him forever." This is the consolation of Christianity and the only honest consolation that Christianity can have for the widow and orphans of an unbeliever. Suppose, however, that the Christian minister has too tender a heart to tell what he believes to be the truth then he can say to the sorrowing friends: "Perhaps the man repented before he died; perhaps he is not in hell, perhaps you may meet him in heaven"; and this "perhaps" is a consolation not growing out of Christianity, but out of the politeness of the preacher – out of paganism.

Q.   Do you not think that the Bible has consolation for those who have lost their friends?

A.   There is about the Old Testament this strange fact – I find in it no burial service. There is in it, I believe, from the first mistake in Genesis to the last curse in Malachi, not one word said over the dead as to their place and state. When Abraham died, nobody said: "He is still alive – he is in another world." When the prophets passed away, not one word was said as to the heaven to which they had gone. In the Old Testament, Saul inquired of the witch, and Samuel rose. Samuel did not pretend that he had been living, or that he was alive, but asked: "Why hast thou disquieted me?" He did not pretend to have come from some other world. And when David speaks of his son, saying that he could not come back to him, but that he, David, could go to his son, that is but saying that he, too, must die. There is not in the Old Testament one hope of immortality. It is expressly asserted that there is no difference between the man and beast – that as the one dieth so dieth the other. There is one little passage in Job which commentators have endeavored to twist into a hope of immortality. Here is a book of hundreds and hundreds of pages, and hundreds and hundreds of chapters – a revelation from God – and in it one little passage, which, by a mistranslation, is tortured into saying something about another life. And this is the Old Testament. I have sometimes thought that the Jews, when slaves in Egypt, were mostly occupied in building tombs for mummies, and that they became so utterly disgusted with that kind of work, that the moment they founded a nation for themselves they went out of the tomb business. The Egyptians were believers in immortality, and spent almost their entire substance on the dead. The living were impoverished to enrich the dead. The grave absorbed the wealth of Egypt. The industry of a nation was buried. Certainly the Old Testament has nothing clearly in favor of immortality. In the New Testament we are told about the "kingdom of heaven" – that it is at hand – and about who shall be worthy, but it is hard to tell what is meant by the kingdom of heaven. The kingdom of heaven was apparently to be in this world, and it was about to commence. The devil was to be chained for a thousand years, the wicked were to be burned up, and Christ and his followers were to enjoy the earth. This certainly was the doctrine of Paul when he says:

"Behold, I shew you a mystery; We shall not all *sleep,* but we shall all be *changed.* In a moment, in the twinkling of an eye, at the last trump; for the trumpet shall sound, and the *dead* shall be *raised* incorruptible, and we shall be *changed.* For this corruptible must put on incorruption, and this mortal must put on immortality." According to this doctrine, those who were alive were to be changed, and those who had died were to be raised from the dead. Paul certainly did not refer to any other world beyond this. All these things were to happen here. The New Testament is made up of the fragments of many religions. It is utterly inconsistent with itself; and there is not a particle of evidence of the resurrection and ascension of Christ – neither in the nature of things could there be. It is a thousand times more probable that people were mistaken than that such things occurred. If Christ really rose from the dead, he should have shown himself, not simply to his disciples, but to the very men who crucified him – to Herod, to the high priest, to Pilate. He should have made a triumphal entry into Jerusalem after his resurrection, instead of before. He should have shown himself to the Sadducees – to those who denied the existence of spirit. Take from the New Testament its doctrine of eternal pain – the idea that we can please God by acts of self-denial that can do no good to others – take away all its miracles, and I have no objection to all the good things in it – no objection to the hope of a future life, if such a hope is expressed – not the slightest. And I would not for the world say anything to take from any mind a hope in which dwells the least comfort; but a doctrine that dooms a large majority of mankind to eternal flames ought not to be called a consolation. What I say is that the writers of the New Testament knew no more about the future state than I do, and no less. The horizon of life has never been pierced. The veil between time and what is called eternity has never been raised, so far as I know; and I say of the dead what all others must say if they say only what they know. There is no particular consolation in a guess. Not knowing what the future has in store for the human race, it is far better to prophesy good than evil. It is better to hope that the night has a dawn, that the sky has a star, than to build a heaven for the few and a hell for the many. It is better to leave your dead in doubt than in fire – better that they should sleep in shadow than in the lurid flames of perdition. And so I say, and always have said, let us hope for the best. The minister asks: "What right have you to hope? It is sacrilegious in you." But, whether the clergy like it or not, I shall always express my real opinion, and shall always be glad to say to those who mourn: "There is in death, as I believe, nothing worse than sleep. Hope for as much better as you can. Under the seven-hued arch let the dead rest." Throw away the Bible, and you throw away the fear of hell, but the hope of another life remains, because the hope does not depend on a book – it depends on the heart – on human affection. The fear, so far as this generation is concerned, is born of the book, and that part of the book was born of savagery. Whatever of hope is in the book is born, as said before, of human affection, and the higher our civilization the greater the affection. I had rather rest my hope of something beyond the grave on the human heart than on what they call the Scriptures, because there I find mingled with the hope of something good the threat of infinite evil. Among the thistles, thorns, and briers of the Bible is one pale and sickly flower of hope. Among all its wild beasts and fowls, only one bird flies heavenward. I prefer the hope without the thorns, without the briers, thistles, hyenas, and serpents.

Q. Do you not know that it is claimed that immortality was brought to light in the New Testament, that that, in fact, was the principal mission of Christ?

A. I know that Christians claim that the doctrine of immortality was first taught in the New Testament. They also claim that the highest morality was found there. Both these claims are utterly without foundation. Thousands of years before Christ was born – thousands of years before Moses saw the light – the doctrine of immortality was preached by the priests of Osiris and Isis. Funeral discourses were pronounced over the dead, ages before Abraham existed. When a man died in Egypt, before he was taken across the sacred lake, he had a trial. Witnesses appeared, and if he had done anything wrong for which he had not made restitution, he was not taken across the lake. The living friends, in disgrace, carried the body back, and it was buried outside of what might be called consecrated ground, while the ghost was supposed to wander for 100 years. Often the children of the dead would endeavor to redeem the poor ghost by acts of love and kindness. When he came to the spirit world there was the god Anubis who weighed his heart in the scales of eternal justice, and if the good deeds preponderated he entered the gates of paradise; if the evil, he had to go back to the world and be born in the bodies of animals for the purpose of final purification. At last, the good deeds would

66

outweigh the evil, and, according to the religion of Egypt, the latch-string of heaven would never be drawn in until the last wanderer got home. Immortality was also taught in India, and, in fact, in all the countries of antiquity. Wherever men have loved, wherever they have dreamed, wherever hope has spread its wings, the idea of immortality promised in the New Testament – admitting that it is so promised – eternal joy side by side with eternal pain. Think of living forever, knowing that countless millions are suffering infinite pain! How much better it would be for God to commit suicide and let all life and motion cease! Christianity has no consolation except for the Christian, and if a Christian minister endeavors to console the widow of an unbeliever he must resort, not to his religion, but to his sympathy – to the natural promptings of the heart. He is compelled to say: "After all, maybe God is not so bad as we think," or, "Maybe your husband was better than he appeared; perhaps somehow, in some way, the dear man has squeezed in; he was a good husband, he was a kind father, and even if he is in hell, maybe he is in the temperate zone, where they have occasional showers, and, where, if the days are hot, the nights are reasonably cool." All I ask of Christian ministers is to tell what they believe to be the truth – not to borrow ideas from the pagans – not to preach the mercy born of unregenerate sympathy. Let them tell their real doctrines. If they will do that, they will not have much influence. If orthodox Christianity is true, a large majority of the men who have made this world fit to live in are now in perdition. A majority of the Revolutionary soldiers have been damned. A majority of the men who fought for the integrity of this Union – a majority who were starved at Libby and Andersonville are now in hell.

Q.   Do you deny the immortality of the soul?

A.   I never have denied the immortality of the soul. I have simply been honest. I have said: "I do not know." Long ago, in my lecture on "The Ghosts," I used the following language: "The idea of immortality, that like a sea has ebbed and flowed in the human heart, with its countless waves of hope and fear beating against the shores and rocks of time and fate, was not born of any book, nor of any creed, nor of any religion. It was born of human affection, and it will continue to ebb and flow beneath the mists and clouds of doubt and darkness as long as love kisses the lips of death. It is the rainbow hope, shining upon the tears of grief."

— *The Post,* Washington, D.C., April 30, 1883.

THE INTERVIEWER

Q. What do you think of newspaper interviewing?

A. I believe that James Redpath claims to have invented the "interview." This system opens all doors, does away with political pretense, batters down the fortifications of dignity and official importance, pulls masks from solemn faces, compels everybody to show his hand. The interviewer seems to be omnipresent. He is the next man after the accident. If a man should be blown up he would likely fall on an interviewer. He is the universal interrogation point. He asks questions for a living. If the interviewer is fair and honest he is useful, if the other way, he is still interesting. On the whole, I regard the interviewer as an exceedingly important person. But whether he is good or bad, he has come to stay. He will interview us until we die, and then ask the "friends" a few questions just to round the subject off.

Q. What do you think the tendency of newspapers is at present?

A. The papers of the future, I think, will be "news" papers The editorial is getting shorter and shorter. The paragraphist is taking the place of the heavy man. People rather form their own opinions from the facts. Of course, good articles will always find readers, but the dreary, doleful, philosophical dissertation has had its day. The magazines will fall heir to such articles; then religious weeklies will take them up, and then they will cease altogether.

Q. Do you think the people lead the newspapers, or do the newspapers lead them?

A. The papers lead and are led. Most papers have for sale what people want to buy. As a rule the people who buy determine the character of the thing sold. The reading public grow more discriminating every year, and, as a result, are less and less "led." Violent papers – those that most freely attack private character – are becoming less hurtful, because they are losing their own reputations. Evil tends to correct itself. People do not believe all they read, and there is a growing tendency to wait and hear from the other side.

Q. Do newspapers today exercise as much influence as they did 25 years ago?

A. More, by the facts published, and less, by editorials. As we become civilized we are governed less by persons and more by principles – less by faith and more by fact. The best of all leaders is the man who teaches people to lead themselves.

Q. What would you define public opinion to be?

A. First, in the widest sense, the opinion of the majority, including all kinds of people. Second, in a narrower sense, the opinion of the majority of the intellectuals. Third, in actual practice, the opinion of those who make the most noise. Fourth, public opinion is generally a mistake, which history records and posterity repeats.

Q. What do you regard as the result of your lectures?

A. In the last fifteen years I have delivered several hundred lectures. The world is growing more and more liberal every day. The man who is now considered orthodox, a few years ago would have been denounced as an Infidel. People are thinking more and believing less. The pulpit is losing influence. In the light of modern discovery the creeds are growing laughable. A theologian is an intellectual mummy, and excites attention only as a curiosity. Supernatural religion has outlived its usefulness. The miracles and wonders of the ancients will soon occupy the same tent. Jonah and Jack the giant killer, Joshua and Red Riding Hood, Noah and Neptune, will all go into the collection of the famous Mother Hubbard. — *The Morning Journal*, New York, July 3, 1883.

POLITICS AND THEOLOGY

Q. What are your present views on theology?

A. Well, I think my views have not undergone any change that I know of. I still insist that observation, reason, and experience are the things to be depended upon in this world. I still deny the existence of the supernatural. I still insist that nobody can be good for you, or bad for you; that you cannot be punished for the crimes of others, nor rewarded for their virtues. I still insist that the consequences of good actions are always good, and those of bad actions are always bad. I insist that nobody can plant thistles and gather figs; neither can they plant figs and gather thistles. I still deny that a finite being can commit an infinite sin; but I continue to insist that a God who would punish a man forever is an infinite tyrant. My views have undergone no change, except that the evidence of that truth constantly increases, and the dogmas of the church look, if possible, a little absurder every day. Theology, you know, is not a science. It stops at the grave; and faith is the end of theology. Ministers have not even the advantage of the doctors; the doctors sometimes can tell by a post-mortem examination whether they killed the man or not; but by cutting a man open after he is dead, the wisest theologians cannot tell what has become of his soul, and whether it was injured or helped by a belief in the inspiration of the Scriptures. Theology depends on assertion for evidence, and on faith for disciples. — *The Tribune,* Denver, Colorado, Jan. 17, 1886.

MORALITY AND IMMORTALITY

Q. I see that the clergy are still making all kinds of charges against you and your doctrines.

A. Yes. Some of the charges are true and some are not. I suppose that they intend to get in the vicinity of veracity, and are probably stating my belief as it is honestly misunderstood by them. I admit that I have said and that I still think that Christianity is a blunder. But the question arises, What is Christianity? I do not mean, when I say Christianity is a blunder, that the morality taught by Christians is a mistake. Morality is not distinctively Christian, any more than it is Mohammedan. Morality is human, it belongs to no ism, and does not depend for a foundation on the supernatural, or on any book, or on any creed. Morality is itself a foundation. When I say that Christianity is a blunder, I mean all those things distinctively Christian are blunders. It is a blunder to say that an infinite being lived in Palestine, learned the carpenter's trade, raised the dead, cured the blind, and cast out devils, and that this God was finally assassinated by the Jews. This is absurd. All these statements are blunders, if not worse. I do not believe that Christ ever claimed that he was of supernatural origin, or that he wrought miracles, or that he would rise from the dead. If he did, he was mistaken – honestly mistaken, perhaps, but still mistaken.

The morality inculcated by Mohammed is good. The immorality inculcated by Mohammed is bad. If Mohammed was a prophet of God, it does not make the morality he taught any better, neither does it make the immorality any better or any worse.

By this time the whole world ought to know that morality does not need to go into partnership with miracles. Morality is based on the experience of mankind. It does not have to learn of inspired writers, or of gods, or divine persons. It is a lesson that the whole human race has been learning and learning from experience. He who upholds, or believes in, or teaches, the miraculous, commits a blunder.

Now, what is morality? Morality is the best thing to do under the circumstances. Anything that tends to the happiness of

71

mankind is moral. Anything that tends to unhappiness is immoral. We apply to the moral world rules and regulations as we do in the physical world. The man who does justice, or tries to do so – who is honest and kind and gives to others what he claims for himself, is a moral man. All actions must be judged by their consequences. Where the consequences are good, the actions are good. Where the consequences are bad, the actions are bad; and all consequences are learned from experience. After we have had a certain amount of experience, we then reason from analogy. We apply our logic and say that a certain course will bring destruction, another course will bring happiness. There is nothing inspired about morality – nothing supernatural. It is simply good common sense, going hand in hand with kindness.

Morality is capable of being demonstrated. You do not have to take the word of anybody; you can observe and examine for yourself. Larceny is the enemy of industry, and industry is good; therefore larceny is immoral. The family is the unit of good government; anything that tends to destroy the family is immoral. Honesty is the mother of confidence; it unites, combines, and solidifies society. Dishonesty is disintegration; it destroys confidence; it brings social chaos; it is therefore immoral.

I also admit that I regard the Mosaic account of the creation as an absurdity – as a series of blunders. Probably Moses did the best he could. He had never talked with Humboldt or Laplace. He knew nothing of geology or astronomy. He had not the slightest suspicion of Kepler's Three Laws. He never saw a copy of Newton's *Principia*. Taking all these things into consideration, I think Moses did the best he could.

The religious people say now that "days" did not mean days. Of these "six days" they make a kind of telescope, which you can push in or draw out at pleasure. If the geologists find that more time was necessary they will stretch them out. Should it turn out that the world is not quite as old as some think, they will push them up. The "six days" can now be made to suit any period of time. Nothing can be more childish, frivolous, or contradictory.

Only a few years ago the Mosaic account was considered true, and Moses was regarded as a scientific authority. Geology and astronomy were measured by the Mosaic standard. The opposite is now true. The church has changed; and instead of trying to prove that modern astronomy and geology are false, because they do not agree with Moses, it is now endeavoring to prove that the account by Moses is true, because it agrees with modern astronomy and geology. In other words, the standard has changed; the ancient is measured by the modern, and where the literal statement in the Bible does not agree with modern discoveries, they do not change the discoveries, but give new meanings to the old account. We are not now endeavoring to reconcile science with the Bible, but to reconcile the Bible with science.

Nothing shows the extent of modern doubt more than the eagerness with which Christians search for some new testimony. Luther answered Copernicus with a passage of Scripture, and he answered him to the satisfaction of orthodox ignorance.

The truth is that the Jews adopted the stories of creation, the Garden of Eden, forbidden fruit, and the fall of man. They were told by older barbarians than they, and the Jews gave them to us.

I never said that the Bible is all bad. I have always admitted that there are many good and splendid things in the Jewish Scriptures, and many bad things. What I insist is that we should have the courage and the common sense to accept the good, and throw away the bad. Evil is not good because found in good company, and truth is still truth, even when surrounded by falsehood.

Q. I see that you are frequently charged with disrespect toward your parents – with lack of reverence for the opinions of your father.

A. I think my father and mother on several religious questions were mistaken. In fact, I have no doubt that they were; but I never felt under the slightest obligation to defend my father's mistakes. No one can defend what he thinks is a mistake, without being dishonest. That is a poor way to show respect for parents. Every Protestant clergyman asks men and women who had Catholic parents to desert the church in which they were raised. They have no hesitation in saying to these people that their fathers and mothers were mistaken, and that they were deceived by priests and popes.

The probability is that we are all mistaken about almost everything; but it is impossible for a man to be respectable enough to make a mistake respectable. There is nothing remarkably holy in a blunder, or praiseworthy in stubbing the toe of the mind against a mistake. Is it possible that logic stands paralyzed in the presence of parental absurdity? Suppose a man has a bad father; is he bound by the bad father's opinion, when he is satisfied that the opinion is wrong? How good does a father have to be in order to put his son under obligation to defend his blunders? Suppose

73

the father thinks one way, and the mother the other; what are the children to do? Suppose the father changes his opinion; what then? Suppose the father thinks one way and the mother the other, and they both die when the boy is young, and the boy is bound out; what is the boy to do? Whose mistakes is he then bound to follow? Our missionaries tell the barbarian boy that his parents are mistaken, that they know nothing, and that the wooden god is nothing but a senseless idol. They do not hesitate to tell this boy that his mother believed lies, and hugged, it may be her dying heart, a miserable delusion. Why should a barbarian boy cast reproach on his parents?

I believe it was Christ who commanded his disciples to leave father and mother; not only to leave them, but to desert them; and not only to desert father and mother, but to desert wives and children. It is also told of Christ that he said that he came to set fathers against children and children against fathers. Strange that a follower of his should object to a man differing in opinion from his parents! The truth is logic knows nothing of consanguinity; facts have no relation but other facts; and these facts do not depend on the character of the person who states them, or on the position of the discoverer. And this leads me to another branch of the same subject.

The ministers are continually saying that certain great men – kings, presidents, statesmen, millionaires – have believed in the inspiration of the Bible. Only the other day, I read a sermon in which Carlyle was quoted as having said that "the Bible is a noble book." That all may be and yet the book not be inspired. But what is the simple assertion of Thomas Carlyle worth? If the assertion is based on a reason, then it is worth simply the value of the reason, and the reason is worth just as much without the assertion, but without the reason the assertion is worthless. Thomas Carlyle thought, and solemnly put the thought in print, that his father was a greater man than Robert Burns. His opinion did Burns no harm, and his father no good. Since reading his *Reminiscences*, I have no great opinion of his opinion. In some respects he was undoubtedly a great man, in others a small one. No man should give the opinion of another as authority and in place of fact and reason, unless he is willing to take all the opinions of that man. An opinion is worth the warp and woof of fact and logic in it and no more. A man cannot add to the truthfulness of truth. In the ordinary business of life we give certain weight to the opinion of specialists – to the opinion of doctors, lawyers, scientists, and historians. Within the domain of the natural we take the opinions of our fellow men; but we do not feel that we are absolutely bound by these opinions. We have the right to reexamine them, and if we find they are wrong we feel at liberty to say so. A doctor is supposed to have studied medicine; to have examined and explored the questions entering into his profession; but we know that doctors are often mistaken. We also know that there are many schools of medicine; that these schools disagree with one another, and that the doctors of each school disagree with one another. We also know that many patients die and, so far as we know, these patients have not come back to tell us whether the doctors killed them or not. The grave generally prevents a demonstration. It is exactly the same with the clergy. They have many schools of theology, all despising each other. Probably no two members of the same church exactly agree. They cannot demonstrate their propositions, because between the premise and the logical conclusion or demonstration stands the tomb. A gravestone marks the end of theology. In some cases, the physician can, by a post-mortem examination, find what killed the patient, but there is no theological post-mortem. It is impossible, by cutting a body open, to find where the soul has gone; or whether baptism, or the lack of it, had the slightest effect on final destiny. The church, knowing that there are no facts beyond the coffin, relies on opinions, assertions, and theories. For this reason it is always asking alms of distinguished people. Some president wishes to be reelected, and thereupon speaks about the Bible as "the cornerstone of American liberty." This sentence is a mouth large enough to swallow any church, and from that time forward the religious people will be citing that remark of the politician to substantiate the inspiration of the Scriptures.

The man who accepts opinions because they have been entertained by distinguished people is a mental snob. When we blindly follow authority we are serfs. When our reason is convinced we are freemen. It is rare to find a fully rounded and complete man. A man may be a great doctor and a poor mechanic, a successful politician and a poor metaphysician, a poor painter and a good poet.

The rarest thing in the world is a logician – that is to say, a man who knows the value of a fact. It is hard to find mental proportion. Theories may be established by names, but facts cannot be demonstrated in that way. Small people are sometimes right, and great people are sometimes wrong. Ministers are sometimes right.

In all the philosophies of the world there are undoubtedly contradictions and absurdities. The mind of man is imperfect and perfect results are impossible. A mirror, in order to reflect a perfect picture, a perfect copy, must itself be perfect. The mind is a little piece of intellectual glass the surface of which is not true, not perfect. In consequence of this every image is more or less distorted. The less we know, the more we imagine that we can know; but the more we know, the smaller seems the sum of knowledge. The less we know, the more we expect, the more we hope for, and the more seems within the range of probability. The less we have, the more we want. There never was a banquet magnificent enough to gratify the imagination of a beggar. The moment people begin to reason about what they call the supernatural, they seem to lose their minds. People seem to have lost their reason in religious matters, much as the dodo is said to have lost its wings; they have been restricted to a little inspired island, and by disuse their reason has been lost.

In the Jewish Scriptures you will find simply the literature of the Jews. You will find there the tears and anguish of captivity, patriotic fervor, national aspiration, proverbs for the conduct of daily life, laws, regulations, customs, legends, philosophy, and folly. These books, of course, were not written by one man, but by many authors. They do not agree, having been written in different centuries, under different circumstances. I see that Mr. Beecher has at last concluded that the Old Testament does not teach the doctrine of immortality. He admits that from Mount Sinai came no hope for the dead. It is curious that we find in the Old Testament no funeral service. No one stands by the dead and predicts another life. In the Old Testament there is no promise of another world. I have sometimes thought that while the Jews were slaves in Egypt, the doctrine of immortality became hateful. They built so many tombs; they carried so many burdens to commemorate the dead; they saw a nation waste its wealth to adorn its graves, and leave the living naked to embalm the dead, that they concluded the doctrine was a curse and never should be taught.

Q. If the Jews did not believe in immortality, how do you account for the allusions made to witches and wizards and things of that character?

A. When Saul visited the witch of Endor, and she, by some magic spell, called up Samuel, the prophet said: "Why hast thou disquieted me, to call me up?" He did not say: "Why have you called me from another world?" The idea expressed is: "I was asleep, why did you disturb that repose which should be eternal?" The ancient Jews believed in witches and wizards and familiar spirits; but they did not seem to think that these spirits had once been men and women. They spoke of them as belonging to another world, a world to which man would never find his way. At that time it was supposed that Jehovah and his angels lived in the sky, but that region was not spoken of as the destined home of man. Jacob saw angels going up and down the ladder, but not the spirits of those he had known. There are two cases where it seems that men were good enough to be adopted into the family of heaven. Enoch was translated, and Elijah was taken up in a chariot of fire. As it is exceedingly cold at the height of a few miles, it is easy to see why the chariot was of fire, and the same fact explains another circumstance – the dropping of the mantle. The Jews probably believed in the existence of other beings – that is to say, in angels and gods and evil spirits – and that they lived in other worlds – but there is no passage showing that they believed in what we call the immortality of the soul.

Q. Do you believe, or disbelieve, in the immortality of the soul?

A. I neither assert nor deny; I simply admit that I do not know. On that subject I am absolutely without evidence. This is the only world that I was ever in. There may be spirits, but I have never met them, and do not know that I would recognize a spirit. I can form no conception of what is called spiritual life. It may be that I am deficient in imagination, and that ministers have no difficulty in conceiving of angels and disembodied souls. I have not the slightest idea how a soul looks, what shape it is, how it goes from one place to another, whether it walks or flies. I cannot conceive of the immaterial having form; neither can I conceive of anything existing without form, and yet the fact that I cannot conceive of a thing does not prove that the thing does not exist, but it does prove that I know nothing about it, and that being so, I ought to admit my ignorance. I am satisfied of a good many things that I do not know. I am satisfied that there is no place of eternal torment. I am satisfied that the doctrine has done more harm than all the religious ideas, other than that, have done good. I do not want to take any hope from any human heart. I have no objection to people believing in any good thing — no objection to their expecting a crown of infinite joy for every human being. Many people imagine that immortality must be an infinite good; but, after all, there is something terrible in the idea of endless life. Think of a river that never reaches the sea; of a bird that never folds its wings; of a journey that never ends. Most people find great pleasure in thinking about and in believing in another world. There the prisoner expects to be free; the slave to find liberty; the poor man expects wealth; the rich man happiness; the peasant dreams of power, and the king of contentment. They expect to find there what they lack here. I do not wish to destroy these dreams. I am endeavoring to put out the everlasting fires. A good cool grave is infinitely better than eternal pain. For my part I would rather be annihilated than to be an angel, with all the privileges of heaven, and yet have within my breast a heart that could be happy while those who had loved me in this world were in perdition.

I most sincerely hope that the future life will fulfill all splendid dreams; but in the religion of the present day there is no joy. Nothing is so devoid of comfort, when bending above our dead, as the assertions of theology unsupported by a single fact. The promises are so far away, and the dead are so near. From words spoken eighteen centuries ago, the echoes are so weak, and the sounds of the clods on the coffin are so loud. Above the grave what can the honest minister say? If the dead were not a Christian, what then? What comfort can the orthodox clergyman give to the widow of the honest unbeliever? If Christianity is true, the other world will be worse than this. There the many will be miserable, only the few happy; there the miserable cannot better their condition; the future has no star of hope, and in the east of eternity there can never be a dawn.

Q. If you take away the idea of eternal punishment, how do you propose to restrain men; in what way will you influence conduct for good?

A. Well, the trouble with religion is that it postpones punishment and reward to another world. Wrong is wrong, because it breeds unhappiness. Right is right, because it tends to the happiness of man. These facts are the basis of what I call the religion of this world. When a man does wrong, the consequences follow, and between the cause and effect, a redeemer cannot step. Forgiveness cannot form a breastwork between act and consequence.

There should be a religion of the body – a religion that will prevent deformity, that will refuse to multiply insanity, that will not propagate disease – a religion that is judged by its consequences in this world. Orthodox Christianity has taught, and still teaches, that in this world the difference between the good and bad is that the bad enjoy themselves, while the good carry the cross of virtue with bleeding brows bound and pierced with the thorns of honesty and kindness. All this, in my judgment, is immoral. The man who does wrong carries a cross. There is no world, no star, in which the result of wrong is real happiness. There is no world, no star, in which the result of right doing is unhappiness. Virtue and vice must be the same everywhere.

Vice must be vice everywhere, because its consequences are evil, and virtue must be virtue everywhere, because its consequences are good. There can be no such thing as forgiveness. These facts are the only restraining influences possible – the innocent man cannot suffer for the guilty and satisfy the law.

Q. How do you answer the argument, or the fact, that the church is constantly increasing, and that there are now 400 millions of Christians?

A. That is what I call the argument of numbers. If that argument is good now, it was always good. If Christians were at any time in the minority, then, according to this argument, Christianity was wrong. Every religion that has succeeded has appealed to the argument of numbers. There was a time when Buddhism was in a majority. Buddha not only had, but has, more followers than Christ. Success is not a demonstration. Mohammed was a success, and a success from the commencement. On a thousand fields he was victor. Of the scattered tribes of the desert he made a nation, and this nation took the fairest part of Europe from the followers of the cross. In the history of the world the success of Mohammed is unparalleled, but this success does not establish that he was the prophet of God.

Now, it is claimed that there are some 400 millions of Christians. To make that total I am counted as a Christian; I am one of 50 or 60 millions of Christians in the United States – excluding Indians, not taxed. By the census report we are all going to heaven – we are all orthodox. At the last great day we can refer with confidence to the ponderous volumes containing the statistics of the United States. As a matter of fact, how many Christians are there in the United States – how many believers in the inspiration of the Scriptures – how many real followers of Christ? I will not pretend to give the number, but I will venture to say that there are not 50 millions. How many in England? Where are the 500 millions found? To make this immense number they have counted all the heretics, all the Catholics, all the Jews, spiritualists, Universalists, and Unitarians, all the babes, all the idiotic and insane, all the Infidels, all the scientists, all the unbelievers. As a matter of fact, they have no right to count any except the orthodox members of the orthodox churches. There may be more "members" now than formerly, and this increase of members is due to a decrease of religion. Thousands of members are only nominal Christians, wearing the old uniform simply because they do not wish to be charged with desertion. The church, too, is a kind of social institution, a club with a creed instead of bylaws, and the creed is never defended unless attacked by an outsider. No objection is made to the minister because he is a liberal, if he says nothing about it in his pulpit. A man like Mr. Beecher draws a congregation, not because he is a Christian, but because he is a genius; not because he is orthodox, but because he has something to say. He is an intellectual athlete. He is full of pathos and poetry. He has more description than divinity; more charity than creed and altogether more common sense than theology. For these reasons thousands of people love to hear him. On the other hand, there are many people who have a morbid desire for the abnormal – for intellectual deformities – for thoughts that have two heads. This accounts for the success of some of Mr. Beecher's rivals. Christians claim that success is a test of truth. Has any church succeeded as well as the Catholic? Was the tragedy of the Garden of Eden a success? Who succeeded there? The last best thought is not a success, if you mean by succeeding that it has won the assent of the majority. Besides there is no time fixed for the test. Is that true which succeeds today, or next year, or in the next century? Once the Copernican system was not a success. There is no time fixed. The result is we have to wait. A thing to exist at all has to be, to a certain extent, a success. A thing cannot even die without having been a success. It certainly succeeded enough to have life. Presbyterians should remember, while arguing the majority argument, that there are far more Catholics than Protestants, and that the Catholics can give a longer list of distinguished names.

My answer to all this, however, is that the history of the world shows that ignorance has always been in the majority. There is one right road; numberless paths that are wrong. Truth is one; error is many. When a great truth has been discovered, one man has pitted himself against the world. A few think; the many believe. The few lead; the many follow. The light of the new day, as it looks over the window sill of the east, falls at first on only one forehead.

There is another thing. A great many people pass for Christian who are not. Only a little while ago a couple of ladies were returning from church in a carriage. They had listened to a good orthodox sermon. One said to the other: "I am going to tell you something – I am going to shock you – I do not believe the Bible." And the other replied: "Neither do I." — *The News*, Detroit, Michigan, Jan. 6, 1884.

MORMONISM AND MR. BEECHER

Q. What do you think of the Mormon question?

A. I do not believe in the bayonet plan. Mormonism must be done away with by the thousand influences of civilization, by education, by the elevation of the people. Of course, a gentleman would rather have one noble woman than 100 females. I hate the system of polygamy. Nothing is more infamous. I admit that the Old Testament upholds it. I admit that the patriarchs were mostly polygamists. I admit that Solomon was mistaken on that subject. But notwithstanding the fact that polygamy is upheld by the Jewish Scriptures, I believe it to be a great wrong. At the same time if you undertake to get that idea out of the Mormons by force you will not succeed. I think a good way to do away with that institution would be for all the churches to unite, bear the expense, and send missionaries to Utah; let these ministers call the people together and read to them the lives of David, Solomon, Abraham, and other patriarchs. Let all the missionaries be called home from foreign fields and teach these people that they should not imitate the only men with whom God ever condescended to hold intercourse. Let these frightful examples be held up to these people, and if it is done earnestly, it seems to me that the result would be good.

Polygamy exists. All laws on the subject should take that fact into consideration, and punishment should be provided for offenses thereafter committed. The children of Mormons should be legitimatized. In other words, in attempting to settle this question, we should accomplish all the good possible, with the least possible harm.

I agree mostly with Mr. Beecher, and I utterly disagree with the Rev. Mr. Newman. Mr. Newman wants to kill and slay. He does not rely on Christianity but on brute force. He has lost his confidence in example and appeals to the bayonet. Mr. Newman had a discussion with one of the Mormon elders, and was put to ignominious flight; no wonder that he appeals to force. Having failed in argument, he calls for artillery; having been worsted in the appeal to Scripture, he asks for the sword. He says, failing to convert, let us kill; and he takes this position in the name of the religion of kindness and forgiveness.

Strange that a minister now should throw away the Bible and yell for a bayonet; that he should desert the Scriptures and call for soldiers; that he should lose confidence in the power of the spirit and trust in the sword. I recommend that Mormonism be done away with by distributing the Old Testament through Utah.

Q. I see that Mr. Beecher is coming round to your views on theology?

A. I would not have the egotism to say that he was coming round to my views, but evidently Mr. Beecher has been growing. His head has been instructed by his heart; and if a man will allow even the poor plant of pity to grow in his heart he will hold in infinite execration all orthodox religion. The moment he will allow himself to think that eternal consequences depend on human life; that the few short years we live in this world determine for an eternity the question of infinite joy or infinite pain; the moment he thinks of that he will see that it is an infinite absurdity. For instance, a man is born in Arkansas and lives there to be 17 or 18 years of age; is it possible that he can be truthfully told at the day of judgment that he had a fair chance? Just imagine a man being held eternally responsible for his conduct in Delaware! Mr. Beecher is a man of great genius – full of poetry and pathos. Every now and then he is driven back by the orthodox members of his congregation toward the old religion, and for the benefit of those weak disciples he will preach what is called "a doctrinal sermon"; but before he gets through with it, seeing it is infinitely cruel, he utters a cry of horror, and protests with all the strength of his nature against the cruelty of the creed. I imagine that he has always thought that he was under great obligation to Plymouth church, but the truth is that that church depends on him; that church gets its character from Mr. Beecher. He has done a vast deal to ameliorate the condition of the average orthodox mind. He excites the envy of the mediocre minister, and he excites the hatred of the really orthodox, but he receives the approbation of good and generous men everywhere. For my part, I have no quarrel with any religion that does not threaten eternal punishment to good people and that does not promise eternal reward to bad people. If orthodox Christianity be true, some of the best people I know are going to hell, and some of the meanest I have ever known are either in heaven or on the road. Of course, I admit that there are thousands and millions of good Christians – honest and noble people, but in my judgment, Mr. Beecher is the greatest man in the world who now occupies a pulpit.

Speaking of a man's living in Delaware, a young man, some time ago, came up to me on the street in an Eastern city and asked for money. "What is your business," I asked. "I am a waiter by profession." "Where do you come from?" "Delaware." "Well, what was the matter – did you drink, or cheat your employer, or were you idle?" "No." "What was the trouble?" "Well, the truth is the state is so small they don't need any waiters; they all reach for what they want."

Q. Do you not think there are some dangerous tendencies in liberalism?

A. I will first state this proposition: The credit system in morals, as in business, breeds extravagance. The cash system in morals, as well as in business, breeds economy. We will suppose a community in which everybody is bound to sell on credit, and in which every creditor can take the benefit of the bankrupt law every Saturday night, and the constable pays the costs. In my judgment that community would be extravagant as long as the merchants lasted. We will take another community in which everybody has to pay cash, and in my judgment that community will be an economical one. Now then, let us apply this to morals. Christianity allows everybody to sin on a credit, and allows a man who has lived, we will say 69 years, what Christians are pleased to call a worldly life, an immoral life. They allow him on his deathbed, between the last dose of medicine and the last breath, to be converted, and that man who has done nothing except evil becomes an angel. Here is another man who has lived the same length of time, doing all the good he possibly could do, but not meeting with what they are pleased to call "a change of heart"; he goes to a world of pain. Now, my doctrine is that everybody must reap exactly what he sows, other things being equal. If he acts badly he will not be happy; if he acts well he will not be sad. I believe in the doctrine of consequences, and that every man must stand the consequences of his own acts. It seems to me that that fact will have a greater restraining influence than the idea that you can, just before you leave this world, shift your burden on to somebody else. I am a believer in the restraining influences of liberty, because responsibility goes hand in hand with freedom. I do not believe that the gallows is the last step between earth and heaven. I do not believe in the conversion and salvation of murderers while their innocent victims are in hell. The church has taught so long that he who acts virtuously carries a cross, and that only sinners enjoy themselves, that it may be that for a little while after men leave the church they may go to extremes until they demonstrate for themselves that the path of vice is the path of thorns, and that only along the wayside of virtue grow the flowers of joy. The church has depicted virtue as a sour wrinkled termagant; an old woman with nothing but skin and bones, and a temper beyond description; and at the same time vice has been painted in all the voluptuous outlines of a Greek statue. The truth is exactly the other way. A thing is right because it pays; a thing is wrong because it does not; and when I use the word "pays," I mean in the highest and noblest sense. — *The Daily News,* Denver, Colorado, Jan. 17, 1884.

CHRISTIANITY

Q. Are you getting nearer to or farther away from God, Christianity, and the Bible?

A. In the first place, as Mr. Locke so often remarked, we will define our terms. If by the word "God" is meant a person, a being, who existed before the creation of the universe, and who controls all that is, except himself, I do not believe in such a being; but if by the word "god" is meant all that is, that is to say, the universe, including every atom and every star, then I am a believer. I suppose the word that would nearest describe me is "pantheist." I cannot believe that a being existed from eternity, and finally created this universe after having wasted an eternity in idleness; but on this subject I know just as little as anybody ever did or ever will, and, in my judgment, just as much. My intellectual horizon is somewhat limited, and, to tell you the truth, this is the only world that I was ever in. I am what might be called a representative of a rural district, and, as a matter of fact, I know little about my district. I believe it was Confucius who said: "How should I know anything about another world when I know so little of this?"

The greatest intellects of the world have endeavored to find words to express their conception of God, of the first cause, or of the science of being, but they have never succeeded. I find in the old confession of faith, in the old catechism, for instance, this description: that God is a being without body, parts or passions. I think it would trouble anybody to find a better definition of nothing. That describes a vacuum, that is to say. that describes the absence of everything. I find that theology is a subject that only the most ignorant are certain about, and that the more a man thinks, the less he knows.

From the Bible God I do not know that I am going farther and farther away. I have been about as far as a man could get for many years. I do not believe in the God of the Old Testament.

Now, as to the next branch of your question, Christianity.

The question arises, What is Christianity? I have no objection to the morality taught as a part of Christianity, no objection to its charity, its forgiveness, its kindness; no objection to its hope for this world and another, not the slightest, but all these things do not make Christianity. Mohammed taught certain doctrines that are good, but the good in the teachings of Mohammed is not Mohammedism. When I speak of Christianity I speak of that which is distinctly Christian. For instance, the idea that the infinite God was born in Palestine, learned the carpenter's trade, disputed with the parsons of his time, excited the wrath of the theological bigots, and was finally crucified; that afterward he was raised from the dead, and that if anybody believes this he will be saved and if he fails to believe it, he will be lost; in other words, that which is distinctly Christian in the Christian system is its supernaturalism, its miracles, its absurdity. Truth does not need to go into partnership with the supernatural. What Christ said is worth the reason it contains. If a man raises the dead and then says twice two are five, that changes no rule in mathematics. If a multiplication table was divinely inspired, that does no good. The question is, is it correct? So I think that in the world of morals we must prove that a thing is right or wrong by experience, by analogy, not by miracles. There is no fact in physical science that can be supernaturally demonstrated. Neither is there any fact in the moral world that could be substantiated by miracles. Now then, keeping in mind that by Christianity I mean the supernatural in that system, of course I am just as far away from it as I can ever get. For the man Christ I have respect. He was an Infidel in his day, and the ministers of his day cried out blasphemy, as they have been crying ever since against every person who has suggested a new thought or shown the worthlessness of an old one.

Now, as to the third part of the question, the Bible. People say that the Bible is inspired. Well, what does inspired mean? Did God write it? No; but the men who did write it were guided by the Holy Spirit. Very well. Did they write exactly what the Holy Spirit wanted them to write? Well, religious people say, yes. At the same time they admit that the gentlemen who were collecting, or taking down in shorthand what was said, had to use their own words. Now, we all know that the same words do not have the same meaning to all people. It is impossible to convey the same thoughts to all minds by the same language, and it is for that reason that the Bible has produced so many sects, not only disagreeing with each other, but disagreeing among themselves.

We find, then, that it is utterly impossible for God (admitting that there is one) to convey the same thoughts by human language to all people. No two persons understand the same language alike. A man's understanding depends on his experience, on his capacity, on the particular bent of his mind – in fact, on the countless influences that have made him what he is. Everything in nature tells everyone who sees it a story, but that story depends on the capacity of the one to whom it is told. The sea says one thing to the ordinary man, and another thing to Shakespeare. The stars have not the same language for all people. The consequence is that no book can tell the same story to any two persons. The Jewish Scriptures are like other books, written by different men in different ages of the world, hundreds of years apart, filled with contradictions. They embody, I presume, fairly enough, the wisdom and ignorance, the reason and prejudice, of the times in which they were written. They are worth the good that is in them, and the question is whether we will take the good and throw the bad away. There are good laws and bad laws. There are wise and foolish sayings. There are gentle and cruel passages, and you can find a text to suit almost any frame of mind; whether you wish to do an act of charity or murder a neighbor's babe, you will find a passage that will exactly fit the case. So that I can say that I am still for the reasonable, for the natural: and am still opposed to the absurd and supernatural.

Q. Is there any better or more ennobling belief than Christianity; if so, what is it?

A. There are many good things, of course, in every religion, or they would not have existed; plenty of good precepts in Christianity, but the thing that I object to more than all others is the doctrine of eternal punishment, the idea of hell for many and heaven for the few. Take from Christianity the doctrine of eternal punishment and I have no particular objection to what is generally preached. If you will take that away, and all the supernatural connected with it, I have no objection; but that doctrine of eternal punishment tends to harden the human heart. It has produced more misery than all the other doctrines in the world. It has shed more blood; it has made more martyrs. It has lighted the fires of persecution and kept the sword of cruelty wet with heroic blood for at least a thousand years. There is no crime that doctrine has not produced. I think it would be impossible for the imagination to conceive of a worse religion than orthodox Christianity – utterly impossible; a doctrine that divides this world, a doctrine that divides families, a doctrine that teaches the son that he can be happy with his mother in perdition; the husband that he can be happy in heaven while his wife suffers the agonies of hell. This doctrine is infinite injustice, and tends to subvert all ideas of justice in the human heart. I think it would be impossible to conceive of a doctrine better calculated to make wild beasts of men than that; in fact, that doctrine was born of all the wild beasts there is in man. It was born of infinite revenge.

Think of preaching that you must believe that a certain being was the son of God, no matter whether your reason is convinced or not. Suppose one should meet, we will say on London Bridge, a man clad in rags, and he should stop us and say, "My friend, I wish to talk with you a moment. I am the rightful king of Great Britain," and you should say to him, "Well, my dinner is waiting; I have no time to bother about who the king of England is," and then he should meet another and insist on his stopping while he pulled out some papers to show that he was the rightful king of England, and the other man should say, "I have got business here, my friend; I am selling goods and I have no time to bother my head about who the king of England is. No doubt you are the king of England, but you don't look like him." And then suppose he stops another man and makes the same statement to him, and the other man should laugh at him and say, "I don't want to hear anything on this subject; you are crazy; you ought to go to some insane asylum, or put something on your head to keep you cool." And suppose, after all it should turn out that the man was king of England and should afterward make his claim good and be crowned in Westminster. What would we think of that king if he should hunt up the gentlemen that he met on London Bridge and have their heads cut off because they had no faith that he was the rightful heir? And what would we think of a God now who would damn a man 1,800 years after the event because he did not believe that he was God at the time he was living in Jerusalem; not only damn the fellow that he met, and who did not believe in him, but gentlemen who lived 1,800 years afterward and who certainly could have known nothing of the facts except from hearsay.

The best religion, after all, is common sense; a religion for this world, one world at a time, a religion for today. We want a religion that will deal in questions in which we are interested. How are we to do away with crime? How are we to do away with pauperism? How are we to do away with the want and misery in every civilized country? England is a Christian nation, and yet about one in six in the city of London dies in almshouses, asylums, prisons, hospitals, and jails. We, I suppose, are a civilized nation, and yet all the penitentiaries are crammed; there is want on every hand, and my opinion is that we had better turn our attention to this world.

Christianity is charitable; Christianity spends a great deal of money; but I am somewhat doubtful as to the good that is accomplished. There ought to be some way to prevent crime; not simply to punish it. There ought to be some way to prevent pauperism, not simply to relieve temporarily a pauper, and if the ministers and good people belonging to the churches would spend their time investigating the affairs of this world and let the new Jerusalem take care of itself, I think it would be far better.

The church is guilty of one great contradiction. The ministers are always talking about worldly people and yet, were it not for worldly people, who would pay the salary? How could the church live a minute unless somebody attended to the affairs of this world? The best religion, in my judgment, is common sense going along hand in hand with kindness, and not troubling ourselves about another world until we get there. I am willing, for one, to wait and see what kind of a country it will be.

Q. Does the question of the inspiration of the Scriptures affect the beauty and benefits of Christianity here and hereafter?

A. A belief in the inspiration of the Scriptures has done, in my judgment, great harm. The Bible has been the breastwork for nearly everything wrong. The defenders of slavery relied on the Bible. The Bible was the real auction block on which every Negro stood when he was sold. I never knew a minister to preach in favor of slavery that did not take his text from the Bible. The Bible teaches persecution for opinion's sake. The Bible – that is the Old Testament — upholds polygamy, and just to the extent that men, through the Bible, have believed that slavery, religious persecution, wars of extermination and polygamy were taught by God, just to that extent the Bible has done great harm. The idea of inspiration enslaves the human mind and debauches the human heart.

Q. Is not Christianity and the belief in God a check on mankind in general and thus a good thing in itself?

A. This, again, brings up the question of what you mean by Christianity; but taking it for granted that you mean by Christianity the church, then I answer, when the church had almost absolute authority, then the world was the worst.

Now, as to the other part of the question, "Is not a belief in God a chuck on mankind in general?" That is owing to what kind of god the man believes in. When mankind believed in the God of the Old Testament, I think that belief was a bad thing; the tendency was bad. I think that John Calvin patterned after Jehovah as nearly as his health and strength would permit. Man makes God in his own image, and bad men are not apt to have a good God if they make him. I believe it is far better to have a real belief in goodness, in kindness, in honesty, and in mankind than in any supernatural being whatever. I do not suppose it would do any harm for a man to believe in a real good God, a God without revenge, a God that was not particular in having a man believe a doctrine whether he could understand it or not. I do not believe that a belief of that kind would do any particular harm.

There is a vast difference between the God of John Calvin and the God of Henry Ward Beecher, and a great difference between the God of Cardinal Pedro Gonzales de Mendoza and the God of Theodore Parker.

Q. Well, Colonel, is the world growing better or worse?

A. I think better in some respects, and worse in others; but on the whole, better. I think that while events, like the pendulum of a clock, go backward and forward, man, like the hands, goes forward. I think there is more reason and less religion, more charity and less creed. I think the church is improving. Ministers are ashamed to preach the old doctrines with the old fervor. There was a time when the pulpit controlled the pews. It is so no longer. The pews know what they want, and if the minister does not furnish it they discharge him and employ another. He is no longer an autocrat; he must bring to the market what his customers are willing to buy.

Q. What are you going to do to be saved?

A. Well, I think I am safe anyway. I suppose I have a right to rely on what Matthew says, that if I will forgive others God will forgive me. I suppose if there is another world I shall be treated much as I treat others. I never expect to find perfect bliss anywhere; maybe I should tire of it if I should. What I have endeavored to do has been to put out the fires of an ignorant and cruel hell; to do what I could to destroy that dogma; to destroy that doctrine that makes the cradle as terrible as the coffin. — *The Denver Republican,* Denver, Colorado, Jan. 17, 1884.

THE OATH QUESTION

Q. I suppose that your attention has been called to the excitement in England over the oath question, and you have probably wondered that so much should have been made of so little.

A. Yes; I have read a few articles on the subject, including one by Cardinal Newman. It is wonderful that so many people imagine that there is something miraculous in the oath. They seem to regard it as a kind of verbal fetish – a charm, an "open sesame" to be pronounced at the door of truth, a spell, a kind of moral thumbscrew, by means of which falsehood itself is compelled to turn informer.

The oath has outlived its brother, "the wager of battle." Both were born of the idea that God would interfere for the right and for the truth. Trial by fire and by water had the same origin. It was once believed that the man in the wrong could not kill the man in the right; but, experience having shown that he usually did, the belief gradually fell into disrepute. So it was once thought that a perjurer could not swallow a piece of sacramental bread; but, the fear that made the swallowing difficult having passed away, the appeal to the corsned [consecrated bread] was abolished. It was found that a brazen or a desperate man could eat himself out of the greatest difficulty with perfect ease, satisfying the law and his own hunger at the same time.

The oath is a relic of barbarous theology, of the belief that a personal god interferes in the affairs of men; that some God protects innocence and guards the right. The experience of the world has sadly demonstrated the folly of that belief. The testimony of a witness ought to be believed, not because it is given under the solemnities of an oath, but because it is reasonable. If unreasonable it ought to be thrown aside. The question ought not to be, "Has this been sworn to?" but, "Is this true?" The moment evidence is tested by the standard of reason, the oath becomes a useless ceremony. Let the man who gives the false evidence be punished as the lawmaking power may prescribe. He should be punished because he commits a crime against society, and he should be punished in this world. All honest men will tell the truth if they can; therefore, oaths will have no effect on them. Dishonest men will not tell the truth unless the truth happens to suit their purpose; therefore, oaths will have no effect on them. We punish them, not for swearing to a lie, but for telling it; and we can make the punishment for telling the falsehood just as severe as we wish. If they are to be punished in another world, the probability is that the punishment there will be for having told the falsehood here. After all, a lie is made no worse by an oath, and the truth is made no better.

Q. You object then to the oath. Is your objection based on any religious grounds, or on any prejudice against the ceremony because of its religious origin; or what is your objection?

A. I care nothing about the origin of the ceremony. The objection to the oath is this: It furnishes a falsehood with a letter of credit. It supplies the wolf with sheep's clothing and covers the hand of Jacob with hair, blows out the light, and in the darkness Leah is taken for Rachel. It puts upon each witness a kind of theological gown. This gown hides the moral rags of the depraved wretch as well as the virtues of the honest man. The oath is a mask that falsehood puts on, and for a moment is mistaken for truth. It gives to dishonesty the advantage of solemnity. The tendency of the oath is to put all testimony on an equality. The obscure rascal and the man of sterling character both "swear," and jurors who attribute a miraculous quality to the oath forget the real difference in the men and give about the same weight to the evidence of each, because both were "sworn." A scoundrel is delighted with the opportunity of going through a ceremony that gives importance and dignity to his story, that clothes him for the moment with respectability, loans him the appearance of conscience, and gives the ring of true coin to the base metal. To him the oath is a shield. He is in partnership, for a moment, with God, and people who have no confidence in the witness credit the firm.

Q. Of course, you know the religionists insist that people are more likely to tell the truth when "sworn," and that to take away the oath is to destroy the foundation of testimony.

A. If the use of the oath is defended on the ground that religious people need a stimulus to tell the truth, then I am compelled to say that religious people have been so badly educated that they mistake the nature of the crime.

They should be taught that to defeat justice by falsehood is the real offense. Besides, fear is not the natural foundation of virtue.

Even with religious people fear cannot always last. Ananias and Sapphira have been dead so long, and since their time so many people have sworn falsely without affecting their health that the fear of sudden divine vengeance no longer pales the cheek of the perjurer. If the vengeance is not sudden, then, according to the church, the criminal will have plenty of time to repent; so that the oath no longer affects even the fearful. Would it not be better for the church to teach that telling the falsehood is the real crime, and that taking the oath neither adds to nor takes from its enormity? Would it not be better to teach that he who does wrong must suffer the consequences, whether God forgives him or not?

He who tries to injure another may or may not succeed, but he cannot by any possibility fail to injure himself. Men should be taught that there is no difference between truth-telling and truth-swearing. Nothing is more vicious than the idea that any ceremony or form of words – hand-lifting or book-kissing – can add, even in the slightest degree, to the perpetual obligation every human being is under to speak the truth.

The truth, plainly told, naturally commends itself to the intelligent. Every fact is a genuine link in the infinite chain, and will agree perfectly with every other fact. A fact asks to be inspected, asks to be understood. It needs no oath, no ceremony, no supernatural aid. It is independent of all the gods. A falsehood goes in partnership with theology and depends on the partner for success.

To show how little influence for good has been attributed to the oath, it is only necessary to say that for centuries, in the Christian world, no person was allowed to testify who had the slightest pecuniary interest in the result of a suit.

The expectation of a farthing in this world was supposed to outweigh the fear of God's wrath in the next. All the pangs, pains, and penalties of perdition were considered as nothing when compared with the pounds, shillings, and pence in this world.

Q. You know that in nearly all deliberative bodies – in parliaments and congresses – an oath or an affirmation is required to support what is called the Constitution; and that all officers are required to swear or affirm that they will discharge their duties; do these oaths and affirmations, in your judgment, do any good?

A. Men have sought to make nations and institutions immortal by oaths. Subjects have sworn to obey kings, and kings have sworn to protect subjects, and yet the subjects have sometimes beheaded a king; and the king has often plundered the subjects.

The oaths enabled them to deceive each other. Every absurdity in religion, and all tyrannical institutions, have been patched, buttressed, and reinforced by oaths; and yet the history of the world shows the utter futility of putting in the coffin of an oath the political and religious aspirations of the race.

Revolutions and reformations care little for "So help me God." Oaths have riveted shackles and sanctified abuses. People swear to support a constitution, and they will keep the oath so long as the constitution supports them. In 1776 the colonists cared nothing for the fact that they had sworn to support the British crown. All the oaths to defend the Constitution of the United States did not prevent the Civil War. We have at last learned that states may be kept together for a little time, by force; permanently only by mutual interests. We have found that the Delilah of superstition cannot bind with oaths the secular Samson.

Why should a member of parliament or of congress swear to maintain the Constitution? If he is a dishonest man, the oath will have no effect; if he is an honest patriot, it will have no effect. In both cases it is equally useless. If a member fails to support the Constitution the probability is that his constituents will treat him as he does the Constitution. In this country, after all the members of Congress have sworn or affirmed to defend the Constitution, each political party charges the other with a deliberate endeavor to destroy that "sacred instrument." Possibly the political oath was invented to prevent the free and natural development of a nation. Kings and nobles and priests wished to retain the property they had filched and clutched, and for that purpose they compelled the real owners to swear that they would support and defend the law under color of which the theft and robbery had been accomplished.

So, in the church, creeds have been protected by oaths. Priests and laymen solemnly swore that they would, under no circumstances, resort to reason; that they would overcome facts by faith, and strike down demonstrations with the "sword of the spirit." Professors of the theological seminary at Andover, Massachusetts, swear to defend certain dogmas and to attack others. They swear sacredly to keep and guard the ignorance they have. With them, philosophy leads to perjury, and reason is the road to crime. While theological professors are not likely to make an intellectual discovery, still it is unwise, by taking an oath, to render that certain which was only improbable.

If all witnesses sworn to tell the truth did so, if all members of Parliament and Congress, in taking the oath, became intelligent, patriotic, and honest, I should be in favor of retaining the ceremony; but we find that men who have taken the same oath advocate opposite ideas, and entertain different opinions as to the meaning of constitutions and laws. The oath adds nothing to their intelligence; does not even tend to increase their patriotism, and certainly does not make the dishonest honest.

Q. Are not persons allowed to testify in the United States whether they believe in future rewards and punishments or not?

A. In this country, in most of the states, witnesses are allowed to testify whether they believe in perdition and paradise or not. In some states they are allowed to testify even if they deny the existence of God. We have found that religious belief does not compel people to tell the truth, and that an utter denial of every Christian creed does not even tend to make them dishonest. You see, a religious belief does not affect the senses. Justice should not shut any door that leads to truth. No one will pretend that because you do not believe in hell your sight is impaired, or your hearing dulled, or your memory rendered less retentive. A witness in a court is called on to tell what he has seen, what he has heard, what he remembers, not what he believes about gods and devils and hells and heavens. A witness substantiates not a faith, but a fact. In order to ascertain whether a witness will tell the truth, you might with equal propriety examine him as to his ideas about music, painting or architecture, as theology. A man may have no ear for music, and yet remember what he hears. He may care nothing about painting, and yet be able to tell what he sees. So he may deny every creed, and yet be able to tell the facts as he remembers them.

Thomas Jefferson was wise enough so to frame the Constitution of Virginia that no person could be deprived of any civil right on account of his religious or irreligious belief. Through the influence of men like Paine, Franklin, and Jefferson, it was provided in the federal Constitution that officers elected under its authority could swear or affirm. This was the natural result of the separation of church and state.

Q. I see that your presidents and governors issue their proclamations calling on the people to assemble in their churches and offer thanks to God. How does this happen in a government where church and state are not united?

A. Jefferson, when president, refused to issue what is known as the "Thanksgiving Proclamation," on the ground that the federal government had no right to interfere in religious matters; that the people owed no religious duties to the government; that the government derived its powers, not from priests or gods, but from the people, and was responsible alone to the source of its power. The truth is the framers of our Constitution intended that the government should be secular in the broadest and best sense; and yet there are thousands and thousands of religious people in this country who are greatly scandalized because there is no recognition of God in the federal Constitution; and for several years a great many ministers have been endeavoring to have the Constitution amended so as to recognize the existence of God and the divinity of Christ. A man by the name of Pollock was once superintendent of the mint at Philadelphia. He was almost insane about having God in the Constitution. Failing in that, he got the inscription on our money, "In God We Trust." As our silver dollar is now, in fact, worth only 85¢, it is claimed that the inscription means that we trust in God for the other 15¢.

There is a constant effort on the part of many Christians to have their religion in some way recognized by law. Proclamations are now issued calling on the people to give thanks, and directing attention to the fact that, while God has scourged or neglected other nations, he has been remarkably attentive to the wants and wishes of the United States. Governors of states issue these documents written in a tone of pious insincerity. The year may or may not have been prosperous, yet the degree of thankfulness called for is always precisely the same.

A few years ago the governor of Iowa issued an exceedingly rhetorical proclamation in which the people were requested to thank God for the unparalleled blessings he had showered on them. A private citizen, fearing that the Lord might be misled by official correspondence, issued his proclamation, in which he recounted with great particularity the hardships of the preceding year. He insisted that the weather had been of the poorest quality; that the crops had generally failed; that the spring came late, and the frost early; that the people were in debt; that the farms were mortgaged; that the merchants were bankrupt; and that everything was in the worst possible condition. He concluded by sincerely hoping that the Lord would pay no attention to the proclamation of the governor, but would, if he had any doubt on the subject, come down and examine the state for himself.

These proclamations have always appeared to me absurdly egotistical. Why should God treat us any better than he does the rest of his children? Why should he send pestilence and famine to China, and health and plenty to us? Why give us corn, and Egypt cholera? All these proclamations grow out of egotism and selfishness, or ignorance and superstition, and are based on the idea that God is a capricious monster; that he loves flattery; that he can be coaxed and cajoled.

The conclusion of the whole matter with me is this: For truth in courts we must depend on the trained intelligence of judges, the right of cross-examination, the honesty and common sense of jurors, and on an enlightened public opinion. As for members of Congress, we will trust to the wisdom and patriotism, not only of the members, but of their constituents. In religion we will give to all the luxury of absolute liberty.

The alchemist did not succeed in finding any stone the touch of which transmuted baser things to gold; and priests have not invented yet an oath with power to force from falsehood's desperate lips the pearl of truth. — *Secular Review,* London, England, 1884.

GENERAL SUBJECTS

Q. Do you enjoy lecturing?

A. Of course, I enjoy lecturing. It is a great pleasure to drive the fiend of fear out of the hearts of men, women, and children. It is a positive joy to put out the fires of hell.

Q. Where do you meet with the bitterest opposition?

A. I meet with the bitterest opposition where the people are the most ignorant, where there is the least thought, where there are the fewest books. The old theology is becoming laughable. Few ministers have the impudence to preach in the old way. They give new meanings to old words. They subscribe to the same creed, but preach exactly the other way. The clergy are ashamed to admit that they are orthodox, and they ought to be.

Q. Do liberal books, such as the works of Paine and Infidel scientists, sell well?

A. Yes, they are about the only books on serious subjects that do sell well. The works of Darwin, Buckle, Draper, Haeckel, Tyndall, Humboldt, and hundreds of others are read by intelligent people the world over. Works of a religious character die on the shelves. The people want facts. They want to know about this world, about all the forms of life. They want the mysteries of every day solved. They want honest thoughts about sensible questions. They are tired of the follies of faith and the falsehoods of superstition. They want a heaven here. In a few years the old theological books will be sold to make paper on which to print the discoveries of science.

Q. In what section of the country do you find the most liberality?

A. I find great freedom of thought in Boston, New York, Chicago, San Francisco, in fact, all over what we call the North. The West, of course, is liberal. The truth is that all the intelligent part of the country is liberal. The railroad, the telegraph, the daily paper, electric light, the telephone, and freedom of thought belong together.

Q. Is it true that you were once threatened with a criminal prosecution for libel on religion?

99

A. Yes, in Delaware. Chief Justice Comegys instructed the grand jury to indict me for blasphemy. I have taken my revenge on the state by leaving it in ignorance. Delaware is several centuries behind the times. It is as bigoted as it is small. Compare Kansas City with Wilmington and you will see the difference between liberalism and orthodoxy.

Q. Will liberalism ever organize in America?

A. I hope not. Organization means creed, and creed means petrifaction and tyranny. I believe in individuality. I will not join any society except an anti-society society.

Q. Do you consider the religion of Bhagavat Purana of the East as good as the Christian?

A. It is far more poetic. It has greater variety and shows vastly more thought. Like the Hebrew, it is poisoned with superstition, but it has more beauty. Nothing can be more barren than the theology of the Jews and Christians. One lonely God, a heaven filled with thoughtless angels, a hell with unfortunate souls. Nothing can be more desolate. The Greek mythology is infinitely better.

Q. What do you think of Beecher?

A. He is a great man, but the habit of his mind and the bent of his early education oppose his heart. He is growing and has been growing every day for many years. He has given up the idea of eternal punishment, and that of necessity destroys it all. The Christian religion is founded on hell. When the foundation crumbles the fabric falls. Beecher was to have answered my article in the *North American Review,* but when it appeared and he saw it, he agreed with so much of it that he concluded that an answer would be useless. — *The Times,* Kansas City, Missouri, Feb. 23, 1884.

REPLY TO KANSAS CITY CLERGY

Q. Will you take any notice of Mr. Magrath's challenge?

A. I do not think it worthwhile to discuss with Mr. Magrath. I do not say this in disparagement of his ability, as I do not know the gentleman. He may be one of the greatest of men. I think, however, that Mr. Magrath might better answer what I have already said. If he succeeds in that, then I will meet him in public discussion. Of course, he is an eminent theologian or he would not think of discussing these questions with anybody. I have never heard of him, but for all that he may be the most intelligent of men.

Q. How have the recently expressed opinions of our local clergy impressed you?

A. I suppose you refer to the preachers who have given their opinion of me. In the first place I am obliged to them for acting as my agents. I think Mr. Hogan has been imposed on. Tacitus is a poor witness – about like Josephus. I say again that we have not a word about Christ written by any human being who lived in the time of Christ – not a solitary word, and Mr. Hogan ought to know it.

The Rev. Mr. Mathews is mistaken. If the Bible proves anything, it proves that the world was made in six days and that Adam and eve were built on Saturday. The Bible gives the age of Adam when he died, and then gives the ages of others down to the flood, and then from that time at least to the return from captivity. If the genealogy of the Bible is true, it is about 6,000 years since Adam was made, and the world is only five days older than Adam. It is nonsense to say the days were long periods of time. If that is so, away goes the idea of Sunday. The only reason for keeping Sunday given in the Bible is that God made the world in six days and rested on the seventh. Mr. Mathews is not candid. He knows that he cannot answer the arguments I have urged against the Bible. He knows that the ancient Jews were barbarians and that the Old Testament is a barbarous book. He knows that it upholds slavery and polygamy, and he probably feels ashamed of what he is compelled to preach.

Mr. Jardine takes a cheerful view of the subject. He expects the light to dawn on the unbelievers. He speaks as though he were

101

the superior of all Infidels. He claims to be a student of the evidences of Christianity. There are no evidences, consequently Mr. Jardine is a student of nothing. It is amazing how dignified some people can get on a small capital.

Mr. Haley has sense enough to tell the ministers not to attempt to answer me. That is good advice. The ministers had better keep still. It is the safer way. If they try to answer what I say, the "sheep" will see how foolish the "shepherds" are. The best way is for them to say, "that has been answered."

Mr. Wells agrees with Mr. Haley. He, too, thinks that silence is the best weapon. I agree with him. Let the clergy keep still; that is the best way. It is better to say nothing than to talk absurdity. I am delighted to think that at last the ministers have concluded that they had better not answer Infidels.

Mr. Woods is fearful only for the young. He is afraid that I will hurt the children. He thinks that the mother ought to stoop over the cradle and in the ears of the babe shout, "Hell!" So he thinks in all probability that the same word ought to be repeated at the grave as a consolation to mourners.

I am glad that Mr. Mann thinks that I am doing neither good nor harm. This gives me great hope. If I do no harm, certainly I ought not to be eternally damned. It is consoling to have an orthodox minister solemnly assert that I am doing no harm. I wish I could say as much for him.

The truth is all these ministers kept back their real thoughts. They do not tell their doubts – they know that orthodoxy is doomed – they know that the old doctrine excites laughter and scorn. They know that the fires of hell are dying out; that the Bible is ceasing to be an authority, and that the pulpit is growing feebler and feebler every day. Poor parsons!

Q. Would the Catholicism of General Sherman's family affect his chances for the presidency?

A. I do not think the religion of the family should have any weight one way or the other. It would make no difference with me; although I hate Catholicism with all my heart, I do not hate Catholics. Some people might be so prejudiced that they would not vote for a man whose wife belongs to the Catholic Church; but such people are too narrow to be consulted. General Sherman says that he wants no office. In that he shows his good sense. He is a great man and a great soldier. He has won laurels enough for one brow. He has the respect and admiration of the nation and does not need the presidency to finish his career. He wishes to enjoy the honors he has won and the rest he deserves.

Q. What is your opinion of Matthew Arnold?

A. He is a man of talent, well educated, a little fussy, somewhat sentimental, but he is not a genius. He is not creative. He is not a critic – not an originator. He will not compare with Emerson. — *The Journal,* Kansas City, Missouri, Feb. 23, 1884.

SWEARING AND AFFIRMING

Q. What is the difference in the parliamentary oath of this country which saves us from such a squabble as they have had in England over the Bradlaugh case?

A. Our Constitution provides that a member of Congress may swear or affirm. The consequence is that we can have no such controversy as they have had in England. The framers of our Constitution wished forever to divorce church and state. They knew that it made no possible difference whether a man swore or affirmed, or whether he swore and affirmed to support the Constitution. All the federal officers who went into the rebellion had sworn or affirmed to support the Constitution. All that did no good. The entire oath business is a mistake. I think it would be a thousand times better to abolish all oaths in courts of justice. The oath allows a rascal to put on the garments of solemnity, the mask of piety, while he tells a lie. In other words, the oath allows the villain to give falsehood the appearance of truth. I think it would be far better to let each witness tell his story and leave his evidence to the intelligence of the jury and judge. The trouble about the oath is that its tendency is to put all witnesses on an equality; the jury says, "Why, he swore to it." Now, if the oath were abolished, the jury would judge all testimony according to the witness, and then the evidence of one man of good reputation would outweigh the lies of thousands of nobodies.

It was at one time believed that there was something miraculous in the oath, that it was a kind of thumbscrew that would torture the truth out of a rascal, and at one time they believed that if a man swore falsely he might be struck by lightning or be paralyzed. But so many people have sworn to lies without having their health injured that the old superstition has little weight with the average witness. I think it would be far better to let every man tell his story; let him be cross-examined, let the jury find out as much as they can of his character, of his standing among his neighbors – then weigh his testimony in the scale of reason. The oath is born of superstition, and everything born of superstition is bad. The oath gives the lie currency; it gives it for a moment the ring of true metal, and the ordinary average juror is imposed on and justice in many instances defeated. Nothing can be more absurd than the swearing of a man to support the Constitution. Let him do what he likes. If he does not support the Constitution, the probability is that his constituents will refuse to support him. Every man who swears to support the Constitution swears to support it as he understands it, and no two understand it exactly alike. Now, if the oath brightened a man's intellect or added to his information or increased his patriotism or gave him a little more honesty, it would be a good thing – but it doesn't. And as a consequence it is a useless and absurd proceeding. Nothing amuses me more in a court than to see one calf kissing the tanned skin of another.

— *The Courier*, Buffalo, New York, May 19, 1884.

REPLY TO A BUFFALO CRITIC

Q. What have you to say in reply to the letter in today's *Times* signed R. H. S.?

A. I find that I am accused of "four flagrant wrongs," and while I am not as yet suffering from the qualms of conscience, nor do I feel called upon to confess and be forgiven, yet I have something to say in self-defense.

As to the first objection made by your correspondent, namely that my doctrine deprives people of the hope that after this life is ended they will meet their fathers, mothers, sisters, and brothers, long since passed away in the land beyond the grave and there enjoy their company forever, I have this to say: If Christianity is true we are not quite certain of meeting our relatives and friends where we can enjoy their company forever. If Christianity is true most of our friends will be in hell. The ones I love best and whose memory I cherish will certainly be among the lost. The trouble about Christianity is that it is infinitely selfish. Each man thinks that if he can save his own little shriveled microscopic soul, that is enough. No matter what becomes of the rest. Christianity has no consolation for a generous man. I do not wish to go to heaven if the ones who have given me joy are to be lost. I would much rather go with them. The only thing that makes life endurable in this world is human love, and yet, according to Christianity, that is the very thing we are not to have in the other world. We are to be so taken up with Jesus and the angels that we shall care nothing about our brothers and sisters that have been damned. We shall be so carried away with the music of the harp that we shall not even hear the wail of father or mother. Such a religion is a disgrace to human nature.

As to the second objection – that society cannot be held together in peace and good order without hell and a belief in eternal torment, I would ask why an infinitely wise and good God should make people of so poor and mean a character that society cannot be held together without scaring them. Is it possible that God has so made the world that the threat of eternal punishment is necessary for the preservation of society?

106

The writer of the letter also says that it is necessary to believe that if a man commits murder here he is destined to be punished in hell for the offense. This is Christianity. Yet nearly every murderer goes directly from the gallows to God. Nearly every murderer takes it on himself to lecture the assembled multitude who have gathered to see him hanged and invite them to meet him in heaven. When the rope is about his neck he feels the wings growing. That is the trouble with the Christian doctrine. Every murderer is told he may repent and go to heaven and have the happiness of seeing his victim in hell. Should heaven at any time become dull, the vein of pleasure can be rethrilled by the sight of his victim wriggling on the gridiron of God's justice. Really, Christianity leads men to sin on credit. It sells rascality on time and tells all the devils they can have the benefit of the Gospel Bankrupt Act.

The next point in the letter is that I do not preach for the benefit of mankind, but for the money which is the price of blood. Of course, it makes no difference whether I preach for money or not. That is to say, it makes no difference to the preached. The arguments I advance are either good or bad. If they are bad, they can easily be answered by argument. If they are not, they cannot be answered by personalities or by ascribing to me selfish motives. It is not a personal matter. It is a matter of logic, of sense – not a matter of slander, vituperation or hatred. The writer of the letter, R. H. S., may be an exceedingly good person, yet that will add no weight to his or her argument. He or she may be a bad person, but that would not weaken the logic of the letter, if it had any logic to begin with. It is not for me to say what my motives are in what I do or say; it must be left to the judgment of mankind. I presume I am about as bad as most folks, and as good as some, but my goodness or badness has nothing to do with the question. I may have committed every crime in the world, yet that does not make the story of the flood reasonable, nor does it even tend to show that the three gentlemen in the furnace were not scorched. I may be the best man in the world, yet that does not go to prove that Jonah was swallowed by the whale. Let me say right here that if there is another world I believe that every soul who finds the way to that shore will have an everlasting opportunity to do right – of reforming. My objection to Christianity is that it is infinitely cruel, infinitely selfish, and I might add, infinitely absurd. I deprive no one of any hope unless you call the expectation of eternal pain a hope.

Q. Have you read the Rev. Father Lambert's *Notes on Ingersoll,* and if so, what have you to say of them or in reply to them?

A. I have read a few pages or paragraphs of that pamphlet, and do not feel called on to say anything. Mr. Lambert has the same right to publish his ideas that I have, and the readers must judge. People who believe his way will probably think that he has succeeded in answering me. After all, he must leave the public to decide. I have no anxiety about the decision. Day by day the people are advancing, and in a little while the sacred superstitions of today will be cast aside with the foolish myths and fables of the pagan world.

As a matter of fact there can be no argument in favor of the supernatural. Suppose you should ask if I had read the work of that gentleman who says that twice two are five. I should answer you that no gentleman can prove that twice two are five; and yet this is exactly as easy as to prove the existence of the supernatural. There are no arguments in favor of the supernatural. There are theories and fears and mistakes and prejudices and guesses, but no arguments – plenty of faith, but no facts; plenty of divine revelation, but no demonstration. The supernatural, in my judgment, is a mistake. I believe in the natural. — *The Times,* Buffalo, New York, May 19, 1884.

BLASPHEMY

"If Robert G. Ingersoll indulges in blasphemy tonight in his lecture, as he has in other places and in this city before, he will be arrested before he leaves the city." So spoke Rev. Irwin H. Torrence, general secretary of the Pennsylvania Bible Society, yesterday afternoon to a Press reporter. "We have consulted counsel; the law is with us, and Ingersoll has but to do what he has done before, to find himself in a cell. Here is the act of March 31, 1860:

> *If any person shall willfully, premeditatedly, and despitefully blaspheme or speak loosely and profanely of almighty God, Christ Jesus, the Holy Spirit, or the Scriptures of truth, such person, on conviction thereof, shall be sentenced to pay a fine not exceeding one hundred dollars, and undergo an imprisonment not exceeding three months, or either, at the discretion of the court."*

Last evening Colonel Ingersoll sat in the dining room of Guy's Hotel, just in from New York City. When told of the plans of Mr. Torrence and his friends, he laughed and said:

> *I did not suppose that anybody was idiotic enough to want me arrested for blasphemy. It seems to me that an infinite being can take care of himself without the aid of any agent of a Bible society. Perhaps it is wrong for me to be here while the Methodist conference is in session. Of course, no one who differs from the Methodist ministers should ever visit Philadelphia while they are here. I most humbly hope to be forgiven.*

Q. What do you think of the law of 1860?

A. It is exceedingly foolish. Surely, there is no need for the legislature of Pennsylvania to protect an infinite God, and why should the Bible be protected by law? The most ignorant priest can hold Darwin up to orthodox scorn. This talk of the Rev. Mr. Torrence shows that my lectures are needed; that religious people do not know what real liberty is. I presume that the law of 1860 is an old one reenacted. It is a survival of ancient ignorance and bigotry, and no one in the legislature thought it worthwhile to fight it. It is the same as the law against swearing, both are dead letters and amount to nothing. They are not enforced and should not be. Public opinion will regulate such matters. If all who take the name of God in vain were imprisoned there would not be room in the jails to hold the ministers. They speak of God in the most flippant and snap-your-fingers way that can be conceived of. They speak to him as though he were an intimate chum, and metaphorically slap him on the back in the most familiar manner possible.

Q. Have you ever had any similar experience before?

A. Oh, yes – threats have been made, but I never was arrested. When Mr. Torrence gets cool he will see that he has made a mistake. People in Philadelphia have been in the habit of calling the citizens of Boston bigots – but there is more real freedom of thought and expression in Boston than in almost any other city in the world. I think that as I am to suffer in hell forever, Mr. Torrence ought to be satisfied and let me have a good time here. He can amuse himself through all eternity by seeing me in hell, and that ought to be enough to satisfy, not only an agent, but the whole Bible society. I never expected any trouble in this state and most sincerely hope that Mr. Torrence will not trouble me and make the city a laughingstock.

Philadelphia has no time to waste in such foolish things. Let the Bible take its chances with other books. Let everybody feel that he has the right freely to express his opinions, provided he is decent and kind about it. Certainly the Christians now ought to treat Infidels as well as Penn did Indians.

Nothing could be more perfectly idiotic than in this day and generation to prosecute any man for giving his conclusions on any religious subject. Mr. Torrence would have had Huxley and Haeckel and Tyndall arrested; would have had Humboldt and John Stuart Mill and Harriet Martineau and George Eliot locked up in the city jail. Mr. Torrence is a fossil from the Old Red Sandstone of a mistake. Let him rest. To hear these people talk you would suppose that God is some petty king, some Liliputian prince, who was about to be dethroned, and who was nearly wild for recruits.

Q. But what would you do if they should make an attempt to arrest you?

A. Nothing, except to defend myself in court. — *Philadelphia Press*, May 24, 1884.

INGERSOLL CATECHIZED

Q. Does Christianity advance or retard civilization?

A. If by Christianity you mean the orthodox church, then I unhesitatingly answer that it does retard civilization, always has retarded it, and always will. I can imagine no man who can be benefited by being made a Catholic or a Presbyterian or a Baptist or a Methodist – or, in other words, by being made an orthodox Christian. But by Christianity I do not mean morality, kindness, forgiveness, justice. Those virtues are not distinctively Christian. They are claimed by Mohammedans and Buddhists, by Infidels and Atheists – and practiced by some of all classes. Christianity consists in the miraculous, the marvelous, and the impossible.

The one thing that I most seriously object to in Christianity is the doctrine of eternal punishment. That doctrine subverts every idea of justice. It teaches the infinite absurdity that a finite offense can be justly visited by eternal punishment. Another serious objection I have is that Christianity endeavors to destroy intellectual liberty. Nothing is better calculated to retard civilization than to subvert the idea of justice. Nothing is better calculated to retain barbarism than to deny to every human being the right to think. Justice and liberty are the two wings that bear man forward. The church, for a thousand years, did all within its power to prevent the expression of honest thought; and when the church had power, there was in this world no civilization. We have advanced just in the proportion that Christianity has lost power. Those nations in which the church is still powerful are still almost savage – Portugal, Spain, and many others I might name. Probably no country is more completely under the control of the religious idea than Russia. The czar is the direct representative of God. He is the head of the church, as well as of the state. In Russia every mouth is a bastille, and every tongue a convict. This Russian pope, this representative of God, has on earth his hell (Siberia), and he imitates the orthodox God to the extent of his health and strength.

Everywhere man advances as the church loses power. In my judgment, Ireland can never succeed until it ceases to be Catholic;

and there can be no successful uprising while the confessional exists. At one time in New England the church had complete power. There was then no religious liberty. And so we might make a tour of the world and find that superstition always has been, is, and forever will be, inconsistent with human advancement.

Q. Do not the evidences of design in the universe prove a creator?

A. If there were any evidences of design in the universe, certainly they would tend to prove a designer, but they would not prove a creator. Design does not prove creation. A man makes a machine. That does not prove that he made the material out of which the machine is constructed. You find the planets arranged in accordance with what you call a plan. That does not prove that they were created. It may prove that they are governed, but it certainly does not prove that they were created. Is it consistent to say that a design cannot exist without a designer, but that a designer can? Does not a designer need a design as much as a design needs a designer? Does not a creator need a creator as much as the thing we think has been created? In other words, is not this simply a circle of human ignorance? Why not say that the universe has existed from eternity? And do you not thus avoid at least one absurdity by saying that the universe has existed from eternity, instead of saying that it was created by a creator who existed from eternity? Because if your creator existed from eternity, and created the universe, there was a time when he commenced; and back of that, according to Shelley, is "an eternity of idleness."

Some people say that God existed from eternity, and has created eternity. It is impossible to think of an act coequal with eternity. If you say that God has existed forever, and has always acted, then you make the universe eternal, and you make the universe as old as God; and if the universe be as old as God, he certainly did not create it.

These questions of origin and destiny – of infinite gods – are beyond the powers of the human mind. They cannot be solved. We might as well try to travel fast enough to get beyond the horizon. It is like a man trying to run away from his girdle. Consequently, I believe in turning our attention to things of importance – to questions that may by some possibility be solved. It is of no importance to me whether God exists or not. I exist, and it is important to me to be happy while I exist. Therefore I had better turn my attention to finding out the secret of happiness instead of trying to ascertain the secret of the universe.

112

I say with regard to God, I do not know; and therefore I am accused of being arrogant and egotistic. Religious papers say that I do know, because Webster told me. They use Webster as a witness to prove the divinity of Christ. They say that Webster was on the God side, and therefore I ought to be. I can hardly afford to take Webster's ideas of another world, when his ideas about this were so bad. When bloodhounds were pursuing a woman through the tangled swamps of the South – she hungry for liberty – Webster took the side of the bloodhounds. Such a man is no authority for me. Bacon denied the Copernican system of astronomy; he is an unsafe guide. Wesley believed in witches; I cannot follow him. No man should quote a name instead of an argument; no man should bring forward a person instead of a principle, unless he is willing to accept all the ideas of that person.

Q. Is not a pleasant illusion preferable to dreary truth – a future life being in question?

A. I think it is. I think that a pleasant illusion is better than a terrible truth, so far as its immediate results are concerned. I would rather think the one I love living, than to think her dead. I would rather think that I had a large balance in the bank than that my account was overdrawn. I would rather think I was healthy than to know that I had cancer. But if we have an illusion, let us have it pleasing. The orthodox illusion is the worst that can possibly be conceived. Take hell out of that illusion, take eternal pain away from that dream, and say that the whole world is to be happy forever – then you might have an excuse for calling it a pleasant illusion; but it is, in fact, a nightmare – a perpetual horror – a cross, on which the happiness of man has been crucified.

Q. Are not religion and morals inseparable?

A. Religion and morality have nothing in common, and yet there is no religion except the practice of morality. But what you call religion is simply superstition. Religion as it is now taught teaches our duties toward God – our obligations to the infinite, and the results of a failure to discharge those obligations. I believe that we are under no obligations to the infinite; that we cannot be. All our obligations are to each other, and to sentient beings. "Believe in the Lord Jesus Christ, and thou shalt be saved," has nothing to do with morality. "Do unto others as ye would that others should do unto you" has nothing to do with believing in the Lord Jesus Christ. Baptism has nothing to do with morality. "Pay your honest debts." That has nothing to do with baptism. What is

113

called religion is simple superstition, with which morality has nothing to do.

The churches do not prevent people from committing natural offenses, but restrain them from committing artificial ones – as, for instance, the Catholic Church can prevent one of its members from eating meat on Friday, but not from whipping his wife. The Episcopal church can prevent dancing, it may be, in Lent, but not slander. The Presbyterian can keep a man from working on Sunday, but not from practicing deceit on Monday. And so I might go through the churches. They lay the greater stress on the artificial offenses. Those countries that are the most religious are the most immoral. When the world was under the control of the Catholic Church, it reached the very pit of immorality, and nations have advanced in morals just in proportion that they have lost Christianity.

Q. It is frequently asserted that there is nothing new in your objections against Christianity. What is your reply to such assertions?

A. Of course, the editors of religious papers will say this. In my opinion, an argument is new until it has been answered. An argument is absolutely fresh, and has upon its leaves the dew of morning, until it has been refuted. All men have experienced, it may be, in some degree, what we call love. Millions of men have written about it. The subject, of course, is old. It is only the presentation that can be new. Thousands of men have attacked superstition. The subject is old, but the manner in which the facts are handled, the arguments grouped – these may be forever new. Millions of men have preached Christianity. Certainly there is nothing new in the original ideas. Nothing can be new except the presentation, the grouping. The ideas may be old, but they may be clothed in new garments of passion; they may be given additional human interest. A man takes a fact, or an old subject, as a sculptor takes a rock; the rock is not new. Of this rock he makes a statue; the statue is new. And yet some orthodox man might say there is nothing new about that statue: "I know the man that dug the rock; I know the owner of the quarry." Substance is eternal; forms are new. So in the human mind certain ideas, or in the human heart certain passions, are forever old; but genius forever gives them new forms, new meanings; and this is the perpetual originality of genius.

Q. Do you consider that churches are injurious to the community?

A. In the exact proportion that churches teach falsehood; in the exact proportion that they destroy liberty of thought, the free action of the human mind; in the exact proportion that they teach the doctrine of eternal pain, and convince people of its truth – they are injurious. In the proportion that they teach morality and justice, and practice kindness and charity – in that proportion they are a benefit. Every church, therefore, is a mixed problem – part good and part bad. In one direction it leads toward and sheds light; in the other direction its influence is entirely bad.

Now, I would like to civilize the churches, so that they will be able to do good deeds without building bad creeds. In other words, take out the superstitious and the miraculous and leave the human and the moral.

Q. Why do you not respond to the occasional clergyman who replies to your lectures?

A. In the first place, no clergyman has ever replied to my lectures. In the second place, no clergyman ever will reply to my lectures. He does not answer my arguments – he attacks me; and the replies that I have seen are not worth answering. They are far below the dignity of the question under discussion. Most of them are ill-mannered, as abusive as illogical, and as malicious as weak. I cannot reply without feeling humiliated. I cannot use their weapons, and my weapons they do not understand. I attack Christianity because it is cruel, and they account for all my actions by putting behind them base motives. They make it at once a personal question. They imagine that epithets are good enough arguments with which to answer an Infidel. A few years ago they would have imprisoned me. A few years ago before that they would have burned me. We have advanced. Now they only slander; and I congratulate myself on the fact that even that is not believed. Ministers do not believe each other about each other. The truth has never yet been ascertained in any trial by a church. The longer the trial lasts, the obscurer is the truth. They will not believe each other, even on oath; and one of the most celebrated ministers of this country has publicly announced that there is no use in answering a lie started by his own church; that if he does answer it – if he does kill it – forty more lies will come to the funeral.

In this connection we must remember that the priests of one religion never credit the miracles of another religion. Is this because priests instinctively know priests? Now, when a Christian

115

tells a Buddhist some of the miracles of the Testament, the Buddhist smiles. When a Buddhist tells a Christian the miracles performed by Buddha, the Christian laughs. This reminds me of an incident. A man told a most wonderful story. Everybody present expressed surprise and astonishment, except one man. He said nothing; he did not even change countenance. One who noticed that the story had no effect on this man said to him: "You do not seem to be astonished in the least at this marvelous tale." The man replied, "No; I am a liar myself."

You see, I am not trying to answer individual ministers. I am attacking the whole body of superstition. I am trying to kill the entire dog, and I do not feel like wasting any time killing fleas on that dog. When the dog dies, the fleas will be out of provisions, and in that way we shall answer them all at once.

So, I do not bother myself answering religious newspapers. In the first place, they are not worth answering; and in the second place, to answer would only produce a new crop of falsehoods. You know, the editor of a religious newspaper, as a rule, is one who has failed in the pulpit; and you can imagine the brains necessary to edit a religious weekly from this fact. I have known some good religious editors. By some I mean one. I do not say that there are others, but I do say I do not know them. I might add here that the one I did know is dead.

Since I have been in this city there have been some "replies" to me. They have been almost idiotic. A Catholic priest asked me how I had the impudence to differ with Newton. Newton, he says, believed in a God; and I ask this Catholic priest how he has the impudence to differ with Newton. Newton was a Protestant. This simply shows the absurdity of using men's names for arguments. This same priest proves the existence of God by a pagan orator. Is it possible that God's last witness died with Cicero? If it is necessary to believe in a God now, the witnesses ought to be on hand now.

Another man, pretending to answer me, quotes Le Conte, a geologist; and according to this geologist we are "getting near to the splendors of the great white throne." Where is the great white throne? Can anyone, by studying geology, find the locality of the great white throne? To what stratum does it belong? In what geologic period was the great white throne formed? What on earth has geology to do with the throne of God?

The truth is there can be no reply to the argument that man should be governed by his reason; that he should depend on observation and experience; that he should use the faculties he has for his own benefit, and the benefit of his fellow men. There is no answer. It is not within the power of man to substantiate the supernatural. It is beyond the power of evidence.

Q. Why do the theological seminaries find it difficult to get students?

A. I was told last spring, at New Haven, that the "theologs," as they call the young men there being fitted for the ministry, were not regarded as intellectual by all the other students. The orthodox pulpit has no rewards for genius. It has rewards only for stupidity, for belief – not for investigation, not for thought; and the consequence is that young men of talent avoid the pulpit. I think I heard the other day that of all the students at Harvard only nine are preparing for the ministry. The truth is the ministry is not regarded as an intellectual occupation. The average church now consists of women and children. Men go to please their wives, or stay at home and subscribe to please their wives; and the wives are beginning to think, and many of them are staying at home. Many of them now prefer the theater or the opera or the park or the seashore or the forest or the companionship of their husbands and children at home.

Q. How does the religious state of California compare with the rest of the Union?

A. I find that sensible people everywhere are about the same, and the proportion of freethinkers depends on the proportion of sensible folks. I think that California has her full share of sensible people. I find everywhere the best people and the brightest people – the people with the most heart and the best brain – all tending toward freethought. Of course, a man of brain cannot believe the miracles of the Old and New Testaments. A man of heart cannot believe in the doctrine of eternal pain. We have found that other religions are like ours, with precisely the same basis, the same idiotic miracles, the same martyrs, the same early fathers, and, as a rule, the same Christ or savior. It will hardly do to say that all others like ours are false, and ours the only true one, when others substantially like it are thousands of years older. We have at last found that a religion is simply an effort on the part of man to account for what he sees, what he hopes. Every savage has his philosophy. That is his religion and his science.

The religions of today are the sciences of the past; and it may be that the sciences of today will be the religions of the future, and that other sciences will be as far beyond them as the science of today is beyond the religion of today. As a rule, religion is a sanctified mistake, and heresy a slandered fact. In other words, the human mind grows – and as it grows it abandons the old, and the old gets its revenge by maligning the new. — *The San Franciscan,* San Francisco, Oct. 4, 1884.

RELIGIOUS PREJUDICE

Q. Will a time ever come when political campaigns will be conducted independently of religious prejudice?

A. As long as men are prejudiced, they will probably be religious, and certainly as long as they are religious they will be prejudiced, and every religionist who imagines the next world infinitely more important than this, and who imagines that he gets his orders from God instead of from his own reason or from his fellow-citizens, and who thinks that he should do something for the glory of God instead of for the benefit of his fellow-citizens – just as long as they believe these things, just so long their prejudices will control their votes. Every good, ignorant, orthodox Christian places his Bible above laws and constitutions. Every good, sincere and ignorant Catholic puts pope above king and president, as well as above the legally expressed will of a majority of his countrymen. Every Christian believes God to be the source of all authority. I believe that the authority to govern comes from the consent of the governed. Man is the source of power, and to protect and increase human happiness should be the object of government. I think that religious prejudices are growing weaker because religious belief is growing weaker. And these prejudices – should men ever become really civilized – will finally fade away. I think that a Presbyterian, today, has no more prejudice against an Atheist than he has against a Catholic. A Catholic does not dislike an Infidel any more than he does a Presbyterian, and I believe, today, that most of the Presbyterians would rather see an Atheist president than a pronounced Catholic.

Q. Is Agnosticism gaining ground in the United States?

A. Of course, there are thousands and thousands of men who have now advanced intellectually to the point of perceiving the limit of human knowledge. In other words, at last they are beginning to know enough to know what can and what cannot be known. Sensible men know that nobody knows whether an infinite God exists or not. Sensible men know that an infinite personality cannot, by human testimony, be established. Sensible men are giving up trying to answer the questions of origin and destiny, and are paying more attention to what happens between these

119

questions – that is to say, to this world. Infidelity increases as knowledge increases, as fear dies, and as the brain develops. After all, it is a question of intelligence. Only cunning performs a miracle, only ignorance believes it.

Q. Do you think that evolution and revealed religion are compatible – that is to say, can a man be an evolutionist and a Christian?

A. Evolution and Christianity may be compatible, provided you take the ground that Christianity is only one of the links in the chain, one of the phases of civilization. But if you mean by Christianity what is generally understood, of course that and evolution are absolutely incompatible. Christianity pretends to be not only the truth, but, so far as religion is concerned, the whole truth. Christianity pretends to give a history of religion and a prophecy of destiny. As a philosophy, it is an absolute failure. As a history, it is false. There is no possible way by which Darwin and Moses can be harmonized. There is an irrepressible conflict between Christianity and science, and both cannot long inhabit the same brain. You cannot harmonize evolution and the atonement. The survival of the fittest does away with original sin.

Q. From your knowledge of the religious tendency in the United States, how long will orthodox religion be popular?

A. I do not think that orthodox religion is popular today. The ministers dare not preach the creed in all its naked deformity and horror. They are endeavoring with the vines of sentiment to cover up the caves and dens in which crawl the serpents of their creed. Few ministers care now to speak of eternal pain. They leave out the lake of fire and brimstone. They are not fond of putting in the lips of Christ the loving words, "Depart from me, ye cursed." The miracles are avoided. In short, what is known as orthodoxy is already unpopular. Most ministers are endeavoring to harmonize what they are pleased to call science and Christianity, and nothing is now so welcome to the average Christian as some work tending to show that, after all, Joshua was an astronomer.

Q. What section of the United States, East, West, North, or South, is the most advanced in liberal religious ideas?

A. That section of the country in which there is the most intelligence is the most liberal. That section of the country where there is the most ignorance is the most prejudiced. The least brain is the most orthodox. There possibly is no more progressive city in the world, no more liberal, than Boston. Chicago is full of liberal people. So is San Francisco. The brain of New York is liberal.

Every town, every city, is liberal in the precise proportion that it is intelligent.

Q. Will the religion of humanity be the religion of the future?

A. Yes; it is the only religion now. All other is superstition. What they call religion rests on a supposed relation between man and God. In what they call religion man is asked to do something for God. As God wants nothing, and can by no possibility accept anything, such a religion is simply superstition. Humanity is the only possible religion. Whoever imagines that he can do anything for God is mistaken. Whoever imagines that he can add to his happiness in the next world by being useless in this is also mistaken. And whoever thinks that any God cares how he cuts his hair or his clothes, or what he eats, or whether he fasts, or rings a bell, or puts holy water on his breast, or counts beads, or shuts his eyes and says words to the clouds, is laboring under a great mistake.

Q. A man in the Swaim court martial case was excluded as a witness because he was an Atheist. Do you think the law in the next decade will permit the affirmative oath?

A. If belief affected your eyes, your ears, any of your senses, or your memory, then, of course, no man ought to be a witness who had not the proper belief. But unless it can be shown that Atheism interferes with the sight, the hearing, or memory, why should justice shut the door to truth?

In most of the states of this Union I could not give testimony. Should a man be murdered before my eyes I could not tell a jury who did it. Christianity endeavors to make an honest man an outlaw. Christianity has such a contemptible opinion of human nature that it does not believe a man can tell the truth unless frightened by a belief in God. No lower opinion of the human race has ever been expressed.

Q. Do you think that bigotry would persecute now for religious opinion's sake, if it were not for the law and the press?

A. I think that the church would persecute today if it had the power, just as it persecuted in the past. We are indebted for nearly all our religious liberty to the hypocrisy of the church. The church does not believe. Some in the church do, and if they had the power, they would torture and burn as of yore. Give the Presbyterian church the power, and it would not allow an Infidel to live. Give the Methodist church the power and the result would be the same. Give the Catholic church the power – just the same. No church in the United States would be willing that any other church should

121

have the power. The only men who are to be angels in the next world are the ones who cannot be trusted with human liberty in this; and the men who are destined to live forever in hell are the only gentlemen with whom human liberty is safe. Why should Christians refuse to persecute in this world, when their God is going to in the next? — *Mail and Express,* New York, Jan. 12, 1885.

RELIGION, PROHIBITION
AND GENERAL GRANT

Q. What do you think of prohibition, and what do you think of its success in this state?

A. Few people understand the restraining influence of liberty. Moderation walks hand in hand with freedom. I do not mean the freedom springing from the sudden rupture of restraint. That kind of freedom usually rushes to extremes.

People must be educated to take care of themselves, and this education must commence in infancy. Self-restraint is the only kind that can always be depended on. Of course, intemperance is a great evil. It causes immense suffering – clothes wives and children in rags, and is accountable for many crimes, particularly those of violence. Laws to be of value must be honestly enforced. Laws that sleep had better be dead. Laws to be enforced must be honestly approved of and believed in by a large majority of the people. Unpopular laws make hypocrites, perjurers, and official shirkers of duty. And if to the violation of such laws severe penalties attach, they are rarely enforced. Laws that create artificial crimes are the hardest to carry into effect. You can never convince a majority of people that it is as bad to import goods without paying the legal duty as to commit larceny. Neither can you convince a majority of people that it is a crime or a sin, or even a mistake to drink a glass of wine or beer. Thousands and thousands of people in this state honestly believe that prohibition is an interference with their natural rights, and they feel justified in resorting to almost any means to defeat the law.

In this way the people become somewhat demoralized. It is unfortunate to pass laws that remain unenforced on account of their unpopularity. People who would on most subjects swear to the truth do not hesitate to testify falsely on a prohibition trial. In addition to this, every known device is resorted to, to sell in spite of the law, and when some want to sell and a great many want to buy, considerable business will be done, while there are fewer saloons and less liquor sold in them. The liquor is poorer and the price is higher. The consumer has to pay for the extra risk. More liquor finds its way to homes, more men buy by the bottle and gallon.

123

In old times nearly everybody kept a little rum or whiskey on the sideboard. The great Washingtonian temperance movement drove liquor out of the home and increased the taverns and saloons. Now we are driving liquor back to the homes. In my opinion there is a vast difference between distilled spirits and the lighter drinks, such as wine and beer. Wine is a fireside and whiskey a conflagration. These lighter drinks are not unhealthful and do not, as I believe, create a craving for stronger beverages. You will, I think, find it almost impossible to enforce the present law against wine and beer. I was told yesterday that there are some sixty places in Cedar Rapids where whiskey is sold. It takes about as much ceremony to get a drink as it does to join the Masons, but they seem to like the ceremony. People seem to take delight in outwitting the state when it does not involve the commission of any natural offense, and when about to be caught, may not hesitate to swear falsely to the extent of "don't remember," or "can't say positively," or "can't swear whether it was whiskey or not."

One great trouble in Iowa is that the politicians, or many of them who openly advocate prohibition, are really opposed to it. They want to keep the German vote, and they do not want to lose native Republicans. They feel a "divided duty" to ride both horses. This causes the contrast between their conversation and their speeches. A few years ago I took dinner with a gentleman who had been elected governor of one of our states on the Prohibition ticket. We had four kinds of wine during the meal, and a pony of brandy at the end. Prohibition will never be a success until it prohibits the Prohibitionists. And yet I most sincerely hope and believe that the time will come when drunkenness shall have perished from the earth. Let us cultivate the love of home. Let husbands and wives and children be companions. Let them seek amusements together. If it is a good place for father to go, it is a good place for mother and the children. I believe that a home can be made more attractive than a saloon. Let the boys and girls amuse themselves at home – play games, study music, read interesting books, and let the parents be their playfellows. The best temperance lecture, in the fewest words, you will find in Victor Hugo's great novel *Les Miserables*. The grave digger is asked to take a drink. He refuses and gives this reason: "The hunger of my family is the enemy of my thirst."

Q. Do you think that the American people are seeking after truth, or do they want to be amused?

A. We have all kinds. Thousands are earnestly seeking for the truth. They are looking over the old creeds, they are studying the Bible for themselves, they have the candor born of courage, they are depending on themselves instead of on the clergy. They have found out that the clergy do not know; that their sources of information are not reliable; that, like the politician, many ministers preach one way and talk another. The doctrine of eternal pain has driven millions from the church. People with good hearts cannot get consolation out of that cruel lie. The ministers themselves are getting ashamed to call that doctrine "the tidings of great joy." The American people are a serious people. They want to know the truth. They feel that whatever the truth may be they have the courage to hear it. The American people also have a sense of humor. They like to see old absurdities punctured and solemn stupidity held up to laughter. They are, on the average, the most intelligent people on the earth. They can see the point. Their wit is sharp, quick, and logical. Nothing amuses them more than to see the mask pulled from the face of sham. The average American is generous, intelligent, level-headed, manly, good-natured.

Q. What, in your judgment, is the source of the greatest trouble among men?

A. Superstition. That has caused more agony, more tears, persecution, and real misery than all other causes combined. The other name for superstition is ignorance. When men learn that all sin is a mistake, that all dishonesty is a blunder, that even intelligent selfishness will protect the rights of others, there will be vastly more happiness in this world. Shakespeare says that "There is no darkness but ignorance." Sometime man will learn that when he steals from another, he robs himself – that the way to be happy is to make others so, and that it is far better to assist his fellow man than to fast, say prayers, count beads or build temples to the unknown. Some people tell us that selfishness is the only sin, but selfishness grows in the soil of ignorance. After all, education is the great lever, and the only one capable of raising mankind. People ignorant of their own rights are ignorant of the rights of others. Every tyrant is the slave of ignorance.

Q. How soon do you think we would have the millennium, if every person attended strictly to his own business?

A. Now, if every person were intelligent enough to know his own business – to know just where his rights ended and the rights of other commenced, and then had the wisdom and honesty to act

125

accordingly, we should have a happy world. Most people like to control the conduct of others. They love to write rules, and pass laws for the benefit of their neighbors, and the neighbors are pretty busy at the same business. People, as a rule, think that they know the business of other people better than they do their own. A man watching others play checkers or chess always thinks he sees better moves than the players make. When all people attend to their own business they know that a part of their own business is to increase the happiness of others.

Q. What is causing the development of this country?

A. Education, the free exchange of ideas, inventions by which the forces of nature become our servants, intellectual hospitality, a willingness to hear the other side, the richness of our soil, the extent of our territory, the diversity of climate and production, our system of government, the free discussion of political questions, our social freedom, and above all, the fact that labor is honorable.

Q. What is your opinion of the religious tendency of the people of this country?

A. Using the word religion in its highest and best sense, the people are becoming more religious – using the word in its best sense – than when we believed in human slavery, but we are not as orthodox as we were then. We have more principle and less piety. We care more for the right and less for the creed. The old orthodox dogmas are moldy. You will find moss on their backs. They are only brought out when a new candidate for the ministry is to be examined. Only a little while ago in New York a candidate for the Presbyterian pulpit was examined and the following is a part of the examination:

Q. "Do you believe in eternal punishment, as set forth in the confession of faith?"

A. (With some hesitation) "Yes, I do."

Q. "Have you preached on that subject lately?"

A. "No. I prepared a sermon on hell, in which I took the ground that the punishment of the wicked will be endless, and have it with me.

Q. "Did you deliver it?"

A. "No. I thought that my congregation would not care to hear it. The doctrine is rather unpopular where I have been preaching, and I was afraid I might do harm, so I have not delivered it yet."

Q. "But you believe in eternal damnation, do you not?"

A. "Oh yes, with all my heart."

He was admitted, and the admission proves the dishonesty of the examiners and the examined. The new version of the Old and

New Testaments has done much to weaken confidence in the doctrine of inspiration. It has occurred to a good many that if God took the pains to inspire men to write the Bible, he ought to have inspired others to translate it correctly. The general tendency today is toward science, toward naturalism, toward what is called infidelity, but is in fact fidelity. Men are in a transition state, and the people, on the average, have more real good, sound sense today than ever before. The church is losing its power for evil. The old chains are wearing out, and new ones are not being made. The tendency is toward intellectual freedom, and that means the final destruction of the orthodox bastille.

Q. What is your opinion of General Grant as he stands before the people today?

A. I have always regarded General Grant as the greatest soldier this continent has produced. He is today the most distinguished son of the Republic. The people have the greatest confidence in his ability, his patriotism, and his integrity. The financial disaster impoverished General Grant but did not stain the reputation of the grand soldier who led to many victories the greatest army that ever fought for the liberties of man. — *Iowa State Register,* May 23, 1885.

HELL OR SHEOL AND OTHER SUBJECTS

Q. Colonel, have you read the revised Testament?

A. Yes, but I don't believe the work has been fairly done. The clergy are not going to scrape the butter off their own bread. The clergy are offensive partisans, and those of each denomination will interpret the Scriptures their way. No Baptist minister would countenance a "Revision" that favored sprinkling, and no Catholic priest would admit that any version would be correct that destroyed the dogma of the "real presence." So I might go through all the denominations.

Q. Why was the word *sheol* introduced in place of *hell*, and how do you like the substitute?

A. The civilized world has outgrown the vulgar and brutal hell of their fathers and founders of the churches. The clergy are ashamed to preach about sulfurous flames and undying worms. The imagination of the world has been developed, the heart has grown tender, and the old dogma of eternal pain shocks all civilized people. It is becoming disgraceful either to preach or believe in such a beastly lie. The clergy are beginning to think that it is hardly manly to frighten children with a detected falsehood. Sheol is a great relief. It is not so hot as the old place. The nights are comfortable, and the society is quite refined. The worms are dead, and the air reasonably free from noxious vapors. It is a much worse word to hold a revival with, but much better for everyday use. It will hardly take the place of the old word when people step on tacks, put up stoves, or sit on pins; but for use at church fairs and mite societies it will do about as well. We do not need revision; excision is what we want. The barbarism should be taken out of the Bible. Passages upholding polygamy, wars of extermination, slavery, and religious persecution should not be attributed to a perfect God. The good that is in the Bible will be saved for man, and man will be saved from the evil that is in that book. Why should we worship in God what we detest in man?

Q. Do you think the use of the word "sheol" will make any difference to the preachers?

A. Of course, it will make no difference with Talmage. He will

128

make sheol just as hot and smoky and uncomfortable as hell, but the congregation will laugh instead of tremble. The old shudder has gone. Beecher had demolished hell before sheol was adopted. According to his doctrine of evolution, hell has been slowly growing cool. The cindered souls do not even perspire. Sheol is nothing to Mr. Beecher but a new name for an old mistake. As for the effect it will have on Heber Newton, I cannot tell, neither can he, until he asks his bishop. There are people who believe in witches and madstones and fiat money, and centuries hence it may be that people will exist who will believe as firmly in hell as Dr. Shedd does now.

Q. What about Beecher's sermons on "Evolution"?

A. Beecher's sermons on "Evolution" will do good. Millions of people believe that Mr. Beecher knows at least as much as the other preachers, and if he regards the atonement as a dogma with a mistake for a foundation, they may conclude that the whole system is a mistake. But whether Mr. Beecher is mistaken or not, people know that honesty is a good thing, that gratitude is a virtue, that industry supports the world, and that whatever they believe about religion they are bound by every conceivable obligation to be just and generous. Mr. Beecher can no more succeed in reconciling science and religion than he could in convincing the world that triangles and circles are exactly the same. There is the same relation between science and religion that there is between astronomy and astrology, between alchemy and chemistry, between orthodoxy and common sense.

Q. Have you read Miss Cleveland's book? She condemns George Eliot's poetry on the ground that it has no faith in it, nothing beyond. Do you imagine she would condemn Burns or Shelley for that reason?

A. I have not read Miss Cleveland's book; but, if the author condemns the poetry of George Eliot, she has made a mistake. There is no poem in our language more beautiful than "The Lovers," and none loftier or purer than "The Choir Invisible." There is no poetry in the "beyond." The poetry is here – here in this world, where love is in the heart. The poetry of the beyond is too far away, a little too general. Shelley's "Skylark" was in our sky, the daisy of Burns grew on our ground, and between that lark and that daisy is room for all the real poetry of the earth.

— *Evening Record,* Boston, Massachusetts, 1885.

INTERVIEWING AND SPIRITUALISM

Q. What is your opinion of the peculiar institution of American journalism known as interviewing?

A. If the interviewers are fair, if they know how to ask questions of a public nature, if they remember what is said, or write it at the time, and if the interviewed knows enough to answer questions in a way to amuse or instruct the public, then interviewing is a blessing. But if the representative of the press asks questions, either impudent or unimportant, and the answers are like the questions, then the institution is a failure. When the journalist fails to see the man he wishes to interview, or when the man refuses to be interviewed, and thereupon the aforesaid journalist writes up an interview, doing the talking for both sides, the institution is a success. Such interviews are always interesting, and, as a rule, the questions are to the point and the answers perfectly responsive. There is probably a little too much interviewing, and too many persons are asked questions on subjects about which they know nothing. Mr. Smith makes some money in stocks or pork, visits London, and remains in that city for several weeks. On his return he is interviewed as to the customs of the British Empire. Of course, such an interview is exceedingly instructive. Lord Affanaff lands at the dock in North River, is driven to a hotel in a closed carriage, is interviewed a few minutes after by a representative of the *Herald* as to his view of the great Republic based on what he has seen. Such an interview is also instructive. Interviews with candidates as to their chances of election is another favorite way of finding out their honest opinion, but people who rely on those interviews generally lose their bets. The most interesting interviews are generally denied. I have been expecting to see an interview with the Rev. Dr. Leonard on the medicinal properties of champagne and toast, or the relation between old ale and modern theology, and as to whether prohibition prohibits the Prohibitionists.

Q. Have you ever been misrepresented in an interview?

A. Several times. As a general rule, the clergy have selected these misrepresentations when answering me. I never blamed them, because it is much easier to answer something that I did not say. Most reporters try to give my real words, but it is difficult to remember. They try to give the substance, and in that way change or destroy the sense. You remember the Frenchman who translated Shakespeare's great line in *Macbeth* – "Out, brief candle!" – into "Short candle, go out!" Another man, trying to give the last words of Webster – "I still live" – said "I ain't dead yit." So that when they try to do their best they often make mistakes. Now and then interviews appear not one word of which I ever said, and sometimes when I really had an interview, another one has appeared. But generally the reporters treat me well, and most of them succeed in telling about what I said. Personally I have no cause for complaint.

Q. We have been having the periodical revival of interest in spiritualism. What do you think of "spiritualism," as it is popularly termed?

A. I do not believe in the supernatural. One who does not believe in gods would hardly believe in ghosts. I am not a believer in any of the "wonders" and "miracles" whether ancient or modern. There may be spirits, but I do not believe there are. They may communicate with some people, but thus far they have been successful in avoiding me. Of course, I know nothing for certain on the subject. I know a great many excellent people who are thoroughly convinced of the truth of spiritualism. Christians laugh at the "miracles" today, attested by folks that they know, but believe the miracles of long ago, attested by folks that they did not know. This is one of the contradictions in human nature. Most people are willing to believe that wonderful things happened long ago and will happen again in the far future; with them the present is the only time in which nature behaves herself with becoming sobriety.

In old times nature did all kinds of juggling tricks, and after a long while will do some more, but now she is attending strictly to business, depending on cause and effect.

Q. Who, in your opinion, is the greatest leader of the "opposition" yclept the Christian religion?

A. I suppose that Mr. Beecher is the greatest man in the pulpit, but he thinks more of Darwin than does he of David and has an idea that the Old Testament is just a little too old. He has put evolution in the place of the atonement – has thrown away the Garden of Eden, snake, apples and all, and is endeavoring to save enough of the orthodox wreck to make a raft. I know of no other genius in the pulpit. There are plenty of theological doctors and bishops and all kinds of titled humility in the sacred profession, but men of genius are scarce. All the ministers, except Messrs. Moody and Jones, are busy explaining away the contradictions between inspiration and demonstration.

Q. What books would you recommend for the perusal of a young man of limited time and culture with reference to helping him in the development of intellect and good character?

A. The works of Darwin, Ernst Haeckel, Draper's *Intellectual Development of Europe,* Buckle's *History of Civilization in England,* Lecky's *History of European Morals,* Voltaire's *Philosophical Dictionary,* Buchner's *Force and Matter, The History of the Christian Religion* by Waite; Paine's *Age of Reason,* D'Holbach's *System of Nature,* and, above all, Shakespeare. Do not forget Burns, Shelley, Dickens, and Hugo.

Q. Will you lecture the coming winter?

A. Yes, about the same as usual. Woe is me if I preach not my gospel.

Q. Have you been invited to lecture in Europe? If so, do you intend to accept the "call"?

A. Yes, often. The probability is that I shall go to England and Australia. I have not only had invitations but most excellent offers from both countries. There is, however, plenty to do here. This is the best country in the world and our people are eager to hear the other side.

The old kind of preaching is getting superannuated. It lags superfluous in the pulpit. Our people are outgrowing the cruelties and absurdities of the ancient Jews. The idea of hell has become shocking and vulgar. Eternal punishment is eternal injustice. It is infinitely infamous. Most ministers are ashamed to preach the doctrine, and the congregations are ashamed to hear it preached. It is the essence of savagery. — *Plain Dealer,* Cleveland, Ohio, Sept. 5, 1885.

MY BELIEF

Q. It is said that in the past four or five years you have changed or modified your views on the subject of religion; is this so?

A. It is not so. The only change, if that can be called a change, is that I am more perfectly satisfied that I am right – satisfied that what is called orthodox religion is a simple fabrication of mistaken men; satisfied that there is no such thing as an inspired book and never will be; satisfied that a miracle never was and never will be performed; satisfied that no human being knows whether there is a God or not, whether there is another life or not; satisfied that the scheme of atonement is a mistake, that the innocent cannot, by suffering for the guilty, atone for the guilt; satisfied that the doctrine that salvation depends on belief, is cruel and absurd; satisfied that the doctrine of eternal punishment is infamously false; satisfied that superstition is of no use to the human race; satisfied that humanity is the only true and real religion.

No, I have not modified my views. I detect new absurdities every day in the popular belief. Every day the whole thing becomes more and more absurd. Of course, there are hundreds and thousands of most excellent people who believe in orthodox religion; people for whose good qualities I have the greatest respect; people who have good ideas on most other subjects; good citizens, good fathers, husbands, wives, and children – good in spite of their religion. I do not attack people. I attack the mistakes of people. Orthodoxy is getting weaker every day.

Q. Do you believe in the existence of a supreme being?

A. I do not believe in any supreme personality or in any supreme being who made the universe and governs nature. I do not say that there is no such being – all I say is that I do not believe that such a being exists. I know nothing on the subject, except that I know that I do not know and that nobody else knows. But if there be such a being, he certainly never wrote the Old Testament. You will understand my position. I do not say that a supreme being does not exist, but I do say that I do not believe such a being exists. The universe – embracing all that is – all atoms, all stars, each grain of sand and all the constellations, each thought and dream of animal and man, all matter and all force, all doubt and all belief, all virtue and all crime, all joy and all pain, all growth and all decay – is all there is. It does not act because it is moved from without. It acts from within. It is actor and subject, means and end.

It is infinite; the infinite could not have been created. It is indestructible and that which cannot be destroyed was not created. I am a pantheist.

Q. Don't you think the belief of the Agnostic is more satisfactory to the believer than that of the Atheist?

A. There is no difference. The Agnostic is an Atheist. The Atheist is an Agnostic. The Agnostic says: "I do not know, but I do not believe there is any God." The Atheist says the same. The orthodox Christian says he knows there is a God; but we know that he does not know. He simply believes. He cannot know. The Atheist cannot know that God does not exist.

Q. Haven't you just the faintest glimmer of a hope that in some future state you will meet and be reunited to those who are dear to you in this?

A. I have no particular desire to be destroyed. I am willing to go to heaven if there be such a place, and enjoy myself forever and ever. It would give me infinite satisfaction to know that all mankind are to be happy forever. Infidels love their wives and children as well as Christians do theirs. I have never said a word against heaven – never said a word against the idea of immortality. On the contrary, I have said all I could truthfully say in favor of the idea that we shall live again. I most sincerely hope that there is another world, better than this, where all the broken ties of love will be united. It is the other place I have been fighting. Better that all of us should sleep the sleep of death forever than that some should suffer pain forever. If in order to have a heaven there must be a hell, then I say away with them both. My doctrine puts the bow of hope over every grave; my doctrine takes from every mother's heart the fear of hell. No good man would enjoy himself in heaven with his friends in hell. No good God could enjoy himself in heaven with millions of his poor, helpless mistakes in hell. The orthodox idea of heaven – with God an eternal inquisitor, a few heartless angels, and some redeemed orthodox, all enjoying themselves, while the vast multitude will weep in the rayless gloom of God's eternal dungeon – is not calculated to make man good or happy. I am doing what I can to civilize the churches, humanize the preachers and get the fear of hell out of the human heart. In this business I am meeting with great success. — *Philadelphia Times,* Sept. 25, 1885.

SOME LIVE TOPICS

Q. Will you attend the Albany Freethought Convention?

A. I have agreed to be present not only, but to address the convention, on Sunday, the 13th of September. I am greatly gratified to know that the interest in the question of intellectual liberty is growing from year to year. Everywhere I go it seems to be the topic of conversation. No matter on what subject people begin to talk, in a little while the discussion takes a religious turn, and people who a few moments before had not the slightest thought of saying a word about the churches, or about the Bible, are giving their opinions in full. I hear discussions of this kind in all the public conveyances, at the hotels, on the piazzas at the seaside – and they are not discussions in which I take any part, because I rarely say anything on these questions except in public, unless I am directly addressed.

There is a general feeling that the church has ruled the world long enough. People are beginning to see that no amount of eloquence, or faith, or erudition, or authority, can make the records of barbarism satisfactory to the heart and brain of this century. They have also found that a falsehood in Hebrew is no more credible than in plain English. People at last are beginning to be satisfied that cruel laws were never good laws, no matter whether inspired or uninspired. The Christian religion, like every other religion depending on inspired writings, is wrecked on the facts of nature. So long as inspired writers confined themselves to the supernatural world; so long as they talked about angels and gods and heavens and hells; so long as they described only things that man has never seen, and never will see, they were safe, not from contradiction, but from demonstration. But these writings had to have a foundation, even for their falsehoods, and that foundation was in Nature. The foundation had to be something about which somebody knew something, or supposed they knew something. They told something about this world that agreed with the then general opinion. Had these inspired writers told the truth about Nature – had they said that the world revolved on its axis, and made a circuit about the sun – they could have gained no credence for their statements about other worlds. They were forced to agree with their contemporaries about this world, and there is where they made the fundamental mistake. Having grown in knowledge, the world has discovered that these inspired men knew nothing about this earth; that the inspired books are filled with mistakes – not only mistakes that we can contradict, but mistakes that we can demonstrate to be mistakes. Had they told the truth in their day, about this earth, they would not have been believed about other worlds, because their contemporaries would have used their own knowledge about this world to test the knowledge of these inspired men. We pursue the same course; and what we know about this world we use as the standard, and by that standard we have found that the inspired men knew nothing about nature as it is. Finding that they were mistaken about this world, we have no confidence in what they have said about another. Every religion has had its philosophy about this world, and everyone has been mistaken. As education becomes general, as scientific modes are adopted, this will become clearer and clearer, until "ignorant as inspiration" will be a comparison.

Q. Have you seen the memorial to the New York legislature, to be presented this winter, asking for the repeal of such laws as practically unite church and state?

A. I have seen a memorial asking that church property be taxed like other property; that no more money should be appropriated from the public treasury for the support of institutions managed by and in the interest of sectarian denominations; for the repeal of all laws compelling the observance of Sunday as a religious day. Such memorials ought to be addressed to the legislature of all the states. The money of the public should only be used for the benefit of the public. Public money should not be used for what a few gentlemen think is for the benefit of the public. Personally, I think it would be for the benefit of the public to have Infidel or scientific – which is the same thing – lectures delivered in every town, in every state, on every Sunday; but knowing that a great many men disagree with me on this point, I do not claim that such lectures ought to be paid for with public money. The Methodist church ought not to be sustained by taxation, nor the Catholic, nor any other church. To relieve their property from taxation is to appropriate money, to the extent of that tax, for the support of that church. Whenever a burden is lifted from one piece of property, it is distributed over the rest of the property of the state, and to release one kind of property is to increase the tax on all other kinds.

There was a time when people really supposed that churches were saving souls from the eternal wrath of a God of infinite love. Being engaged in such a philanthropic work, and at that time nobody having the courage to deny it – the church being all-powerful – all other property was taxed to support the church; but now the more civilized part of the community, being satisfied that a God of infinite love will not be eternally unjust, feel as though the church should support herself. To exempt the church from taxation is to pay a part of the priest's salary. The Catholic now objects to being taxed to support a school in which his religion is not taught. He is not satisfied with the school that says nothing on the subject of religion. He insists that it is an outrage to tax him to support a school where the teacher simply teaches what he knows. And yet this same Catholic wants his church exempted from taxation, and the tax of an Atheist or of a Jew increased, when he teaches in his untaxed church that the Atheist and Jew will both be eternally damned! Is it possible for impudence to go further?

I insist that no religion should be taught in any school supported by public money; and by religion I mean superstition. Only that should be taught in a school that somebody can learn and that somebody can know. In my judgment, every church should be taxed precisely the same as other property. The church may claim that it is one of the instruments of civilization and therefore should be exempt. If you exempt that which is useful, you exempt every trade and every profession. In my judgment, theaters have done more to civilize mankind than churches; that is to say, theaters have done something to civilize mankind – churches nothing. The effect of all superstition has been to render man barbarous. I do not believe in the civilizing effects of falsehood.

There was a time when ministers were supposed to be in the employ of God, and it was thought that God selected them with great care – that their profession had something sacred about it. These ideas are no longer entertained by sensible people. Ministers should be paid like other professional men, and those who like their preaching should pay for the preach. They should depend, as actors do, on their popularity, on the amount of sense, or nonsense, that they have for sale. They should depend on the market like other people, and if people do not want to hear sermons badly enough to build churches and pay for them, and pay the taxes on them, and hire the preacher, let the money be diverted to some other use. The pulpit should no longer be a pauper. I do not believe in carrying on any business with the contribution box. All the sectarian institutions ought to support themselves. There should be no Methodist or Catholic or Presbyterian hospitals or orphan asylums. All these should be supported by the state. There is no such thing as Catholic charity, or Methodist charity. Charity belongs to humanity, not to any particular form of faith or religion. You will find as charitable people who never heard of religion as you can find in any church. The state should provide for those who ought to be provided for. A few Methodists beg of everybody they meet – send women with subscriptions papers, asking money from all classes of people, and nearly everybody gives something from politeness, or to keep from being annoyed; and when the institution is finished, it is pointed at as the result of Methodism.

Probably a majority of the people in this country suppose that there was no charity in the world until the Christian religion was founded. Great men have repeated this falsehood, until ignorance and thoughtlessness believe it. There were orphan asylums in China, in India, and in Egypt thousands of years before Christ was born; and there certainly never was a time in the history of the whole world when there was less charity in Europe than during the centuries when the church of Christ had absolute power. There were hundreds of Mohammedan asylums before Christianity had built ten in the entire world.

All institutions for the care of unfortunate people should be secular – should be supported by the state. The money for the purpose should be raised by taxation, to the end that the burden may be borne by those able to bear it. As it is now, most of the money is paid, not by the rich, but by the generous, and those most able to help their needy fellow-citizens are the ones who do nothing. If the money is raised by taxation, then the burden will fall where it ought to fall, and these institutions will no longer be supported by the generous and emotional, and the rich and stingy will no longer be able to evade the duties of citizenship and humanity.

Now, as to the Sunday laws, we know that they are only spasmodically enforced. Now and then a few people are arrested for selling papers or cigars. Some unfortunate barber is grabbed by a policeman because he has been caught shaving a Christian, Sunday morning. Now and then some poor fellow with a hack, trying to make a dollar or two to feed his horses, or to take care of his wife and children, is arrested as though he were a murderer. But in a few days the public are inconvenienced to that degree that the arrests stop and business goes on in its accustomed channels, Sunday and all.

Now and then society becomes so pious, so virtuous, that people are compelled to enter saloons by the back door; others are compelled to drink beer with the front shutters up; but otherwise the stream that goes down the thirsty throats is unbroken. The ministers have done their best to prevent all recreation on the Sabbath. They would like to stop all the boats on the Hudson, and on the sea – stop all the excursion trains. They would like to compel every human being that lives in the city of New York to remain within its limits 24 hours each Sunday. They hate the parks; they hate music; they hate anything that keeps a man away from church. Most of the churches are empty during the summer, and now most of the ministers leave themselves, and give over the entire city to the devil and his emissaries. And yet if the ministers had their way, there would be no form of human enjoyment except prayer, signing subscription papers, putting money in contribution boxes, listening to sermons, reading the cheerful histories of the Old Testament, imagining the joys of heaven and the torments of hell. The church is opposed to the theater, is the enemy of the opera, looks on dancing as a crime, hates billiards, despises cards, opposes roller-skating, and even entertains a certain kind of prejudice against croquet.

Q. Do you think that the orthodox church gets its ideas of the Sabbath from the teachings of Christ?

A. I do not hold Christ responsible for these idiotic ideas concerning the Sabbath. He regarded the Sabbath as something made for man – which was a sensible view. The holiest day is the happiest day. The most sacred day is the one in which have been done the most good deeds. There are two reasons given in the Bible for keeping the Sabbath. One is that God made the world in six days, and rested on the seventh. Now that all the ministers admit that he did not make the world in six days, but that he made it in six "periods," this reason is no longer applicable. The other reason is that he brought the Jews out of Egypt with a "mighty hand." This may be a good reason still for the observance of the Sabbath by the Jews, but the real Sabbath, that is to say, the day to be commemorated, is our Saturday, and why should we commemorate the wrong day? That disposes of the second reason.

140

Nothing can be more inconsistent than the theories and practice of the churches about the Sabbath. The cars run Sundays, and out of the profits hundreds of ministers are supported. The great iron and steel works fill with smoke and fire the Sabbath air, and the proprietors divide the profits with the churches. The printers of the city are busy Sunday afternoons and evenings, and the presses during the nights, so that the sermons of Sunday can reach the heathen on Monday. The servants of the rich are denied the privileges of the sanctuary. The coachman sits on the box outdoors, while his employer kneels in church preparing himself for the heavenly chariot. The iceman goes about on the holy day, keeping believers cool, they knowing at the same time that he is making it hot for himself in the world to come. Christians cross the Atlantic, knowing that the ship will pursue its way on the Sabbath. They write letters to their friends knowing that they will be carried in violation of Jehovah's law, by wicked men. Yet they hate to see a pale-faced sewing girl enjoying a few hours by the sea; a poor mechanic walking in the fields; or a tired mother watching her children playing on the grass. Nothing ever was, nothing ever will be, more utterly absurd and disgusting than a Puritan Sunday. Nothing ever did make a home more hateful than the strict observance of the Sabbath. It fills the house with hypocrisy and the meanest kind of petty tyranny. The parents look sour and stern, the children sad and sulky. They are compelled to talk on subjects about which they feel no interest, or to read books that are thought good only because they are stupid.

Q. What have you to say about the growth of Catholicism, the activity of the Salvation Army, and the success of revivalists like the Rev. Samuel Jones? Is Christianity really gaining a stronghold on the masses?

A. Catholicism is growing in this country, and it is the only country in which it is growing. Its growth here depends entirely on immigration, not on intellectual conquest. Catholic emigrants who leave their homes in the Old World because they have never had any liberty, and who are Catholics for the same reason, add to the number of Catholics here, but their children's children will not be Catholics. Their children will not be good Catholics, and even the immigrants themselves, in a few years, will not grovel quite so low in the presence of a priest. The Catholic Church is gaining no ground in Catholic countries.

The Salvation Army is the result of two things – the general belief in what are known as the fundamentals of Christianity and

141

the heartlessness of the church. The Church in England – that is to say, the Church of England – having succeeded – that is to say, being supported by general taxation that is to say, being a successful, well-fed parasite – naturally neglected those who did not in any way contribute to its support. It became aristocratic. Splendid churches were built; younger sons with good voices were put in the pulpits; the pulpit became the asylum for aristocratic mediocrity, and in that way the Church of England lost interest in the masses and the masses lost interest in the Church of England. The neglected poor, who really had some belief in religion, and who had not been absolutely petrified by form and patronage, were ready for the Salvation Army. They were not at home in the church. They could not pay. They preferred the freedom of the street. They preferred to attend a church where rags were no objection. Had the church loved and labored with the poor the Salvation Army never would have existed. These people are simply giving their idea of Christianity, and in their way endeavoring to do what they consider good. I don't suppose the Salvation Army will accomplish much. To improve mankind you must change conditions. It is not enough to work simply on the emotional nature. The surroundings must be such as naturally produce virtuous actions. If we are to believe recent reports from London, the Church of England, even with the assistance of the Salvation Army, has accomplished but little. It would be hard to find any savage country with less morality. You would search long in the jungles of Africa to find greater depravity.

I account for revivalists like the Rev. Samuel Jones in the same way. There is in every community an ignorant class – what you might call a literal class – who believe in the real blood atonement; who believe in heaven and hell, and harps, and gridirons; who have never had their faith weakened by reading commentators or books harmonizing science and religion. They love to hear the good old doctrine; they want hell described; they want it described so that they can hear the moans and shrieks: they want heaven described; they want to see God on a throne, and they want to feel that they are finally to have the pleasure of looking over the battlements of heaven and seeing all their enemies among the damned. The Rev. Mr. Munger has suddenly become a revivalist. According to the papers he is sought for in every direction. His popularity seems to rest on the fact that he brutally beat a girl twelve years old because she did not say her prayers to suit him. Muscular Christianity is what the ignorant people want. I regard all these efforts including those made by Mr. Moody and Mr. Hammond – as evidence that Christianity, as an intellectual factor, has almost spent its force. It no longer governs the intellectual world.

Q. Are not the Catholics the least progressive? And are they not, in spite of their professions to the contrary, enemies to republican liberty?

A. Every church that has a standard higher than human welfare is dangerous. A church that puts a book above the laws and constitution of its country, that puts a book above the welfare of mankind, is dangerous to human liberty. Every church that puts itself above the legally expressed will of the people is dangerous. Every church that holds itself under greater obligation to a pope than to a people is dangerous to human liberty. Every church that puts religion above humanity – above the well-being of man in this world is dangerous. The Catholic Church may be more dangerous, not because its doctrines are more dangerous, but because, on the average, its members more sincerely believe its doctrines, and because that church can be hurled as a solid body in any given direction. For these reasons it is more dangerous than other churches; but its doctrines are no more dangerous than those of the Protestant churches. The man who would sacrifice the well-being of man to please an imaginary phantom that he calls God is also dangerous. The only safe standard is the well-being of man in this world. Whenever this world is sacrificed for the sake of another, a mistake has been made. The only God that man can know is the aggregate of all beings capable of suffering and of joy within the reach of his influence. To increase the happiness of such beings is to worship the only God that man can know.

Q. What have you to say to the assertion of Dr. Deems that there were never so many Christians as now?

A. I suppose that the population of the earth is greater now than at any other time within the historic period. This being so, there may be more Christians, so-called, in the world than there were 100 years ago. Of course, the reverend doctor, in making up his aggregate of Christians, counts all kinds and sects – Unitarians, Universalists, and all the other "ans" and "ists" and "ics" and "ites" and "ers." But Dr. Deems must admit that only a few years ago most of the persons he now calls Christians would have been burnt as heretics and infidels. Let us compare the average New York Christian with the Christian of 200 years ago. It is probably safe to say that there is not now in the city of New York a genuine Presbyterian outside of an insane asylum. Probably no one could be found who will today admit that he believes absolutely in the Presbyterian confession of faith. There is probably not an Episcopalian who believes in the thirty-nine articles. Probably there is not an intelligent minister in the city of New York, outside of the Catholic Church, who believes that everything in the Bible is true. Probably no clergyman, of any standing, would be willing to take the ground that everything in the Old Testament – leaving out the question of inspiration – is actually true. Few ministers now preach the doctrine of eternal punishment. Most of them would be ashamed to utter that brutal falsehood. A large majority of gentlemen who attend church take the liberty of disagreeing with the preacher. They would have been poor Christians 200 years ago. A majority of the ministers take the liberty of disagreeing, in many things, with their Presbyteries and synods. They would have been poor preachers 200 years ago. Dr. Deems forgets that most Christians are only nominally so. Few believe their creeds. Few even try to live in accordance with what they call Christian doctrines. Nobody loves his enemies. No Christian when smitten on one cheek turns the other. Most Christians do take a little thought for the morrow. They do not depend entirely on the providence of God. Most Christians now have greater confidence in the average life insurance company than in God – feel easier when dying to know that they have a policy, through which they expect the widow will receive $10,000, than when thinking of all the Scripture promises. Even church-members do not trust in God to protect their own property. They insult heaven by putting lightning rods on their temples. They insure the churches against the act of God. The experience of man has shown the wisdom of relying on something that we know something about, instead of on the shadowy supernatural. The poor wretches today in Spain, depending on their priests, die like poisoned flies; die with prayers between their pallid lips; die in their filth and faith.

Q. What have you to say on the Mormon question?

A. The institution of polygamy is infamous and disgusting beyond expression. It destroys what we call, and what all civilized people call, "the family." It pollutes the fireside, and, above all, as Burns would say, "petrifies the feeling." It is, however, one of the institutions of Jehovah. It is protected by the Bible. It has inspiration on its side. Sinai, with its barren, granite peaks, is a

144

perpetual witness in its favor. The beloved of God practiced it, and, according to the sacred word, the wisest man had, I believe, about 700 wives. This man received his wisdom directly from God. It is hard for the average Bible-worshiper to attack this institution without casting a certain stain on his own book.

Only a few years ago slavery was upheld by the same Bible. Slavery having been abolished, the passages in the inspired volume upholding it have been mostly forgotten; but polygamy lives, and the polygamists, with great volubility, repeat the passages in their favor. We send our missionaries to Utah, with their Bibles, to convert the Mormons.

The Mormons show, by these very Bibles, that God is on their side. Nothing remains now for the missionaries except to get back their Bibles and come home. The preachers do not appeal to the Bible for the purpose of putting down Mormonism. They say: "Send the army" If the people of this country could only be honest; if they would only admit that the Old Testament is but the record of a barbarous people; if the Samson of the 19th century would not allow its limbs to be bound by the Delilah of superstition, it could with one blow destroy this monster. What shall we say of the moral force of Christianity, when it utterly fails in the presence of Mormonism? What shall we say of a Bible that we dare not read to a Mormon as an argument against legalized lust, or as an argument against illegal lust? I am opposed to polygamy. I want it exterminated by law; but I hate to see the exterminators insist that God, only a few thousand years ago, was as bad as the Mormons are today. In my judgment, such a God ought to be exterminated.

Q. What do you think of men like the Rev. Henry Ward Beecher and the Rev. R. Heber Newton? Do they deserve any credit for the course they have taken?

A. Mr. Beecher is evidently endeavoring to shore up the walls of the falling temple. He sees the cracks; he knows that the building is out of plumb; he feels that the foundation is insecure. Lies can take the place of stones only so long as they are thoroughly believed. Mr. Beecher is trying to do something to harmonize superstition and science. He is reading between the lines. He has discovered that Darwin is only a later St. Paul, or that St. Paul was the original Darwin. He is endeavoring to make the New Testament a scientific textbook. Of course, he will fail. But his intentions are good. Thousands of people will read the New

Testament with more freedom than heretofore. They will look for new meanings; and he who looks for new meanings will not be satisfied with the old ones. Mr. Beecher, instead of strengthening the walls, will make them weaker.

There is no harmony between religion and science. When science was a child, religion sought to strangle it in the cradle. Now that science has attained its youth, and superstition is in its dotage, the trembling, palsied wreck says to the athlete: "Let us be friends." It reminds me of the bargain the cock wished to make with the horse: "Let's agree not to step on each other's feet." Mr. Beecher, having done away with hell, substitutes annihilation. His doctrine at present is that only a fortunate few are immortal, and that the great mass return to dreamless dust. This, of course, is far better than hell, and is a great improvement on the orthodox view. Mr. Beecher cannot believe that God would make such a mistake as to make men doomed to suffer eternal pain. Why, I ask, should God give life to men whom he knows are unworthy of life? Why should he annihilate his mistakes? Why should he make mistakes that need annihilation?

It can hardly be said that Mr. Beecher's idea is a new one. It was taught, with an addition, thousands of years ago, in India, and the addition almost answers my objection. The old doctrine was that only the soul that bursts into blossom will at the death of the body rejoin the infinite, and that all other souls – souls not having blossomed – will go back into low forms and make the journey up to man once more and, should they then blossom and bear fruit, will be held worthy to join the infinite, but should they again fail, they again go back; and this process is repeated until they do blossom, and in this way all souls at last become perfect. I suggest that Mr. Beecher make at least this addition to his doctrine.

But allow me to say that, in my judgment, Mr. Beecher is doing great good. He may not convince many people that he is right, but he will certainly convince a great many people that Christianity is wrong.

ATHEISM AND CITIZENSHIP

Q. Have you noticed the decision of Nathaniel Jarvis, Jr., clerk of the Naturalization Bureau of the Court of Common Pleas, that an Atheist cannot become a citizen?

A. Yes, but I do not think it necessary for a man to be a theist in order to become or to remain a citizen of this country. The various laws, from 1790 up to 1828, provided that the person wishing to be naturalized might make oath or affirmation. The first exception you will find in the Revised Statutes of the United States passed in 1873-74, § 2,165, as follows: "An alien may be admitted to become a citizen of the United States in the following manner, and not otherwise: First, he shall declare on oath, before a circuit or district court of the United States, etc." I suppose Mr. Jarvis felt it to be his duty to comply with this section. In this section there is nothing about affirmation – only the word "oath" is used – and Mr. Jarvis came to the conclusion that an Atheist could not take an oath, and, therefore, could not declare his intention legally to become a citizen of the United States. Undoubtedly Mr. Jarvis felt it his duty to stand by the law and to see to it that nobody should become a citizen of this country who had not a well-defined belief in the existence of a being that he could not define and that no man has ever been able to define. In other words, that he should be perfectly convinced that there is a being "without body, parts, or passions," who presides over the destinies of this world, and more especially those of New York in and about that part known as City Hall Park.

Q. Was not Mr. Jarvis right in standing by the law?

A. If Mr. Jarvis is right, neither Humboldt nor Darwin could have become a citizen of the United States. Wagner, the greatest of musicians, not being able to take an oath, would have been left an alien. Under this ruling, Haeckel, Spencer, and Tyndall would be denied citizenship – that is to say, the six greatest men produced by the human race in the 19th century, were and are unfit to be citizens of the United States. Those who have placed the human race in debt cannot be citizens of the Republic. On the other hand, the ignorant wife beater, the criminal, the pauper raised in the workhouse, could take the necessary oath and would be welcomed by New York "with arms outstretched as she would fly."

Q. You have quoted one statute. Is there no other applicable to this case?

A. I am coming to that. If Mr. Jarvis will take the pains to read not only the law of naturalization in § 2,165 of the Revised Statutes of the United States, but the very first chapter in the book, "Title I.," he will find in the very first section this sentence: "The requirement of any 'oath' shall be deemed complied with by making affirmation in official form." This applies to § 2,165. Of course, an Atheist can affirm, and the statute provides that wherever an oath is required affirmation may be made.

Q. Did you read the recent action of judge O'Gorman, of the Superior Court, in refusing naturalization papers to an applicant because he had not read the Constitution of the United States?

A. I did. The United States Constitution is an important document, a good, sound document, but it is talked about a great deal more than it is read. I'll venture that you may commence at the Battery to interview merchants and other businessmen about the Constitution and you will talk with 100 before you will find one who has ever read it. — *New York Herald,* Aug. 8, 1886.

PROHIBITION

Q. How much importance do you attach to the present prohibition movement?

A. No particular importance. I am opposed to prohibition and always have been, and hope always to be. I do not want the legislature to interfere in these matters. I do not believe that the people can be made temperate by law. Men and women are not made great and good by the law. There is no good in the world that cannot be abused. Prohibition fills the world with spies and tattlers, and, besides that, where a majority of the people are not in favor of it the law will not be enforced; and where a majority of the people are in favor of it there is not much need of the law. Where a majority are against it, juries will violate their oath, and witnesses will get around the truth, and the result is demoralization. Take wine and malt liquors out of the world and we shall lose a vast deal of good fellowship; the world would lose more than it would gain. There is a certain sociability about wine that I should hate to have taken from the earth. Strong liquors the folks had better let alone. If prohibition succeeds, and wines and malt liquors go, the next thing will be to take tobacco away, and the next thing all other pleasures, until prayer meetings will be the only places of enjoyment.

REPLY TO THE REV. B. F. MORSE

At the usual weekly meeting of the Baptist ministers at the Publication Rooms yesterday, the Rev. Dr. B. F. Morse read an essay on "Christianity vs. Materialism." His contention was that all nature showed that design, not evolution, was its origin.

In his concluding remarks Dr. Morse said that he knew from unquestionable authority that Robert G. Ingersoll did not believe what he uttered in his lectures, and that to get out of financial embarrassment he looked around for a money-making scheme that could be put into immediate execution. To lecture against Christianity was the most rapid way of giving him the needed cash and, what was quite as acceptable to him, at the same time, notoriety.

This aquatic or web-footed theologian who expects to go to heaven by diving is not worth answering. Nothing can be more idiotic than to answer an argument by saying he who makes it does not believe it. Belief has nothing to do with the cogency or worth of an argument. There is another thing. This man, or rather this minister, says that I attacked Christianity simply to make money. Is it possible that, after preachers have had the field for 1,800 years, the way to make money is to attack the clergy? Is this intended as a slander against me or the ministers?

The trouble is that my arguments cannot be answered. All the preachers in the world cannot prove that slavery is better than liberty. They cannot show that all have not an equal right to think. They cannot show that all have not an equal right to express their thoughts. They cannot show that a decent God will punish a decent man for making the best guess he can. This is all there is about it. — *The Herald,* New York, Dec. 14, 1886.

INGERSOLL ON McGLYNN

The attitude of the Roman Catholic Church in Dr. McGlynn's case is consistent with the history and constitution of the Catholic Church – perfectly consistent with its ends, its objects, and its means, and just as perfectly consistent with intellectual liberty and the real civilization of the human race.

When a man becomes a Catholic priest, he has been convinced that he ought not to think for himself on religious questions. He has become convinced that the church is the only teacher – that he has a right to think only to enforce its teachings. From that moment he is a moral machine. The chief engineer resides at Rome, and he gives his orders through certain assistant engineers until the one is reached who turns the crank, and the machine has nothing to do one way or the other. This machine is paid for giving up his liberty by having machines under him who have also given up theirs. While somebody else turns his crank, he has the pleasure of turning a crank belonging to somebody below him.

Of course, the Catholic Church is supposed to be the only perfect institution on earth. All others are not only imperfect, but unnecessary. All others have been made either by man, or by the devil, or by a partnership, and consequently cannot be depended on for the civilization of man.

The Catholic Church gets its power directly from God, and is the only institution now in the world founded by God. There was never any other, so far as I know, except polygamy and slavery and a crude kind of monarchy, and they have been, for the most part, abolished.

The Catholic Church must be true to itself. It must claim everything, and get what it can. It alone is infallible. It alone has all the wisdom of this world. It alone has the right to exist. All other interests are secondary. To be a Catholic is of the first importance. Human liberty is nothing. Wealth, position, food, clothing, reputation, happiness – all these are less than worthless compared with what the Catholic Church promises to the man who will throw all these away.

A priest must preach what his bishop tells him. A bishop must preach what his archbishop tells him. The pope must preach what he says God tells him.

Dr. McGlynn cannot make a compromise with the Catholic Church. It never compromises when it is in the majority.

I do not mean by this that the Catholic Church is worse than any other. All are alike in this regard. Every sect, no matter how insignificant; every church, no matter how powerful, asks precisely the same thing from every member – that is to say, a surrender of intellectual freedom. The Catholic Church wants the same as the Baptist, the Presbyterian, and the Methodist – it wants the whole earth. It is ambitious to be the one supreme power. It hopes to see the world on its knees, with all its tongues thrust out for wafers. It has the arrogance of humility and the ferocity of universal forgiveness. In this respect it resembles every other sect. Every religion is a system of slavery.

Of course, the religionists say that they do not believe in persecution; that they do not believe in burning and hanging and whipping, or loading with chains a man simply because he is an Infidel. They are willing to leave all this with God, knowing that a being of infinite goodness will inflict all these horrors and tortures upon an honest man who differs with the church.

In case Dr. McGlynn is deprived of his priestly functions, it is hard to say what effect it will have on his church and the labor party in this country.

So long as a man believes that a church has eternal joy in store for him, so long as he believes that a church holds within its hand the keys of heaven and hell, it will be hard to make him trade off the hope of everlasting happiness for a few good clothes and a little good food and higher wages here. He finally thinks that, after all, he had better work for less and go a little hungry, and be an angel forever.

I hope, however, that a good many people who have been supporting the Catholic Church by giving tithes of the wages of weariness will see, and clearly see, that Catholicism is not their friend; that the church cannot and will not support them; that, on the contrary, they must support the church. I hope they will see that all the prayers have to be paid for, although not one has ever been answered. I hope they will perceive that the church is on the side of wealth and power, that the mitre is the friend of the crown, that the altar is the sworn brother of the throne. I hope they will finally know that the church cares infinitely more for the money of the millionaire than for the souls of the poor.

Of course, there are thousands of individual exceptions. I am speaking of the church as an institution, as a corporation – and when I say the church, I include all churches. It is said of corporations in general that they have no soul, and it may truthfully be said of the church that it has less than any other. It lives on alms. It gives nothing – for what it gets. It has no sympathy. Beggars never weep over the misfortunes of other beggars.

Nothing could give me more pleasure than to see the Catholic Church on the side of human freedom, nothing more pleasure than to see the Catholics of the world – those who work and weep and toil – sensible enough to know that all the money paid for superstition is worse than lost. I wish they could see that the counting of beads, and the saying of prayers and celebrating of masses, and all the kneelings and censerswingings and fastings and bell-ringing, amount to less than nothing that all these things tend only to the degradation of mankind. It is hard, I know, to find an antidote for a poison that was mingled with a mother's milk.

The laboring masses, so far as the Catholics are concerned, are filled with awe and wonder and fear about the church. This fear began to grow while they were being rocked in their cradles, and they still imagine that the church has some mysterious power; that it is in direct communication with some infinite personality that could, if it desired, strike dead or damn their souls forever. Persons who have no such belief, who care nothing for popes or priests, or churches or heavens or hells or devils or gods, have little idea of the power of fear.

The old dogmas filled the brain with strange monsters. The soul of the orthodox Christian gropes and wanders and crawls in a kind of dungeon, where the strained eyes see fearful shapes, and the frightened flesh shrinks from the touch of serpents.

The good part of Christianity – that is to say, kindness, morality – will never go down. The cruel part ought to go down. And by the cruel part I mean the doctrine of eternal punishment – of allowing the good to suffer for the bad – allowing innocence to pay the debt of guilt. So the foolish part of Christianity – that is to say, the miraculous – will go down. The absurd part must perish. But there will be no war about it as there was in France. Nobody believes enough in the foolish part of Christianity now to fight for it. Nobody believes with intensity enough in miracles to shoulder a musket. There is probably not a Christian in New York willing to fight for any story, no matter if the story is so old that it is covered with moss. No mentally brave and intelligent man believes in miracles, and no intelligent man cares whether there was a miracle or not, for the reason that every intelligent man knows that the miraculous has no possible connection with the moral. "Thou shalt not steal," is just as good a commandment if it should turn out that the flood was a drought. "Thou shalt not murder," is a good and just and righteous law, and whether any particular miracle was ever performed or not has nothing to do with the case. There is no possible relation between these things.

I am on the side not only of the physically oppressed, but of the mentally oppressed. I hate those who put lashes on the body, and I despise those who put the soul in chains. In other words, I am in favor of liberty. I do not wish that any man should be the slave of his fellow men, or that the human race should be the slaves of any god, real or imaginary. Man has the right to think for himself, to work for himself, to take care of himself, to get bread for himself, to get a home for himself. He has a right to his own opinion about God, and heaven and hell; the right to learn any art or mystery or trade; the right to work for whom he will, for what he will, and when he will.

The world belongs to the human race. There is to be no war in this country on religious opinions, except a war of words – a conflict of thoughts, of facts; and in that conflict the hosts of superstition will go down. They may not be defeated today, or tomorrow, or next year, or during this century, but they are growing weaker day by day.

This priest, McGlynn, has the courage to stand up against the propaganda. What would have been his fate a few years ago? What would have happened to him in Spain, in Portugal, in Italy – in any other country that was Catholic – only a few years ago? Yet he stands here in New York, he refuses to obey God's vicegerent; he freely gives his mind to an archbishop; he holds the Holy Inquisition in contempt. He has done a great thing. He is undoubtedly an honest man. He never should have been a Catholic. He has no business in that church. He has ideas of his own – theories, and seems to be governed by principles. The Catholic Church is not his place. If he remains, he must submit, he must kneel in the humility of abjectness; he must receive on the back of his independence the lashes of the church. If he remains, he must ask the forgiveness of slaves for having been a man. If he refuses to submit, the church will not have him. He will be driven to take his choice to remain a member, humiliated, shunned, or go out into the great, free world a citizen of the Republic, with the rights, responsibilities, and duties of an American citizen.

I believe that Dr. McGlynn is an honest man and that he really believes in the land theories of Henry George. I have no confidence in his theories, but I have confidence that he is actuated by the best and noblest motives.

Q. Are you to go on the lecture platform again?

A. I expect to after a while. I am now waiting for the church to catch up. I got so far ahead that I began almost to sympathize with the clergy. They looked so helpless and talked in such a weak, wandering, and wobbling kind of way that I felt as though I had been cruel. From the papers I see that they are busy trying to find out who the wife of Cain was. I see that the Rev. Dr. Robinson of New York is now wrestling with that problem. He begins to be in doubt whether Adam was the first man, whether Eve was the first woman; suspects that there were other races, and that Cain did not marry his sister, but somebody else's sister, and that the somebody else was not Cain's brother. One can hardly overestimate the importance of these questions, they have such a direct bearing on the progress of the world. If it should turn out that Adam was the first man, or that he was not the first man, something might happen – I am not prepared to say what, but it might.

It is curious kind of a spectacle to see a few hundred people paying a few thousand dollars a year for the purpose of hearing these great problems discussed: "Was Adam the first man?" "Who was Cain's wife?" "Has anyone seen a map of the land of Nod?" "Where are the four rivers that ran murmuring through the groves of paradise?" "Who was the snake? How did he walk? What language did he speak?" This turns a church into a kind of nursery, makes a cradle of each pew, and gives to each member a rattle with which he can amuse what he calls his mind.

The great theologians of Andover – the gentlemen who wear the brass colors furnished by the dead founder – have been disputing among themselves as to what is to become of the heathen who fortunately died before meeting any missionary from the institution. One can almost afford to be damned hereafter for the sake of avoiding the dogmas of Andover here. Nothing more

155

absurd and childish has ever happened – not in the intellectual, but in the theological world.

There is no need of the freethinkers saying anything at present. The work is being done by the church members themselves. They are beginning to ask questions of the clergy. They are getting tired of the old ideas – tired of the consolations of eternal pain – tired of hearing about hell – tired of hearing the Bible quoted or talked about – tired of the scheme of redemption – tired of the trinity, of the plenary inspiration of the barbarous records of a barbarous people – tired of the patriarchs and prophets – tired of Daniel and the goats with three horns, and the image with the clay feet, and the little stone that rolled downhill – tired of the mud man and the rib woman – tired of the flood of Noah, of the astronomy of Joshua, the geology of Moses – tired of Kings and Chronicles and Lamentations – tired of the lachrymose Jeremiah – tired of the monstrous, the malicious, and the miraculous. In short, they are beginning to think. They have bowed their necks to the yoke of ignorance and fear and impudence and superstition, until they are weary. They long to be free. They are tired of the services – tired of the meaningless prayers – tired of hearing each other say, "Hear us, good Lord" – tired of the texts, tired of the sermons, tired of the lies about spontaneous combustion as a punishment for blasphemy, tired of the bells, and they long to hear the doxology of superstition. They long to have Common Sense lift its hands in benediction and dismiss the congregation. — *Brooklyn Citizen,* April, 1886.

TRIAL OF THE CHICAGO ANARCHIST

Q. What do you think of the trial of the Anarchists and their chances for a new trial?

A. I have paid some attention to the evidence and to the rulings of the court, and I have read the opinion of the Supreme Court of Illinois, in which the conviction is affirmed. Of course, these men were tried during a period of great excitement – tried when the press demanded their conviction – when it was asserted that society was on the edge of destruction unless these men were hanged. Under such circumstances, it is not easy to have a fair and impartial trial. A judge should either sit beyond the reach of prejudice, in some calm that storms cannot invade, or he should be a kind of oak so that before any blast he would stand erect. It is hard to find such a place as I have suggested, and not easy to find such a man. We are all influenced more or less by our surroundings, by the demands and opinions and feelings and prejudices of our fellow-citizens. There is a personality made up of many individuals known as society. This personality has prejudices like an individual. It often becomes enraged, acts without the slightest sense, and repents at its leisure. It is hard to reason with a mob whether organized or disorganized, whether acting in the name of the law or of simple brute force. But in any case, where people refuse to be governed by reason, they become a mob.

Q. Do you not think that these men had a fair trial?

A. I have no doubt that the court endeavored to be fair – no doubt that Judge Gary is a perfectly honest, upright man, but I think his instructions were wrong. He instructed the jury to the effect that where men have talked in a certain way, and where the jury believed that the result of such talk might be the commission of a crime, that such men are responsible for that crime. Of course, there is neither law nor sense in an instruction like this. I hold that it must have been the intention of the man making the remark, or publishing the article, or doing the thing – it must have been his intention that the crime should be committed. Men differ as to the effect of words, and a man may say a thing with the best intentions the result of which is a crime, and he may say a thing with the worst of intentions and the result may not be a crime. The Supreme Court of Illinois seemed to have admitted that the instruction was wrong, but took the ground that it made no difference with the verdict. This is a dangerous course for the court of last resort to pursue; neither is it complimentary to the judge who tried the case that his instructions had no effect on the jury. Under the instructions of the court below, any man who had been arrested with the seven Anarchists and of whom it could be proved that he ever said a word in favor of any change in government, or of other peculiar ideas, no matter whether he knew of the meeting at the Haymarket or not, would have been convicted.

I am satisfied that the defendant Fielden never intended to harm a human being. As a matter of fact, the evidence shows that he was making a speech in favor of peace at the time of the occurrence. The evidence also shows that he was an exceedingly honest, industrious, and a poor and philanthropic man.

Q. Do you then uphold the Anarchists?

A. Certainly not. There is no place in this country for the Anarchist. The source of power here is the people, and to attack the political power is to attack the people. If the laws are oppressive, it is the fault of the oppressed. If the laws touch the poor and leave them without redress, it is the fault of the poor. They are in a majority. The men who work for their living are the very men who have the power to make every law that is made in the United States. There is no excuse for any resort to violence in this country. The boycotting by trades unions and by labor organizations is all wrong. Let them resort to legal methods and to no other. I have not the slightest sympathy with the methods that have been pursued by Anarchists, or by Socialists, or by any other class that has resorted to force or intimidation. The ballot-box is the place to assemble. The will of the people can be made known in that way, and their will can be executed. At the same time, I think I understand what has produced the Anarchist, the Socialist, and the agitator. In the old country, a laboring man, poorly clad, without quite enough to eat, with a wife in rags, with a few children asking for bread – this laboring man sees the idle enjoying every luxury of this life; he sees on the breast of "my lady" a bonfire of diamonds; he sees "my Lord" riding in his park; he sees thousands of people who from the cradle to the grave do no useful act; add nothing to the intellectual or the physical wealth of the world; he sees labor living in the tenement house, in the hut; idleness and nobility

158

in the mansion and the palace; the poor man a trespasser everywhere except on the street, where he is told to "move on," and in the dusty highways of the country. That man naturally hates the government – the government of the few, the government that lives on the unpaid labor of the many, the government that takes the child from the parents and puts him in the army to fight the child of another poor man and woman in some other country. These Anarchists, these Socialists, these agitators, have been naturally produced. All the things of which I have spoken sow in the breast of poverty the seeds of hatred and revolution. These poor men, hunted by the officers of the law, cornered, captured, imprisoned, excite the sympathy of other poor men, and if some are dragged to the gallows and hanged, or beheaded by the guillotine, they become saints and martyrs, and those who sympathize with them feel that they have the power, and only the power of hatred – the power of riot, of destruction – the power of the torch, of revolution, that is to say, of chaos and anarchy. The injustice of the higher classes makes the lower criminal. Then there is another thing. The misery of the poor excites in many noble breasts sympathy, and the men who thus sympathize wish to better the condition of their fellows. At first they depend on reason, on calling the attention of the educated and powerful to the miseries of the poor. Nothing happens, no result follows. The juggernaut of society moves on, and the wretches are still crushed beneath the great wheels. These men who are really good at first, filled with sympathy, now become indignant – they are malicious, then destructive and criminal. I do not sympathize with these methods, but I do sympathize with the general object that all good and generous people seek to accomplish – namely, to better the condition of the human race. Only the other day, at Boston, I said that we ought to take into consideration the circumstances under which the Anarchists were reared; that we ought to know that every man is necessarily produced; that man is what he is, not by accident, but necessity; that society raises its own criminals – that it plows the soil and cultivates and harvests the crop. And it was telegraphed that I had defended anarchy. Nothing was ever further from my mind. There is no place, as I said before, for anarchy in the United States. In Russia it is another question; in Germany another question. Every country that is governed by the one man, or governed by the few, is the victim of anarchy. That is anarchy. That is the worst possible form of socialism. The definition of socialism given

159

by its bitterest enemy is that idlers wish to live on the labor and on the money of others. Is not this definition – a definition given in hatred – a perfect definition of every monarchy and of nearly every government in the world? That is to say: the idle few live on the labor and the money of others.

Q. Will the Supreme Court take cognizance of this case and prevent the execution of the judgment?

A. Of course, it is impossible for me to say. At the same time, judging from the action of Justice Miller in the case of *The People v. Maxwell,* it seems probable that the Supreme Court may interfere, but I have not examined the question sufficiently to form an opinion. My feeling about the whole matter is this: that it will not tend to answer the ideas advanced by these men, to hang them. Their execution will excite sympathy among thousands and thousands of people who have never examined and know nothing of the theories advanced by the Anarchists, or the Socialists, or other agitators. In my judgment, supposing the men to be guilty, it is far better to imprison them. Less harm will be done the cause of free government. We are not on the edge of any revolution. No other government is as firmly fixed as ours. No other government has such a broad and splendid foundation. We have nothing to fear. Courage and safety can afford to be generous – can afford to act without haste and without the feeling of revenge. So, for my part, I hope that the sentence may be commuted, and that these men, if found guilty at last, may be imprisoned. This course is, in my judgment, the safest to pursue. It may be that I am led to this conclusion because of my belief that every man does as he must. This belief makes me charitable toward all the world. This belief makes me doubt the wisdom of revenge. This belief, so far as I am concerned, blots from our language the word 'punishment.' Society has a right to protect itself, and it is the duty of society to reform, in so far as it may be possible, any member who has committed what is called a crime. Where the criminal cannot be reformed, and the safety of society can be secured by his imprisonment, there is no possible excuse for destroying his life. After these six or seven men have been, in accordance with the forms of law, strangled to death, there will be a few pieces of clay, and about them will gather a few friends, a few admirers – and these pieces will be buried, and over the grave will be erected a monument, and those who were executed as criminals will be regarded by thousands as saints. It is far better for society to have a little mercy.

The effect on the community will be good. If these men are imprisoned, people will examine their teachings without prejudice. If they are executed, seen through the tears of pity, their virtues, their sufferings, their heroism, will be exaggerated; others may emulate their deeds, and the gulf between the rich and the poor will be widened – a gulf that may not close until it has devoured the noblest and the best. — *Mail and Express,* New York, Nov. 3, 1887.

THE STAGE AND THE PULPIT

Q. What do you think of the Methodist minister at Nashville, Tennessee who, from his pulpit, denounced the theatrical profession, without exception, as vicious, and of the congregation which passed resolutions condemning Miss Emma Abbott for rising in church and contradicting him, and of the Methodist bishop who likened her to a "painted courtesan," and invoked the aid of the law "for the protection of public worship" against "strolling players"?

A. The Methodist minister of whom you speak without doubt uttered his real sentiments. The church has always regarded the stage as a rival, and its utterances have been as malicious as untrue. It has always felt that the money given to the stage was in some way taken from the pulpit. It is on this principle that the pulpit wishes everything, except the church, shut up on Sunday. It knows that it cannot stand free and open competition.

All well-educated ministers know that the Bible suffers by a comparison with Shakespeare. They know that there is nothing within the lids of what they call "the sacred book" that can for one moment stand side by side with *Lear* or *Hamlet* or *Julius Caesar* or *Antony and Cleopatra* or with any other play written by the immortal man. They know what a poor figure the Davids and the Brahmas and the Jeremiads and the Lots, the Jonahs, the Jobs, and the Noahs cut when on the stage with the great characters of Shakespeare. For these reasons, among others, the pulpit is malicious and hateful when it thinks of the glories of the stage. What minister is there now living who could command the prices commanded by Edwin Booth or Joseph Jefferson; and what two clergymen, by making a combination, could contend successfully with Robson and Crane? How many clergymen would it take to command, at regular prices, the audiences that attend the presentation of Wagner's operas?

It is easy to see why the pulpit attacks the stage. Nothing could have been in more wretched taste than for the minister to condemn Miss Emma Abbott for rising in church and defending not only herself, but other good women who are doing honest work for an honest living. Of course, no minister wishes to be answered; no minister wishes to have anyone in the congregation call for the proof. A few questions would break up all the theology in the world. Ministers can succeed only when congregations keep silent. Where superstition succeeds, doubt must be dumb.

The Methodist bishop who attacked Miss Abbott simply repeated the language of several centuries ago. In the laws of England actors were described as "sturdy vagrants," and this bishop calls them "strolling players." If we only had some strolling preachers like Garrick, like Edwin Forrest, or Booth and Barrett, or some crusade sisters like Mrs. Siddons, Madam Ristori, Charlotte Cushman, or Madam Modjeska, how fortunate the church would be!

Q. What is your opinion of the relative merits of the pulpit and the stage, preachers, and actors?

A. We must remember that the stage presents an ideal life. It is a world controlled by the imagination – a world in which the justice delayed in real life may be done, and in which that may happen which according to the highest ideal should happen. It is a world, for the most part, in which evil does not succeed, in which the vicious are foiled, in which the right, the honest, the sincere, and the good prevail. It cultivates the imagination, and in this respect is far better than the pulpit. The mission of the pulpit is to narrow and shrivel the human mind. The pulpit denounces the freedom of thought and of expression; but on the stage the mind is free, and for thousands of years the poor, the oppressed, the enslaved, have been permitted to witness plays wherein the slave was freed, wherein the oppressed became the victor, and where the downtrodden rose supreme.

And there is another thing. The stage has always laughed at the spirit of caste. The low-born lass has loved the prince. All human distinctions in this ideal world have for the moment vanished, while honesty and love have triumphed. The stage lightens the cares of life. The pulpit increases the tears and groans of man. There is this difference: the pretense of honesty and the honesty of pretense.

Q. How do you view the Episcopalian scheme of building a six-million-dollar untaxed cathedral in this city for the purpose of "uniting the sects," and, when that is accomplished, "unifying the world in the love of Christ," and thereby abolishing misery?

A. I regard the building of an Episcopal cathedral simply as a piece of religious folly. The world will never be converted by Christian palaces and temples. Every dollar used in its construction will be wasted. It will have no tendency to unite the various sects; on the contrary, it will excite the envy and jealousy of every other sect. It will widen the gulf between the Episcopalian and the Methodist, between the Episcopalian and the Presbyterian, and this hatred will continue until the other sects build a cathedral just a little larger, and then the envy and the hatred will be on the other side.

Religion will never unify the world, and never will give peace to mankind. There has been more war in the last thousand years than during any similar period within historic times. War will be abolished, if it ever is abolished, not by religion, but by intelligence. It will be abolished when the poor people of Germany, of France, of Spain, of England, and other countries find that they have no interest in war. When those who pay, and those who do the fighting, find that they are simply destroying their own interests, wars will cease.

There ought to be a national court to decide national difficulties. We consider a community civilized when the individuals of that community submit their differences to a legal tribunal; but there being no national court, nations now sustain, as to each other, the relation of savages – that is to say, each one must defend its rights by brute force. The establishment of a national court civilizes nations, and tends to do away with war.

Christianity caused so much war, so much bloodshed, that Christians were forced to interpolate a passage to account for their history, and the interpolated passage is, "I came not to bring peace, but a sword." Suppose that all the money wasted in cathedrals in the Middle Ages had been used for the construction of schoolhouses, academies, and universities; how much better the world would have been! Suppose that instead of supporting hundreds of thousands of idle priests, the money had been given to men of science for the purpose of finding out something of benefit to the human race here in this world.

Q. What is your opinion of "Christian charity" and the "fatherhood of God" as an economic policy for abolishing poverty and misery?

A. Of course, the world is not to be civilized and clothed and fed through charity. Ordinary charity creates more want than it

164

alleviates. The greatest possible charity is the greatest possible justice. When proper wages are paid, when everyone is as willing to give what a thing is worth as he is now willing to get it for less, the world will be fed and clothed.

I believe in helping people to help themselves. I believe that corporations, and successful men, and superior men intellectually, should do all within their power to keep from robbing their fellow men. The superior man should protect the inferior. The powerful should be the shield of the weak. Today it is, for the most part, exactly the other way. The failures among men become the food of success.

The world is to grow better and better through intelligence, through a development of the brain, through taking advantage of the forces of nature, through science, through chemistry, and through the arts. Religion can do nothing except to sow the seeds of discord between men and nations. Commerce, manufacturers, and the arts tend to peace and the well-being of the world. What is known as religion – that is to say, a system by which this world is wasted in preparation for another – a system in which the duties of man are greater to God than to his fellow men – a system that denies the liberty of thought and expression – tends only to discord and retrogression. Of course, I know that religious people cling to the Bible on account of the good that is in it, and in spite of the bad, and I know that Freethinkers throw away the Bible on account of the bad that is in it, in spite of the good. I hope the time will come when that book will be treated like other books, and will be judged on its merits, apart from the fiction of inspiration. The church has no right to speak of charity, because it is an object of charity itself. It gives nothing; all it can do is to receive. At best, it is only a respectable beggar. I never care to hear one who receives alms pay a tribute to charity. The one who gives alms should pay this tribute. The amount of money expended on churches and priests and all the paraphernalia of superstition is more than enough to drive the wolves from the doors of the world.

Q. Have you noticed the progress Catholics are making in the Northwest, discontinuing public schools, and forcing people to send their children to the parochial schools; also, at Pittsburgh, Pennsylvania, a Roman Catholic priest has been elected principal of a public school, and he has appointed nuns as assistant teachers?

A.   Sectarian schools ought not to be supported by public taxation. It is the very essence of religious tyranny to compel a Methodist to support a Catholic school, or to compel a Catholic to support a Baptist academy. Nothing should be taught in the public schools that the teachers do not know. Nothing should be taught about any religion, and nothing should be taught that can, in any way, be called sectarian. The sciences are not religious. There is no such thing as Methodist mathematics or Baptist botany. In other words, no religion has anything to do with facts. The facts are all secular; the sciences are all of this world. If Catholics wish to establish their own schools for the purpose of preserving their ignorance, they have the right to do so; so has any other denomination. But in this country, the state has no right to teach any form of religion whatever. Persons of all religions have the right to become citizens, and citizens have the right to advocate and defend any religion in which they believe, or they have the right to denounce all religions. If the Catholics establish parochial schools, let them support such schools; and if they do, they will simply lessen or shorten the longevity of that particular superstition. It has often been said that nothing will repeal a bad law as quickly as its enforcement. So, in my judgment, nothing will destroy any church as certainly, and as rapidly, as for the members of that church to live squarely up to the creed. The church is indebted to its hypocrisy today for its life. No orthodox church in the United States dare meet for the purpose of revising the creed. They know that the whole thing would fall in pieces.

Nothing could be more absurd than for a Roman Catholic priest to teach a public school, assisted by nuns. The Catholic Church is the enemy of human progress; it teaches every man to throw away his reason, to deny his observation and experience.

Q.   Your opinions have frequently been quoted with regard to the Anarchists – with regard to their trial and execution. Have you any objection to stating your real opinion in regard to the matter?

A.   Not the least. I am perfectly willing that all civilized people should know my opinions on any question in which others than myself can have any interest.

I was anxious, in the first place, that the Anarchists should have a fair and impartial trial. The worst form of anarchy is when a judge violates his conscience and bows to a popular demand. A court should care nothing for public opinion. An honest judge decides the law, not as it ought to be, but as it is, and the state of the public mind throws no light on the question of what the law then is.

I thought that some of the rulings on the trial of the Anarchists were contrary to law. I think so still. I have read the opinion of the Supreme Court of Illinois, and while the conclusion reached by that tribunal is the law of that case, I was not satisfied with the reasons given, and do not regard the opinion as good law. There is no place for an Anarchist in the United States. There is no excuse for any resort to force; and it is impossible to use language too harsh or too bitter in denouncing the spirit of anarchy in this country. But, no matter how bad a man is, he has the right to be fairly tried; and if he cannot be fairly tried, then there is anarchy on the bench. So I was opposed to the execution of those men. I thought it would have been far better to commute the punishment to imprisonment, and I said so; and I not only said so, but I wrote a letter to Governor Oglesby, in which I urged the commutation of the death sentence. In my judgment, a great mistake was made. I am on the side of mercy, and if I ever make mistakes, I hope they will all be made on that side. I have not the slightest sympathy with the feeling of revenge. Neither have I ever admitted, and I never shall, that every citizen has not the right to give his opinion on all that may be done by any servant of the people, by any judge, or by any court, by any officer – however small or however great. Each man in the United States is a sovereign, and a king can freely speak his mind.

Words were put in my mouth that I never uttered with regard to the Anarchists. I never said that they were saints, or that they would be martyrs. What I said was that they would be regarded as saints and martyrs by many people if they were executed, and that has happened which I said would happen. I am, so far as I know, on the side of the right. I wish above all things for the preservation of human liberty. This government is the best, and we should not lose confidence in liberty. Property is of little value in comparison with freedom. A civilization that rests on slavery is utterly worthless. I do not believe in sacrificing all there is of value in the human heart, or in the human brain, for the preservation of what is called property, or rather, on account of the fear that what is called "property" may perish. Property is in no danger while man is free. It is the freedom of man that gives value to property. It is the happiness of the human race that creates what we call value. If we preserve liberty, the spirit of progress, the conditions of development, property will take care of itself.

Q. The Christian press during the past few months has been solicitous as to your health, and has reported you weak and feeble physically, and not only so, but asserts that there is a growing disposition on your part to lay down your arms, and even to join the church.

A. I do not think the Christian press has been solicitous about my *health*. Neither do I think that my health will ever add to theirs. The fact is I am exceedingly well, and my throat is better than it has been for many years. Anyone who imagines that I am disposed to lay down my arms can read my reply to Dr. Field in the November issue of the *North American Review*. I see no particular difference in myself, except this; that my hatred of superstition becomes a little more and more intense; on the other hand, I see more clearly that all the superstitions were naturally produced, and I am now satisfied that every man does as he must, including priests and editors of religious papers.

This gives me hope for the future. We find that certain soil, with a certain amount of moisture and heat, produces good corn, and we find when the soil is poor, or when the ground is too wet, or too dry, that no amount of care can, by any possibility, produce good corn. In other words, we find that the fruit, that is to say, the result, whatever it may be, depends absolutely on the conditions. This being so, we will in time find out the conditions that produce good, intelligent, honest men. This is the hope for the future. We shall know better than to rely on what is called reformation, or regeneration, or a resolution born of ignorant excitement. We shall rely, then, on the eternal foundation – the fact in nature – that like causes produce like results, and that good conditions will produce good people.

Q. Every now and then someone challenges you to a discussion, and nearly everyone who delivers lectures or speeches attacking you or your views says that you are afraid publicly to debate these questions. Why do you not meet these men, and why do you not answer these attacks?

A. In the first place, it would be a physical impossibility to reply to all the attacks that have been made – to all the "answers." I receive these attacks, and these answers, and these lectures almost every day. Hundreds of them are delivered every year. A great many are put in pamphlet form, and, of course, copies are received by me. Some of them I read, at least I look them over, and I have never yet received one worthy of the slightest notice, never one in which the writer showed the slightest appreciation of the questions under discussion. All these pamphlets are about the same, and they could, for that matter, have all been produced by one person. They are impudent, shallow, abusive, illogical, and in most respects, ignorant. So far as the lectures are concerned, I know of no one who has yet said anything that challenges a reply. I do not think a single paragraph has been produced by any of the gentlemen who have replied to me in public that is now remembered by reason of its logic or its beauty. I do not feel called on to answer any argument that does not at least appear to be of value. Whenever any article appears worthy of an answer, written in a kind and candid spirit, it gives me pleasure to reply.

I should like to meet someone who speaks by authority, someone who really understands his creed, but I cannot afford to waste time on little priests or obscure parsons or ignorant laymen. — *The Truth Seeker,* New York, Jan. 14, 1888.

THE CHURCH AND THE STAGE

Q. I have come to talk with you a little about drama. Have you any decided opinions on that subject?

A. Nothing is more natural than imitation. The little child with her doll, telling it stories, putting words in its mouth, attributing to it the feelings of happiness and misery, is the simple tendency toward the drama. Little children always have plays, they imitate their parents, they put on the clothes of their elders, they have imaginary parties, carry on conversation with imaginary persons, have little dishes filled with imaginary food, pour tea and coffee out of invisible pots, receive callers, and repeat what they have heard their mothers say. This is simply the natural drama, an exercise of the imagination which always has been and which, probably, always will be a source of great pleasure. In the early days of the world nothing was more natural than for the people to reenact the history of their country – to represent the great heroes, the great battles, and the most exciting scenes the history of which has been preserved by legend. I believe this tendency to reenact, to bring before the eyes the great, the curious, and pathetic events of history has been universal. All civilized nations have delighted in the theater, and the greatest minds in many countries have been devoted to the drama, and, without doubt, the greatest man about whom we know anything devoted his life to the production of plays.

Q. I would like to ask you why, in your opinion as a student of history, has the Protestant church always been so bitterly opposed to the theater?

A. I believe that the early Christians expected the destruction of the world. They had no idea of remaining here, in the then condition of things, but for a few days. They expected that Christ would come again, that the world would be purified by fire, that all the unbelievers would be burned up and that the earth would become a fit habitation for the followers of the Savior. Protestantism became as ascetic as the early Christians. It is hard to conceive of anybody believing in the "Five Points" of John Calvin going to any place of amusement. The creed of

Protestantism made life infinitely sad and made man infinitely responsible. According to this creed, every man was liable at any moment to be summoned to eternal pain; the most devout Christian was not absolutely sure of salvation. This life was a probationary state. Everybody was considered as waiting on the dock of time, sitting on his trunk, expecting the ship that was to bear him to an eternity of good or evil – probably evil. They were in no state of mind to enjoy burlesque or comedy, and, so far as tragedy was concerned, their own lives and their own creeds were tragic beyond anything that could by any possibility happen in this world. A broken heart was nothing to be compared with a damned soul; the afflictions of a few years, with the flames of eternity. This, to say the least of it, accounts, in part, for the hatred that Protestantism always bore toward the stage. Of course, the churches have always regarded the theater as a rival and have begrudged the money used to support the stage. You know that Macaulay said the Puritans objected to bear-baiting, not because they pitied the bears, but because they hated to see the people enjoy themselves. There is in this at least a little truth. Orthodox religion has always been and always will be the enemy of happiness. This world is not the place for enjoyment. This is the place to suffer. This is the place to practice self-denial, to wear crowns of thorns; the other world is the place for joy, provided you are fortunate enough to travel the narrow grass-grown path. Of course, wicked people can be happy here, people who care nothing for the good of others, who live selfish and horrible lives, are supposed by Christians to enjoy themselves; consequently, they will be punished in another world. But whoever carried the cross of decency, and whoever denied himself to that degree that he neither stole nor forged nor murdered, will be paid for this self-denial in another world. And whoever said that he preferred a prayer-meeting with five or six queer old men and two or three aged women, with one or two candles, and who solemnly affirmed that he enjoyed that far more than he could a play of Shakespeare, was expected with much reason, I think, to be rewarded in another world.

Q. Do you think that church people were justified in their opposition to the drama in the days when Congreve, Wycherley, and Ben Jonson were the popular favorites?

A. In that time there was a great deal of vulgarity in many of the plays. Many things were said on the stage that the people of this age would not care to hear, and there was not often enough wit in the saying to redeem it. My principal objection to Congreve, Wycherley, and most of their contemporaries is that the plays were exceedingly poor and had not much in them of real, sterling value. The Puritans, however, did not object on account of the vulgarity; that was not the honest objection. No play was ever put on the English stage more vulgar than the *Table Talk* of Martin Luther, and many sermons preached in that day were almost unrivaled for vulgarity. The worst passages in the Old Testament were quoted with a kind of unction that showed a love for the vulgar. And, in my judgment, the worst plays were as good as the sermons, and the theater of that time was better adapted to civilize mankind, to soften the human heart, and to make better men and better women, than the pulpit of that day. The actors, in my judgment, were better people than the preachers. They had in them more humanity, more real goodness and more appreciation of beauty, of tenderness, of generosity, and of heroism. Probably no religion was ever more thoroughly hateful than Puritanism. But all religionists who believe in an eternity of pain would naturally be opposed to everything that makes this life better; and, as a matter of fact, orthodox churches have been the enemies of painting, of sculpture, of music, and of the drama.

Q. What, in your estimation, is the value of the drama as a factor in our social life at the present time?

A. I believe that the plays of Shakespeare are the most valuable things in the possession of the human race. No man can read and understand Shakespeare without being an intellectually developed man. If Shakespeare could be as widely circulated as the Bible – if all the Bible societies would break the plates they now have and print Shakespeare, and put Shakespeare in all the languages of the world, nothing would so raise the intellectual standard of mankind. Think of the different influence on men between reading Deuteronomy and *Hamlet* and *King Lear;* between studying Numbers and the *Midsummer Night's Dream;* between pondering over the murderous crimes and assassinations in Judges and studying *The Tempest* or *As You Like It.* Man advances as he develops intellectually. The church teaches obedience. The man who reads Shakespeare has his intellectual horizon enlarged. He begins to think for himself, and he enjoys living in a new world. The characters of Shakespeare become his acquaintances. He admires the heroes, the philosophers; he laughs with the clowns, and he almost adores the beautiful women, the pure, loving and heroic women born of Shakespeare's heart and brain. The stage has amused and instructed the world. It has added to the happiness of mankind. It has kept alive all the arts. It is in partnership with all there is of beauty, of poetry, and expression. It goes hand in hand with music, with painting, with sculpture, with oratory, with philosophy, and history. The stage has humor. It abhors stupidity. It despises hypocrisy. It holds up to laughter the peculiarities, the idiosyncrasies, and the little insanities of mankind. It thrusts the spear of ridicule through the shield of pretense. It laughs at the lugubrious and it has ever taught and will, in all probability, forever teach, that man is more than a title, and that human love laughs at all barriers, at all the prejudices of society and caste that tend to keep apart two loving hearts.

Q. What is your opinion of the progress of the drama in educating the artistic sense of the community as compared with the progress of the church as an educator of the moral sentiment?

A. Of course, the stage is not all good, nor is – and I say this with becoming modesty – the pulpit all bad. There have been bad actors and there have been good preachers. There has been no improvement in plays since Shakespeare wrote. There has been great improvement in theaters, and the tendency seems to me to be toward higher artistic excellence in the presentation of plays. As we become slowly civilized we will constantly demand more artistic excellence. There will always be a class satisfied with the lowest form of dramatic presentation, with coarse wit, with stupid but apparent jokes, and there will always be a class satisfied with almost anything; but the class demanding the highest, the best, will constantly increase in numbers, and the other classes will, in all probability, correspondingly decrease. The church has ceased to be an educator. In an artistic direction it never did anything except in architecture, and that ceased long ago. The followers of today are poor copyists. The church has been compelled to be a friend of, or rather to call in the assistance of, music. As a moral teacher, the church always has been and always will be a failure. The pulpit, to use the language of Frederick Douglass, has always "echoed the cry of the street." Take our own history. The church was the friend of slavery. That institution was defended in nearly every pulpit. The Bible was the auction-block on which the slave-mother stood while her child was sold from her arms. The church, for hundreds of years, was the friend and defender of the slave-trade. I know of no crime that has not been defended by the

173

church, in one form or other. The church is not a pioneer; it accepts a new truth, last of all, and only when denial has become useless. The church preaches the doctrine of forgiveness. This doctrine sells crime on credit. The idea that there is a God who rewards and punishes, and who can reward, if he so wishes, the meanest and vilest of the human race so that he will be eternally happy, and can punish the best of the human race so that he will be eternally miserable, is subversive of all morality. Happiness ought to spring from the seed a man sows himself. It ought not to be a reward; it ought to be a consequence; and there ought to be no idea that there is any being who can step between action and consequence. To preach that a man can abuse his wife and children, rob his neighbors, slander his fellow-citizens, and yet, a moment or two before he dies, by repentance become a glorified angel, is, in my judgment, immoral. And to preach that a man can be a good man, kind to his wife and children, an honest man, paying his debts, and yet, for the lack of a certain belief, the moment after he is dead, be sent to an eternal prison, is also immoral. So that, according to my opinion, while the church teaches men many good things, it also teaches doctrines subversive of morality. If there were not in the whole world a church, the morality of man, in my judgment, would be the gainer.

Q. What do you think of the treatment of the actor by society in his social relations?

A. For a good many years the basis of society has been the dollar. Only a few years ago all literary men were ostracized because they had no money; neither did they have a reading public. If any man produced a book he had to find a patron – some titled donkey, some landed lubber, in whose honor he could print a few well-turned lies on the fly-leaf. If you wish to know the degradation of literature, read the dedication written by Lord Bacon to James I, in which he puts him beyond all kings, living and dead – beyond Caesar and Marcus Aurelius. In those days the literary man was a servant, a hack. He lived in Grub Street. He was only one degree above the sturdy vagrant and the escaped convict. Why was this? He had no money and he lived in an age when money was the foundation of respectability. Let me give you another instance: Mozart, whose brain was a fountain of melody, was forced to eat at a table with coachmen, with footmen, and scullions. He was simply a servant who was commanded to make music for a pudding-headed bishop. The same was true of the great painters, and of almost all other men who rendered the world beautiful by art, and who enriched the languages of mankind. The basis of respectability was the dollar.

Now that the literary man has an intelligent public he cares nothing for the ignorant patron. The literary man makes money. The world is becoming civilized and the literary man stands high. In England, however, if Charles Darwin had been invited to dinner, and there had been present some sprig of nobility, some titled vessel holding the germs of hereditary disease, Darwin would have been compelled to occupy a place beneath him. But I have hopes even for England. The same is true of the artist. The man who can now paint a picture for which he receives from $5,000 to $50,000 is necessarily respectable. The actor who may realize from $1,000 to $2,000 a night, or even more, is welcomed in the stupidest and richest society. So with the singers and with all others who instruct and amuse mankind. Many people imagine that he who amuses them must be lower than they. This, however, is hardly possible. I believe in the aristocracy of brain and heart; in the aristocracy of intelligence and goodness, and not only appreciate but admire the great actor, the great painter, the great sculptor, the marvelous singer. In other words, I admire all people who tend to make this life richer, who give an additional thought to this poor world.

Q. Do you think this liberal movement, favoring the better class of plays, inaugurated by the Rev. Dr. Abbott, will tend to soften the sentiment of the orthodox churches against the stage?

A. I have not read what Dr. Lyman Abbot has written on this subject. From your statement of his position, I think he entertains quite a sensible view, and, when we take into consideration that he is a minister, a miraculously sensible view. It is not the business of the dramatist, the actor, the painter or the sculptor to teach what the church calls morality. The dramatist and the actor ought to be truthful, ought to be natural – that is to say, truthfully and naturally artistic. He should present pictures of life properly chosen, artistically constructed, an exhibition of emotions truthfully done, artistically done. If vice is presented naturally, no one will fall in love with vice. If the better qualities of the human heart are presented naturally, no one can fail to fall in love with them. But they need not be presented for that purpose. The object of the artist is to present truthfully and artistically. He is not a Sunday school teacher. He is not to have the moral effect eternally in his mind. It is enough for him to be truly artistic. Because, as I have said a great many times, the greatest good is done by indirection. For instance, a man lives a good, noble, honest, and lofty life. The value of that life would be destroyed if he kept calling attention to it – if he said to all who met him, "Look at me!" he would become intolerable. The truly artistic speaks of perfection; that is to say, of harmony, not only of conduct, but of harmony and proportion in everything. The pulpit is always afraid of the passions and really imagines that it has some influence on men and women, keeping them in the path of virtue. No greater mistake was ever made. Eternally talking and harping on that one subject, in my judgment, does harm. Forever keeping it in the mind by reading passages from the Bible, by talking about the "corruption of the human heart," of the "power of temptation," of the scarcity of virtue, of the plentifulness of vice – all these platitudes tend to produce exactly what they are directed against.

Q. I fear, Colonel, that I have surprised you into agreeing with a clergyman. The following are the points made by the Rev. Dr. Abbott in his editorial on the theater, and it seems to me that you and he think much alike – on that subject. The points are these:

1. It is not the function of the drama to teach moral lessons.
2. A moral lesson neither makes nor mars either a drama or novel.
3. The moral quality of a play does not depend on the result.
4. The real function of the drama is like that of the novel – not to amuse, not to excite; but to portray life, and so minister to it. And as virtue and vice, goodness and evil, are the great fundamental facts of life, they must, in either serious story or serious play, be portrayed. If they are so portrayed that the vice is alluring and the virtue repugnant, the play or story is immoral; if so portrayed that the vice is repellent and the virtue alluring, the play or story is moral.
5. The church has no occasion to ask the theater to preach; though if it does preach we have a right to demand that its ethical doctrines be pure and high. But we have a right to demand that in its pictures of life it so portrays vice as to make it abhorrent, and so portrays virtue as to make it attractive.

A. I agree in most of what you have read, though I must confess that to find a minister agreeing with me, or to find myself agreeing with a minister, makes me a little uncertain. All art, in my judgment, is for the sake of expression – equally true of the drama as of painting and sculpture. No poem touches the human heart unless it touches the universal. It must, at some point, move in unison with the great ebb and flow of things. The same is true of the play, of a piece of music or a statue. I think that all real artists, in all departments, touch the universal, and when they do the result is good; but the result need not have been a consideration. There is an old story that at first there was a temple erected upon the earth by God himself; that afterward this temple was shivered into countless pieces and distributed over the whole earth, and that all the rubies and diamonds and precious stones since found are parts of that temple. Now, if we could conceive of a building, or of anything involving all art, and that it had been scattered abroad, then I would say that whoever finds and portrays truthfully a thought, an emotion, a truth, has found and restored one of the jewels. — *Dramatic Mirror,* New York, April 21, 1888.

SECULARISM

Q. Colonel, what is your opinion of Secularism? Do you regard it as a religion?

A. I understand that the word Secularism embraces everything that is of any real interest or value to the human race. I take it for granted that everybody will admit that well-being is the only good; that is to say, that it is impossible to conceive of anything of real value that does not tend either to preserve or to increase the happiness of some sentient being. Secularism, therefore, covers the entire territory. It fills the circumference of human knowledge and of human effort. It is, you may say, the religion of this world; but if there is another world, it is necessarily the religion of that as well.

Man finds himself in this world naked and hungry. He needs food, raiment, shelter. He finds himself filled with almost innumerable wants. To gratify these wants is the principal business of life. To gratify them without interfering with other people is the course pursued by all honest men.

Secularism teaches us to be good here and now. I know nothing better than goodness. Secularism teaches us to be just here and now. It is impossible to be juster than just.

Man can be as just in this world as in any other, and justice must be the same in all worlds. Secularism teaches a man to be generous, and generosity is certainly as good here as it can be anywhere else. Secularism teaches a man to be charitable, and certainly charity is as beautiful in this world and in this short life as it could be were man immortal.

But orthodox people insist that there is something higher than Secularism; but, as a matter of fact, the mind of man can conceive of nothing better, nothing higher, nothing more spiritual, than goodness, justice, generosity, charity. Neither has the mind of man been capable of finding a nobler incentive to action than human love. Secularism has to do with every possible relation. It says to the young man and to the young woman: "Don't marry unless you can take care of yourself and your children." It says to the parents: "Live for your children; put forth every effort to the end that your

178

children may know more than you – that they may be better and grander than you." It says: "You have no right to bring children into the world that you are not able to educate and feed and clothe." It says to those who have diseases that can be transmitted to children: "Do not marry; do not become parents; do not perpetuate suffering, deformity, agony, imbecility, insanity, poverty, wretchedness."

Secularism tells all children to do the best they can for their parents – to discharge every duty and every obligation. It defines the relation that should exist between husband and wife; between parent and child; between the citizen and the Nation. And not only that, but between nations.

Secularism is a religion that is to be used everywhere and at all times – that is to be taught everywhere and practiced at all times. It is not a religion that is so dangerous that it must be kept out of the schools; it is not a religion that is so dangerous that it must be kept out of politics. It belongs in the schools; it belongs at the polls. It is the business of Secularism to teach every child; to teach every voter. It is its business to discuss all political problems, and to decide all questions that affect the rights or the happiness of a human being.

Orthodox religion is a firebrand; it must be kept out of the schools; it must be kept out of politics. All the churches unite in saying that orthodox religion is not for everyday use. The Catholics object to any Protestant religion being taught to children. Protestants object to any Catholic religion being taught to children. But the Secularist wants his religion taught to all; and his religion can produce no feeling, for the reason that it consists of facts – of truths. And all of it is important; important for the child, important for the parent, important for the politician – for the president – for all in power; important to every legislator, to every professional man, to every laborer, and to every farmer – that is to say, to every human being.

The great benefit of Secularism is that it appeals to the reason of every man. It asks every man to think for himself. It does not threaten punishment if a man thinks, but offers a reward for fear that he will not think. It does not say, "You will be damned in another world if you think." But it says, "You will be damned in this world if you do not think."

Secularism preserves the manhood and the womanhood of all. It says to each human being: "Stand on your own feet. Count one!

Examine for yourself. Investigate, observe, think. Express your opinion. Stand by your judgment, unless you are convinced you are wrong, and when you are convinced, you can maintain and preserve your manhood or your womanhood only by admitting that you were wrong."

It is impossible that the whole world should agree on one creed. It may be impossible that any two human beings can agree exactly in religious belief. Secularism teaches that each one must take care of himself, that the first duty of man is to himself, to the end that he may be not only useful to himself but to others. He who fails to take care of himself becomes a burden; the first duty of man is not to be a burden.

Every Secularist can give a reason for his creed. First of all, he believes in work – taking care of himself. He believes in the culti- vation of the intellect, to the end that he may take advantage of the forces of nature – to the end that he may be clothed and fed and sheltered.

He also believes in giving to every other human being every right that he claims for himself. He does not depend on prayer. He has no confidence in ghosts or phantoms. He knows nothing of another world, and knows just as little of a "first cause." But what little he does know, he endeavors to use, and to use for the benefit of himself and others.

He knows that he sustains certain relations to other sentient beings, and he endeavors to add to the aggregate of human joy. He is his own church, his own priest, his own clergyman, and his own pope. He decides for himself; in other words, he is a free man.

He also has a Bible, and this Bible embraces all the good and true things that have been written, no matter by whom, or in what language, or in what time. He accepts everything that he believes to be true and rejects all that he thinks is false. He knows that nothing is added to the probability of an event because there has been an account of it written and printed.

All that has been said that is true is part of his Bible. Every splendid and noble thought, every good word, every kind action – all these you will find in his Bible. And, in addition to these, all that is absolutely known – that has been demonstrated – belongs to the Secularist. All the inventions, machines – everything that has been of assistance to the human race – belongs to his religion. The Secularist is in possession of everything that man has. He is deprived only of that which man never had. The orthodox world believes in ghosts and phantoms, in dreams and prayers, in miracles and monstrosities; that is to say, in modern theology. But these things do not exist, or if they do exist, it is impossible for a human being to ascertain the fact. Secularism has no "castles in Spain." It has no glorified fog. It depends on realities, on demonstrations; and its end and aim is to make this world better every day – to do away with poverty and crime, and to cover the world with happy and contented homes.

Let me say, right here, that a few years ago the Secular Hall at Leicester, England, was opened by a speech from George Jacob Holyoake entitled, "Secularism a Religion." I have never read anything better on the subject of Secularism than this address. It is so clear and so manly that I do not see how any human being can read it without becoming convinced and almost enraptured.

Let me quote a few lines from this address:

"The mind of man would die if it were not for Thought, and were Thought suppressed, God would rule over a world of idiots.

"Nature feeds Thought, day and night, with a million hands.

"To think is a duty, because it is a man's duty not to be a fool.

"If man does not think himself, he is an intellectual pauper, living on the truth acquired by others, and making no contribution himself in return. He has no ideas but such as he obtains by "out-door relief," and he goes about the world with a charity mind.

"The more thinkers there are in the world, the more truth there is in the world.

"Progress can only walk in the footsteps of conviction.

"Coercion in thought is not progress, it reduces to ignominious pulp the backbone of the mind.

"By religion I mean the simple creed of deed and duty, by which a man seeks his own welfare in his own way, with an honest and fair regard to the welfare and ways of others.

"In these thinking and practical days, men demand a religion of daily life, which stands on a business footing."

I think nothing could be much better than the following, which shows the exact relation that orthodox religion sustains to the actual wants of human beings:

"The churches administer a system of foreign affairs.

"Secularism dwells in a land of its own. It dwells in a land of certitude.

"In the kingdom of Thought there is no conquest over man, but over foolishness only."

I will not quote more, but hope all who read this will read the address of Mr. Holyoake, who has, in my judgment, defined Secularism with the greatest possible clearness.

Q. What, in your opinion, are the best possible means to spread this gospel or religion of Secularism?

A. This can be done only by the cultivation of the mind – only through intelligence – because we are fighting only the monsters of the mind. The phantoms whom we are endeavoring to destroy do not exist; they are all imaginary. They live in that undeveloped or unexplored part of the mind that belongs to barbarism.

I have sometimes thought that a certain portion of the mind is cultivated so that it rises above the surrounding faculties and is like some peak that has lifted itself above the clouds, while all the valleys below are dark or dim with mist and cloud. It is this valley region, amid these mists, beneath these clouds, that these monsters and phantoms are born. And there they will remain until the mind sheds light – until the brain is developed.

One exceedingly important thing is to teach man that his mind has limitations; that there are walls that he cannot scale – that he cannot pierce, that he cannot dig under. When a man finds the limitations of his own mind, he knows that other people's minds have limitations. Then, instead of believing what the priest says, he asks the priest questions. In a few moments he finds that the priest has been drawing on his imagination for what is beyond the wall. Consequently he finds that the priest knows no more than he, and it is impossible that he should know more than he.

An ignorant man has not the slightest suspicion of what a superior man may do. Consequently, he is liable to become the victim of the intelligent and cunning. A man wholly unacquainted with chemistry, after having been shown a few wonders, is ready to believe anything. But a chemist who knows something of the limitations of that science – who knows what chemists have done and who knows the nature of things – cannot be imposed on. When no one can be imposed on, orthodox religion cannot exist. It is an imposture, and there must be impostors and there must be victims, or the religion cannot be a success.

Secularism cannot be a success, universally, as long as there is an impostor or a victim. This is the difference: the foundation of orthodox religion is imposture. The foundation of Secularism is demonstration. Just to the extent that a man knows, he becomes a Secularist.

Q. What do you think of the action of the Knights of Labor in Indiana in turning out one of their members because he was an Atheist, and because he objected to the reading of the Bible at lodge meetings?

A. In my judgment, the Knights of Labor have made a great mistake. They want liberty for themselves – they feel that, to a certain extent, they have been enslaved and robbed. If they want liberty, they should be willing to give liberty to others. Certainly one of their members has the same right to his opinion with regard to the existence of a God that the other members have to theirs.

I do not blame this man for doubting the existence of a supreme being, provided he understands the history of liberty. When a man takes into consideration the fact that for many thousands of years labor was unpaid, nearly all of it being done by slaves, and that millions and hundreds of millions of human beings were bought and sold the same as cattle, and that during all that time the religions of the world upheld the practice, and the priests of the countless unknown gods insisted that the institution of slavery was divine – I do not wonder that he comes to the conclusion that perhaps, after all, there is no supreme being – at least none who pays any particular attention to the affairs of this world.

If one will read the history of the slave-trade, of the cruelties practiced, of the lives sacrificed, of the tortures inflicted, he will at least wonder why "a God of infinite goodness and wisdom" did not interfere just a little; or, at least, why he did not deny that he was in favor of the trade. Here, in our own country, millions of men were enslaved, and hundreds and thousands of ministers stood up in their pulpits, with their Bibles in front of them, and proceeded to show that slavery was about the only institution that they were absolutely certain was divine. And they proved it by reading passages from this very Bible that the Knights of Labor in Indiana are anxious to have read in their meetings. For their benefit, let me call their attention to a few passages, and suggest that hereafter they read those passages at every meeting for the purpose of convincing all the Knights that the Lord is on the side of those who work for a living:

"Both thy bondmen and thy bondmaids which thou shalt have, shall be of the heathen round about you; of them shall ye buy bondmen and bondmaids.

"Moreover, of the children of the strangers that do sojourn among you of them shall ye buy, and of their families which are with you, which they begat in your land: and they shall be your possession.

"And ye shall take them as an inheritance, for your children after you to inherit them for a possession. They shall be your bondmen forever."

Nothing seems more natural to me than that a man, who believes that labor should be free and that he who works should be free, should come to the conclusion that the passages above quoted are not entirely on his side. I don't see why people should be in favor of free bodies who are not also in favor of free minds. If the mind is to remain in imprisonment, it is hardly worthwhile to free the body. If the man has the right to labor, he certainly has the right to use his mind, because without mind he can do no labor. As a rule, the more mind he has, the more valuable his labor is, and the freer his mind is the more valuable it is.

If the Knights of Labor expect to accomplish anything in this world, they must do it by thinking. They must have reason on their side, and the only way they can do anything by thinking is to allow each other to think. Let all the men who do not believe in the inspiration of the Bible leave the Knights of Labor and I do not know how many would be left. But I am perfectly certain that those left will accomplish little, simply from their lack of sense.

Intelligent clergymen have abandoned the idea of plenary inspiration. The best ministers in the country admit that the Bible is full of mistakes, and while many of them are forced to say that slavery is upheld by the Old Testament they also insist that slavery was and is, and forever will be, wrong. What had the Knights of Labor to do with a question of religion? What business is it of theirs who believes or disbelieves in the religion of the day? Nobody can defend the rights of labor without defending the right to think.

I hope that in time these Knights will become intelligent enough to read in their meetings something of importance; something that applies to this century; something that will throw a little light on questions under discussion at the present time. The idea of men engaged in a kind of revolution reading from Leviticus, Deuteronomy, and Haggai, for the purpose of determining the rights of workingmen in the 19th century! No wonder such men have been swallowed by the whale of monopoly. And no wonder that, while they are in the belly of this fish, they insist on casting out a man with sense enough to understand the situation! The Knights of Labor have made a mistake and the sooner they reverse their action the better for all concerned. Nothing should be taught in this world that somebody does not know. — *Secular Thought,* Toronto, Canada, Aug. 25, 1888.

SUMMER RECREATION — MR. GLADSTONE

From an unfinished interview found among Colonel Ingersoll's papers.

Q. What is the best philosophy of summer recreation?

A. As a matter of fact, no one should be overworked. Recreation becomes necessary only when a man has abused himself or has been absurd. Holidays grew out of slavery. An intelligent man ought not to work so hard today that he is compelled to rest tomorrow. Each day should have its labor and its rest. But in our civilization, if it can be called civilization, every man is expected to devote himself entirely to business for the most of the year and by that means to get into such a state of body and mind that he requires, for the purpose of recreation, the inconveniences, the poor diet, the horrible beds, the little towels, the warm water, the stale eggs, and the tough beef of the average "resort." For the purpose of getting his mental and physical machinery in fine working order, he should live in a room for two or three months that is about 11 by 13; that is to say, he should live in a trunk, fight mosquitoes, quarrel with strangers, dispute bills, and generally enjoy himself; and this is supposed to be the philosophy of summer recreation. He can do this, or he can go to some extremely fashionable resort where his time is taken up in making himself and family presentable.

Seriously, there are few better summer resorts than New York City. If there were no city here it would be the greatest resort for the summer on the continent; with its rivers, its bay, with its wonderful scenery, with the winds from the sea, no better could be found. But we cannot in this age of the world live in accordance with philosophy. No particular theory can be carried out. We must live as we must; we must earn our bread and we must earn it as others do, and, as a rule, we must work when others work. Consequently, if we are to take any recreation we must follow the example of others; go when they go and come when they come. In other words, man is a social being, and if one endeavors to carry individuality to an extreme he must suffer the consequences. So I have made up my mind to work as little as I can and to rest as much as I can.

Q. What is your opinion of Mr. Gladstone as a controversialist?

A. Undoubtedly Mr. Gladstone is a man of great talent, of vast and varied information, and undoubtedly he is, politically speaking, at least, one of the greatest men in England – possibly the greatest. As a controversialist, and I suppose by that you mean on religious questions, he is certainly as good as his cause. Few men can better defend the indefensible than Mr. Gladstone. Few men can bring forward more probabilities in favor of the improbable, or more possibilities in favor of the impossible, than Mr. Gladstone. He is, in my judgment, controlled in the realm of religion by sentiment; he was taught long ago certain things as absolute truths and he has never questioned them. He has had all he can do to defend them. It is of but little use to attack sentiment with argument, or to attack argument with sentiment. A question of sentiment can hardly be discussed; it is like a question of taste. A man is enraptured with a landscape by Corot; you cannot argue him out of his rapture; the sharper the criticism the greater his admiration, because he feels that it is incumbent on him to defend the painter who has given him so much real pleasure. Some people imagine that what they think ought to exist must exist, and that what they really desire to be true is true. We must remember that Mr. Gladstone has been what is called a deeply religious man all his life. There was a time when he really believed it to be the duty of the government to see to it that the citizens were religious; when he really believed that no man should hold any office or any position under the government who was not a believer in the established religion; who was not a defender of the parliamentary faith. I do not know whether he has ever changed his opinions on these subjects or not. There is not the slightest doubt as to his honesty, as to his candor. He says what he believes, and for his belief he gives the reasons that are satisfactory to him. To me it seems impossible that miracles can be defended. I do not see how it is possible to bring forward any evidence that any miracle was ever performed; and unless miracles have been performed, Christianity has no basis as a system. Mr. Hume took the ground that it was impossible to substantiate a miracle for the reason that it is more probable that the witnesses are mistaken or are dishonest than that a fact in nature should be violated. For instance: A man says that at a certain time, in a certain locality, the attraction of gravitation was suspended; that there were several moments during which a cannon ball weighed nothing, during which when dropped from the hand, it refused to fall and remained in the air. It is safe to say that no amount of evidence, no number of witnesses, could convince an intelligent man today that such a thing occurred. We believe too thoroughly in the constancy of nature. While men will not believe witnesses who testify to the happening of miracles now, they seem to have perfect confidence in men whom they never saw, who have been dead for 2,000 years. Of course, it is known that Mr. Gladstone has published a few remarks concerning my religious views and that I have answered him the best I could. I have no opinion to give as to that controversy; neither would it be proper for me to say what I think of the arguments advanced by Mr. Gladstone in addition to what I have already published. I am willing to leave the controversy where it is, or I am ready to answer any further objections that Mr. Gladstone may be pleased to urge.

In my judgment, the "Age of Faith" is passing away. We are living in a time of demonstration.

ROBERT ELSMERE

Why do people read a book like *Robert Elsmere,* and why do they take any interest in it? Simply because they are not satisfied with the religion of our day. The civilized world has outgrown the greater part of the Christian creed. Civilized people have lost their belief in the reforming power of punishment. They find that whips and imprisonment have but little influence for good. The truth has dawned on their minds that eternal punishment is infinite cruelty – that it can serve no useful purpose, and that the eternity of hell makes heaven impossible – that there can be in this universe no perfectly happy place while there is a perfectly miserable place – that no infinite being can be good who knowingly and, as one may say, willfully created myriads of human beings, knowing that they would be eternally miserable. In other words, the civilized man is greater, tenderer, nobler, nearer just than the old idea of God. The ideal of a few thousand years ago is far below the real of today. No good man now would do what Jehovah is said to have done 4,000 years ago, and no civilized human being would now do what, according to the Christian religion, Christ threatens to do at the day of judgment.

Q. Has the Christian religion changed in theory of late years, Colonel Ingersoll?

A. A few years ago the Deists denied the inspiration of the Bible on account of its cruelty. At the same time they worshipped what they were pleased to call the God of nature. Now we are convinced that nature is as cruel as the Bible; so that, if the God of nature did not write the Bible, this God at least has caused earthquakes and pestilence and famine, and this God has allowed millions of his children to destroy one another. So that now we have arrived at the question – not as to whether the Bible is inspired and not as to whether Jehovah is the real God, but whether there is a God or not. The intelligence of Christendom today does not believe in an inspired religion any more than it believes in an inspired art or an inspired literature. If there be an infinite God, inspiration in some particular regard would be a patch – it would be the puttying of a crack, the hiding of a defect – in other words, it would show that the general plan was defective.

189

Q. Do you consider any religion adequate?

A. A good man, living in England, drawing a certain salary for reading certain prayers on stated occasions, for making a few remarks on the subject of religion, putting on clothes of a certain cut, wearing a gown with certain frills and flounces starched in an orthodox manner, and then looking about him at the suffering and agony of the world, would not feel satisfied that he was doing anything of value for the human race. In the first place, he would deplore his own weakness, his own poverty, his inability to help his fellow men. He would long every moment for wealth, that he might feed the hungry and clothe the naked – for knowledge, for miraculous power, that he might heal the sick and the lame and that he might give to the deformed the beauty of proportion. He would begin to wonder how a being of infinite goodness and infinite power could allow his children to die, to suffer, to be deformed by necessity, by poverty, to be tempted beyond resistance; how he could allow the few to live in luxury, and the many in poverty and want, and the more he wondered the more useless and ironical would seem to himself his sermons and his prayers. Such a man is driven to the conclusion that religion accomplishes but little – that it creates as much want as it alleviates, and that it burdens the world with parasites. Such a man would be forced to think of the millions wasted in superstition. In other words, the inadequacy, the uselessness of religion would be forced on his mind. He would ask himself the question: "Is it possible that this is a divine institution? Is this all that man can do with the assistance of God? Is this the best?"

Q. That is a perfectly reasonable question, is it not, Colonel Ingersoll?

A. The moment a man reaches the point where he asks himself this question he has ceased to be an orthodox Christian. It will not do to say that in some other world justice will be done. If God allows injustice to triumph here, why not there?

Robert Elsmere stands in the dawn of philosophy. There is hardly light enough for him to see clearly; but there is so much light that the stars in the night of superstition are obscured.

Q. You do not deny that a religious belief is a comfort?

A. There is one thing that it is impossible for me to comprehend. Why should anyone, when convinced that Christianity is a superstition, have or feel a sense of loss? Certainly a man acquainted with England, with London, having at the same time something like a heart, must feel overwhelmed by the failure of what is known as Christianity. Hundreds of thousands exist there without decent food, dwelling in tenements, clothed with rags, familiar with every form of vulgar vice, where the honest poor eat the crust that the vicious throw away. When this man of intelligence, of heart, visits the courts; when he finds human liberty a thing treated as of no value, and when he hears the judge sentencing girls and boys to the penitentiary – knowing that a stain is being put on them that all the tears of all the coming years can never wash away – knowing, too, and feeling that this is done without the slightest regret, without the slightest sympathy, as a mere matter of form, and that the judge puts this brand of infamy on the forehead of the convict just as cheerfully as a Mexican brands his cattle; and when this man of intelligence and heart knows that these poor people are simply the victims of society, the unfortunate who stumble and over whose bodies rolls the juggernaut – he knows that there is, or at least appears to be, no power above or below working for righteousness – that from the heavens is stretched no protecting hand. And when a man of intelligence and heart in England visits the workhouse, the last resting place of honest labor; when he thinks that the young man, without any great intelligence but with a good constitution, starts in the morning of his life for the workhouse, and that it is impossible for the laboring man, one who simply has his muscle, to save anything; that health is not able to lay anything by for the days of disease – when the man of intelligence and heart sees all this, he is compelled to say that the civilization of today, the religion of today, the charity of today – no matter how much of good there may be behind them or in them – are failures.

A few years ago people were satisfied when the minister said: All this will be made even in another world; a crust-eater here will sit at the head of the banquet there, and the king here will beg for the crumbs that fall from the table there." When this was said, the poor man hoped and the king laughed. A few years ago the church said to the slave: "You will be free in another world and your freedom will be made glorious by the perpetual spectacle of your master in hell." But the people – that is, many of the people are no longer deceived by what once were considered fine phrases. They have suffered so much that they no longer wish to see others suffer and no longer think of the suffering of others as a source of joy to themselves. The poor see that the eternal starvation of kings and queens in another world will be no compensation for what they have suffered here. The old religions appear vulgar and the ideas of rewards and punishments are only such as would satisfy a cannibal chief or one of his favorites.

Q. Do you think the Christian religion has made the world better?

A. For many centuries there has been preached and taught in an almost infinite number of ways a supernatural religion. During all this time the world has been in the care of the infinite, and yet every imaginable vice has flourished, every imaginable pang has been suffered, and every injustice has been done. During all these years the priests have enslaved the minds, and the kings the bodies, of men. The priests did what they did in the name of God, and the kings appeal to the same source of authority. Man suffered as long as he could. Revolution, reformation, was simply a reaction, a cry from the poor wretch that was between the upper and the nether millstone. The liberty of man has increased just in the proportion that the authority of the gods has decreased. In other words, the wants of man, instead of the wishes of God, have inaugurated what we call progress, and there is this difference: Theology is based on the narrowest and intensest form of selfishness. Of course, the theologian knows, the Christian knows, that he can do nothing for God; consequently all that he does must be and is for himself, his object being to win the approbation of this God, to the end that he may become a favorite. On the other side, men touched not only by their own misfortunes, but by the misfortunes of others, are moved not simply by selfishness, but by a splendid sympathy with their fellow men.

Q. Christianity certainly fosters charity?

A. Nothing is more cruel than orthodox theology, nothing more heartless than a charitable institution. For instance, in England, think for a moment of the manner in which charities are distributed, the way in which the crust is flung at Lazarus. If that parable could be now retold, the dogs would bite him. The same is true in this country. The institution has nothing but contempt for the one it relieves. The people in charge regard the pauper as one who has wrecked himself. They feel much as a man would feel rescuing from the water some hare-brained wretch who had endeavored to swim the rapids of Niagara – the moment they reach him they begin to upbraid him for being such a fool. This course makes charity a hypocrite, with every pauper for its enemy.

192

Mrs. Ward compelled Robert Elsmere to perceive, in some slight degree, the failure of Christianity to do away with vice and suffering, with poverty and crime. We know that the rich care but little for the poor. No matter how religious the rich may be, the sufferings of their fellows have but little effect on them. We are also beginning to see that what is called charity will never redeem this world.

The poor man willing to work, eager to maintain his independence, knows that there is something higher than charity – that is to say, justice. He finds that many years before he was born his country was divided out between certain successful robbers, flatterers, cringers, and crawlers, and that in consequence of such division not only himself, but a large majority of his fellow men are tenants, renters, occupying the surface of the earth only at the pleasure of others. He finds, too, that these people who have done nothing and who do nothing, have everything, and that those who do everything have but little. He finds that idleness has the money and that the toilers are compelled to bow to the idlers. He finds also that the young men of genius are bribed by social distinctions – unconsciously it may be – but still bribed in a thousand ways. He finds that the church is a kind of wastebasket into which are thrown the younger sons of titled idleness.

Q. Do you consider that society in general has been made better by religious influences?

A. Society is corrupted because the laurels, the titles, are in the keeping and within the gift of the corrupters. Christianity is not an enemy of this system – it is in harmony with it. Christianity reveals to us a universe presided over by an infinite autocrat – a universe without republicanism, without democracy – a universe where all power comes from one and the same source, and where everyone using authority is accountable, not to the people, but to this supposed source of authority. Kings reign by divine right. Priests are ordained in a divinely appointed way – they do not get their office from man. Man is their servant, not their master.

In the story of Robert Elsmere all there is of Christianity is left except the miraculous. Theism remains, and the idea of a protecting providence is left, together with a belief in the immeasurable superiority of Jesus Christ; that is to say, the miracles are discarded for lack of evidence, and only for lack of evidence; not on the ground that they are impossible, not on the ground that they

193

impeach and deny the integrity of cause and effect, not on the ground that they contradict the self-evident proposition that an effect must have an efficient cause, but like the Scottish verdict, "not proven." It is an effort to save and keep in repair the dungeons of the Inquisition for the sake of the beauty of the vines that have overrun them. Many people imagine that falsehoods may become respectable on account of age, that a certain reverence goes with antiquity, and that if a mistake is covered with the moss of sentiment it is altogether more credible than a parvenu fact. They endeavor to introduce the idea of aristocracy into the world of thought, believing, and honestly believing, that a falsehood long believed is far superior to a truth that is generally denied.

Q. If Robert Elsmere's views were commonly adopted, what would be the effect?

A. The new religion of Elsmere is, after all, only a system of outdoor relief, an effort to get successful piracy to give up a larger percent for the relief of its victims. The abolition of the system is not dreamed of. A civilized minority could not by any possibility be happy while a majority of the world were miserable. A civilized majority could not be happy while a minority were miserable. As a matter of fact, a civilized world could not be happy while one man was really miserable. At the foundation of civilization is justice – that is to say, the giving of an equal opportunity to all the children of men. Secondly, there can be no civilization in the highest sense until sympathy becomes universal. We must have a new definition for success. We must have new ideals. The man who succeeds in amassing wealth, who gathers money for himself, is not a success. It is an exceedingly low ambition to be rich to excite the envy of others, or for the sake of the vulgar power it gives to triumph over others. Such men are failures. So the man who wins fame, position, power, and wins these for the sake of himself, and wields this power not for the elevation of his fellow men, but simply to control, is a miserable failure. He may dispense thousands of millions in charity, and his charity may be prompted by the meanest part of his nature – using it simply as a bait to catch more fish and to prevent the rising tide of indignation that might overwhelm him. Men who steal millions and then give a small percentage to the Lord to gain the praise of the clergy and to bring the salvation of their souls within the possibilities of imagination are all failures.

Robert Elsmere gains our affection and our applause to the extent that he gives up what are known as orthodox views, and his wife Catherine retains our respect in the proportion that she lives the doctrine that Elsmere preaches. By doing what she believes to be right she gains our forgiveness for her creed. One is astonished that she can be as good as she is, believing as she does. The utmost stretch of our intellectual charity is to allow the old wine to be put in a new bottle, and yet she regrets the absence of the old bottle – she really believes that the bottle is the important thing – that the wine is but a secondary consideration. She misses the label, and not having perfect confidence in her own taste, she does not feel quite sure that the wine is genuine.

Q. What, on the whole, is your judgment of the book?

A. I think the book conservative. It is an effort to save something – a few shreds and patches and ravelings – from the wreck. Theism is difficult to maintain. Why should we expect an infinite being to do better in another world than he has done and is doing in this? If he allows the innocent to suffer here, why not there? If he allows rascality to succeed in this world, why not in the next? To believe in God and to deny his personality is an exceedingly vague foundation for a consolation. If you insist on his personality and power, then it is impossible to account for what happens. Why should an infinite God allow some of his children to enslave others? Why should he allow a child of his to burn another child of his under the impression that such a sacrifice was pleasing to him?

Unitarianism lacks the motive power. Orthodox people who insist that nearly everybody is going to hell, and that it is their duty to do what little they can to save their souls, have what you might call a spur to action. We can imagine a philanthropic man engaged in the business of throwing ropes to persons about to go over the falls of Niagara, but we can hardly think of his carrying on the business after becoming convinced that there are no falls, or that people go over them in perfect safety. In this country the question has come up whether all the heathen are bound to be damned unless they believe in the gospel. Many admit that the heathen will be saved if they are good people and that they will not be damned for not believing something that they never heard The really orthodox people – that is to say, the missionaries – instantly see that this doctrine destroys their business. They take the ground that there is but one way to be saved – you must believe on the Lord Jesus Christ – and they are willing to admit, and cheerfully to admit, that the heathen for many generations have gone in an unbroken column down to eternal wrath. And they not only admit this, but insist on it, to the end that subscriptions may not cease. With them salary and salvation are convertible terms.

The tone of this book is not of the highest. Too much stress is laid on social advantages – too much respect for fashionable folly and for ancient absurdity. It is hard for me to appreciate the feelings of one who thinks it difficult to give up the consolations of the gospel. What are the consolations of the Church of England? It is a religion imposed on the people by authority. It is the gospel at the mouth of a cannon, at the point of a bayonet, enforced by all authority, from the beadle to the queen. It is a parasite living on tithes – these tithes being collected by the army and navy. It produces nothing – is simply a beggar – or rather an aggregation of beggars. It teaches nothing of importance. It discovers nothing. It is under obligation not to investigate. It has agreed to remain stationary not only, but to resist all innovation. According to the creed of this church, a large proportion of the human race is destined to suffer eternal pain. This does not interfere with the quiet, with the serenity and repose of the average clergyman. They put on their gowns, they read the service, they repeat the creed and feel that their duty has been done. How anyone can feel that he is giving up something of value when he finds that the Episcopal creed is untrue is beyond my imagination. I should think that every good man and woman would overflow with joy, that every heart would burst into countless blossoms the moment the falsity of the Episcopal creed was established.

Christianity is the most heartless of all religions – the most unforgiving, the most revengeful. According to the Episcopalian belief, God becomes the eternal prosecutor of his own children. I know of no creed believed by any tribe, not excepting the tribes where cannibalism is practiced, that is more heartless, more inhuman than this. To find that the creed is false is like being roused from a frightful dream, in which hundreds of serpents are coiled about you, in which their eyes, gleaming with hatred, are fixed on you, and finding the world bathed in sunshine and the songs of birds in your ears and those you love about you. — *New York World,* Nov. 18, 1888.

LIBERALS AND LIBERALISM

Q. What do you think of the prospects of liberalism in this country?

A. The prospects of liberalism are precisely the same as the prospects of civilization – that is to say, of progress. As the people become educated, they become liberal. Bigotry is the provincialism of the mind. Men are bigoted who are not acquainted with the thoughts of others. They have been taught one thing and have been made to believe that their little mental horizon is the circumference of all knowledge. The bigot lives in an ignorant village, surrounded by ignorant neighbors. This is the honest bigot. The dishonest bigot may know better, but he remains a bigot because his salary depends on it. A bigot is like a country that has had no commerce with any other. He imagines that in his little head there is everything of value. When a man becomes an intellectual traveler, he begins to widen, to grow liberal. He finds that the ideas of others are as good as, and often better than, his own. The habits and customs of other people throw light on his own, and by this light he is enabled to discover at least some of his own mistakes. Now the world has become acquainted. A few years ago, a man knew something of the doctrines of his own church. Now he knows the creeds of others, and not only so, but he has examined to some extent the religions of other nations. He finds in other creeds all the excellencies that are in his own, and most of the mistakes. In this way he learns that all creeds have been produced by men and that their differences have been accounted for by race, climate, heredity – that is to say, by a difference in circumstances. So we now know that the cause of liberalism is the cause of civilization. Unless the race is to be a failure, the cause of liberalism must succeed. Consequently, I have the same faith in that cause that I have in the human race.

Q. Where are the most liberals, and in what section of the country is the best work for liberalism being done?

A. The most liberals are in the most intelligent section of the United States. Where people think the most, you will find the most liberals; where people think the least, you will find the most bigots. Bigotry is produced by feeling – liberalism by thinking – that is to say, the one is a prejudice, the other a principle. Every geologist, every astronomer, every scientist, is doing a noble work for liberalism. Every man who finds a fact, and demonstrates it, is doing work for the cause. All the literature of our time that is worth reading is on the liberal side. All the fiction that really interests the human mind is with us. No one cares to read the old theological works. Essays written by professors of theological colleges are regarded, even by Christians, with a kind of charitable contempt. When any demonstration of science is attacked by a creed or a passage of Scripture, all the intelligent smile. For these reasons I think that the best work for liberalism is being done where the best work for science is being done – where the best work for man is being accomplished. Every legislator that assists in the repeal of theological laws is doing a great work for liberalism.

Q. In your opinion, what relation do liberalism and prohibition bear to each other?

A. I do not think they have anything to do with each other. They have nothing in common except this: the Prohibitionists, I presume, are endeavoring to do what they can for temperance; so all intelligent liberals are doing what they can for the cause of temperance. The Prohibitionist endeavors to accomplish his object by legislation – the liberalist by education, by civilization, by example, by persuasion. The method of the liberalist is good, that of the Prohibitionist chimerical and fanatical.

Q. Do you think that liberals should undertake a reform in the marriage and divorce laws and relations?

A. I think that liberals should do all in their power to induce people to regard marriage and divorce in a sensible light, and without the slightest reference to any theological ideas. They should use their influence to the end that marriage shall be considered as a contract – the highest and holiest that men and women can make. And they should also use their influence to have the laws of divorce based on this fundamental idea – that marriage is a contract. All should be done that can be done by law to uphold the sacredness of this relation. All should be done that can be done to impress on the minds of all men and all women their duty to discharge all the obligations of the marriage contract faithfully and cheerfully. I do not believe that it is to the interest of the state or of the nation that people should be compelled to live together who hate each other, or that a woman should be bound to

198

a man who has been false and who refuses to fulfill the contract of marriage. I do not believe that any man should call on the police, or on the creeds, or on the church, to compel his wife to remain under his roof, or to compel a woman against her will to become the mother of his children. In other words, liberals should endeavor to civilize mankind, and when men and women are civilized, the marriage question and the divorce question will be settled.

Q. Should liberals vote on liberal issues?

A. I think that, other things being anywhere equal, liberals should vote for the men who believe in liberty, men who believe in giving to others the rights they claim for themselves – that is to say, for civilized men, for men of some breadth of mind. Liberals should do what they can to do away with all the theological absurdities.

Q. Can or ought the liberals and spiritualists to unite?

A. All people should unite where they have objects in common. They can vote together and act together without believing the same on all points. A liberal is not necessarily a spiritualist, and a spiritualist is not necessarily a liberal. If spiritualists wish to liberalize the government, certainly liberals would be glad of their assistance; and if spiritualists take any step in the direction of freedom, the liberals should stand by them to that extent.

Q. Which is the more dangerous to American institutions – the National Reform Association (God-in-the-Constitution party) or the Roman Catholic Church?

A. The Association and the Catholic Church are dangerous according to their power. The Catholic Church has far more power than the Reform Association and is consequently far more dangerous. The God-in-the-Constitution Association is weak, fanatical, stupid, and absurd. What God are we to have in the Constitution? Whose God? If we should agree tomorrow to put God in the Constitution, the question would then be: which God? On that question, the religious world would fall out. In that direction there is no danger. But the Roman Catholic Church is the enemy of intellectual liberty. It is the enemy of investigation. It is the enemy of free schools. That church always has been, always will be, the enemy of freedom. It works in the dark. When in a minority it is humility itself – when in power it is the impersonation of arrogance. In weakness it crawls – in power it stands erect and compels its victims to fall upon their faces. The most dangerous institution in this world, so far as the intellectual liberty of man is concerned, is the Roman Catholic Church. Next to that is the Protestant church.

Q. What is your opinion of the Christian religion and the Christian church?

A. My opinion on this subject is certainly well known. The Christian church is founded on miracles – that is to say, on impossibilities. Of course, there is a great deal that is good in the creeds of the churches, and in the sermons delivered by its ministers; but mixed with this good is much that is evil. My principal objection to orthodox religion is the dogma of eternal pain. Nothing can be more infamously absurd. All civilized men should denounce it – all women should regard it with a kind of shuddering abhorrence. — *Secular Thought,* Toronto, Canada, 1888.

POPE LEO XIII

Q. Do you agree with the views of Pope Leo XIII as expressed in *The Herald* of last week?

A. I am not personally acquainted with Leo XIII, but I have not the slightest idea that he loves Americans or their country. I regard him as an enemy of intellectual liberty. He tells us that where the church is free it will increase, and I say to him that where others are free it will not. The Catholic Church has increased in this country by immigration and in no other way. Possibly the pope is willing to use his power for the good of the whole people, Protestants and Catholics, and to increase their prosperity and happiness, because by this he means that he will use his power to make Catholics out of Protestants.

It is impossible for the Catholic Church to be in favor of mental freedom. That church represents absolute authority. Its members have no right to reason – no right to ask questions – they are called on simply to believe and to pay their subscriptions.

Q. Do you agree with the pope when he says that the result of efforts which have been made to throw aside Christianity and live without it can be seen in the present condition of society – discontent, disorder, hatred, and profound unhappiness?

A. Undoubtedly the people in Europe who wish to be free are discontented. Undoubtedly these efforts to have something like justice done will bring disorder. Those in power will hate those who are endeavoring to drive them from their thrones. If the people now, as formerly, would bear all burdens cheerfully placed on their shoulders by church and state – that is to say, if they were so enslaved mentally that they would not even have sense enough to complain, then there would be what the pope might call "peace and happiness" – that is to say, the peace of ignorance, and the happiness of those who are expecting pay in another world for their agonies endured in this.

Of course, the revolutionists of Europe are not satisfied with the Catholic religion; neither are they satisfied with the Protestant. Both of these religions rest on authority. Both discourage reason. Both say "Let him that hath ears to hear, hear," but neither says, "let him that hath brains to think, think."

Christianity has been thoroughly tried, and it is a failure. Nearly every church has upheld slavery, not only of the body, but of the mind. When Christian missionaries invade what they call a heathen country, they are followed in a little while by merchants and traders, and in a few days afterward by the army. The first real work is to kill the heathen or steal their lands, or else reduce them to something like slavery.

I have no confidence in the reformation of this world by churches. Churches for the most part exist, not for this world, but for another. They are founded on the supernatural, and they say: "Take no thought for the morrow; put your trust in your heavenly father and he will take care of you." On the other hand, science says: "You must take care of yourself, live for the world in which you happen to be – if there is another, live for that when you get there."

Q. What do you think of the plan to better the condition of the workingmen by committees headed by bishops of the Catholic Church, in discussing their duties?

A. If the bishops wish to discuss with anybody about duties, they had better discuss with the employers, instead of the employed. This discussion had better take place between the clergy and the capitalist. There is no need of discussing this question with the poor wretches who cannot earn more than enough to keep their souls in their bodies. If the Catholic Church has so much power, and if it represents God on earth, let it turn its attention to softening the hearts of capitalists, and no longer waste its time in preaching patience to the poor slaves who are now bearing the burdens of the world.

Q. Do you agree with the pope that: "Sound rules of life must be founded on religion?"

A. I do not. Sound rules of life must be founded on the experience of mankind. In other words, we must live for this world. Why should men throw away hundreds and thousands of millions of dollars in building cathedrals and churches, and paying the salaries of bishops and priests, and cardinals and popes, and get no possible return for all this money except a few guesses about another world – those guesses being stated as facts – when every pope and priest and bishop knows that no one knows the slightest thing on the subject. Superstition is the greatest burden borne by the industry of the world.

The nations of Europe today all pretend to be Christian, yet millions of men are drilled and armed for the purpose of killing other Christians. Each Christian nation is fortified to prevent other Christians from devastating their fields. There is already a debt of about twenty-five thousand millions of dollars which has been incurred by Christian nations, because each one is afraid of every other, and yet all say: "It is our duty to love our enemies."

This world, in my judgment, is to be reformed through intelligence – through development of the mind – not by credulity, but by investigation; not by faith in the supernatural, but by faith in the natural. The church has passed the zenith of her power. The clergy must stand aside. Scientists must take their places.

Q. Do you agree with the pope in attacking the present governments of Europe and the memories of Mazzini and Saffi?

A. I do not. I think Mazzini was of more use to Italy than all the popes that ever occupied the chair of St. Peter – which, by the way, was not his chair. I have a thousand times more regard for Mazzini, for Garibaldi, for Cavour, than I have for any gentleman who pretends to be the representative of God.

There is another objection I have to the pope, and that is that he was so scandalized when a monument was reared in Rome to the memory of Giordano Bruno. Bruno was murdered about 290 years ago by the Catholic Church, and such has been the development of the human brain and heart that on the very spot where he was murdered a monument rises to his memory.

But the vicar of God has remained stationary, and he regards this mark of honor to one of the greatest and noblest of the human race as an act of blasphemy. The poor old man acts as if America had never been discovered – as if the world were still flat – and as if the stars had been made out of little pieces left over from the creation of the world and stuck in the sky simply to beautify the night.

But, after all, I do not blame this pope. He is the victim of his surroundings. He was never married. His heart was never softened by wife or children. He was born that way, and, to tell you the truth, he has my sincere sympathy. Let him talk about America and stay in Italy. — *The Herald,* New York, April 22, 1890.

THE WESTMINSTER CREED
AND OTHER SUBJECTS

Q. What do you think of the revision of the Westminster Creed?

A. I think that the intelligence and morality of the age demand the revision. The Westminster Creed is infamous. It makes God an infinite monster, and men the most miserable of beings. That creed has made millions insane. It has furrowed countless cheeks with tears. Under its influence the sentiments and sympathies of the heart have withered. This creed was written by the worst of men. The civilized Presbyterians do not believe it. The intelligent clergyman will not preach it, and all good men who understand it hold it in abhorrence. But the fact is that it is just as good as the creed of any orthodox church. All these creeds must be revised. Young America will not be consoled by the doctrine of eternal pain. Yes, the creeds must be revised or the churches will be closed.

Q. What do you think of the influence of the press on religion?

A. If you mean on orthodox religion, then I say the press is helping to destroy it. Just to the extent that the press is intelligent and fearless, it is and must be the enemy of superstition. Every fact in the universe is the enemy of every falsehood. The press furnishes food for and excites thought. This tends to the destruction of the miraculous and absurd. I regard the press as the friend of progress and consequently the foe of orthodox religion. The old dogmas do not make the people happy. What is called religion is full of fear and grief. The clergy are always talking about dying, about the grave and eternal pain. They do not add to the sunshine of life. If they could have their way, all the birds would stop singing, the flowers would lose their color and perfume, and all the owls would sit on dead trees and hoot, "Broad is the road that leads to death."

Q. If you should write your last sentence on religious topics, what would be your closing?

A. I now in the presence of death affirm and reaffirm the truth of all that I have said against the superstitions of the world. I would say at least that much on the subject with my last breath.

Q. What, in your opinion, will be Robert Browning's position in the literature of the future?

A. Lower than at present. Mrs. Browning was far greater than her husband. He never wrote anything comparable to "Mother and Poet." Browning lacked form, and that is as great a lack in poetry as it is in sculpture. He was the author of some great lines, some great thoughts, but he was obscure, uneven, and was always mixing the poetic with the commonplace. To me he cannot be compared with Shelley or Keats, or with our own Walt Whitman. Of course, poetry cannot be well discussed. Each man knows what he likes, what touches his heart, and what words burst into blossom, but he cannot judge for others. After one has read Shakespeare, Burns and Byron, and Shelley and Keats; after he has read the "Sonnets" and the "Daisy" and the "Prisoner of Chillon" and the "Skylark" and the "Ode to the Grecian Urn" – the "Flight of the Duchess" seems a little weak. — *The Post-Express,* Rochester, New York, June 23, 1890.

SHAKESPEARE AND BACON

Q. What is your opinion of Ignatius Donnelly as a literary man irrespective of his Baconian theory?

A. I know that Mr. Donnelly enjoys the reputation of being a man of decided ability and that he is regarded by many as a great orator. He is known to me through his Baconian theory, and in that, of course, I have no confidence. It is nearly as ingenious as absurd. He has spent great time, and has devoted much curious learning to the subject, and has at last succeeded in convincing himself that Shakespeare claimed that which he did not write, and that Bacon wrote that which he did not claim. But to me the theory is without the slightest foundation.

Q. Mr. Donnelly asks: "Can you imagine the author of such grand productions retiring to that mud house in Stratford to live without a single copy of the quarto that has made his name famous?" What do you say?

A. Yes; I can. Shakespeare died in 1616, and the quarto was published in 1623, seven years after he was dead. Under these circumstances I think Shakespeare ought to be excused, even by those who attack him with the greatest bitterness, for not having a copy of the book. There is, however, another side to this. Bacon did not die until long after the quarto was published. Did he have a copy? Did he mention the copy in his will? Did he ever mention the quarto in any letter, essay, or in any way? He left a library, was there a copy of the plays in it? Did he leave any manuscript of the play? Has there ever been found a line from any play or sonnet in his handwriting? Bacon left his writings, his papers, all in perfect order, but no plays, no sonnets, said nothing about plays – claimed nothing in their behalf. This is the other side. Now, there is still another thing. The edition of 1623 was published by Shakespeare's friends, Heminge and Condell. They knew him – had been with him for years, and they collected most of his plays and put them in book form.

Ben Jonson wrote a preface, in which he placed Shakespeare above all other poets – declared that he was for all time.

The edition of 1623 was gotten up by actors, by the friends, and associates of Shakespeare, vouched for by dramatic writers – by those who knew him. That is enough.

Q. How do you explain the figure: "His soul, like Mazeppa, was lashed naked to the wild horse of every fear and love and hate." Mr. Donnelly does not understand you?

A. It hardly seems necessary to explain a thing as simple and plain as that. Men are carried away by some fierce passion – carried away in spite of themselves as Mazeppa was carried by the wild horse to which he was lashed. Whether the comparison is good or bad it is at least plain. Nothing could tempt me to call Mr. Donnelly's veracity in question. He says that he does not understand the sentence and I most cheerfully admit that he tells the exact truth.

Q. Mr. Donnelly says that you said: "Where there is genius, education seems almost unnecessary," and he denounces your doctrine as the most abominable doctrine ever taught. What have you to say to that?

A. In the first place, I never made the remark. In the next place, it may be well enough to ask what education is. Much is taught in colleges that is of no earthly use; much is taught that is hurtful. There are thousands of educated men who never graduated from any college or university. Every observant, thoughtful man is educating himself as long as he lives. Men are better than books. Observation is a great teacher. A man of talent learns slowly. He does not readily see the necessary relation that one fact bears to another. A man of genius, learning one fact, instantly sees hundreds of others. It is not necessary for such a man to attend college. The world is his university. Every man he meets is a book – every woman a volume – every fact a torch – and so without the aid of the so-called schools he rises to the very top. Shakespeare was such a man.

Q. Mr. Donnelly says that: "The biggest myth ever on earth was Shakespeare, and that if Francis Bacon had said to the people, I, Francis Bacon, a gentleman of gentlemen, have been taking in secret my share of the coppers and shillings taken at the door of those low playhouses, he would have been ruined. If he had put the plays forth simply as poetry it would have ruined his legal reputation." What do you think of this?

A. I hardly think that Shakespeare was or is a myth. He was certainly born, married, lived in London, belonged to a company of actors, went back to Stratford, where he had a family, and died. All these things do not as a rule happen to myths. In addition to this, those who knew him believed him to be the author of the plays. Bacon's friends never suspected him. I do not think it would have hurt Bacon to have admitted that he wrote *Lear* and *Othello*, and that he was getting "coppers and shillings" to which he was justly entitled. Certainly not as much as for him to have written this, which, in fact, though not in exact form, he did write: "I, Francis Bacon, a gentleman of gentlemen, have been taking coppers and shillings to which I was not entitled – but which I received as bribes while sitting as a judge." He has been excused for two reasons. First, because his salary was small, and second, because it was the custom for judges to receive presents.

Bacon was a lawyer. He was charged with corruption – with having taken bribes, with having sold his decisions. He knew what the custom was and knew how small his salary was. But he did not plead the custom in his defense. He did not mention the smallness of the salary. He confessed that he was guilty – as charged. His confession was deemed too general and he was called on by the lords to make a specific confession. This he did. He specified the cases in which he had received the money and told how much, and begged for mercy. He did not make his confession, as Mr. Donnelly is reported to have said, to get his fine remitted. The confession was made before the fine was imposed.

Neither do I think that the theater in which the plays of Shakespeare were represented could or should be called a "lowly playhouse." The fact that *Othello, Lear, Hamlet, Julius Caesar,* and the other great dramas were first played in that playhouse made it the greatest building in the world. The gods themselves should have occupied seats in that theater, where for the first time the greatest productions of the human mind were put on the stage. — *The Tribune*, Minneapolis, Minnesota, May 31, 1891.

GROWING OLD GRACEFULLY
AND PRESBYTERIANISM

Q. How have you acquired the art of growing old gracefully?

A. It is hard to live a great while without getting old, and it is hardly worthwhile to die just to keep young. It is claimed that people with certain incomes live longer than those who have to earn their bread. But the income people have a stupid kind of life, and though they may hang on a good many years, they can hardly be said to do much real living. The best you can say is, not that they lived so many years, but that it took them so many years to die. Some people imagine that regular habits prolong life, but that depends somewhat on the habits. Only the other day I read an article written by a physician in which regular habits – good ones – were declared to be quite dangerous.

Where life is perfectly regular, all the wear and tear comes on the same nerves – every blow falls on the same place. Variety, even in a bad direction, is a great relief. But living long has nothing to do with getting old gracefully. Good nature is a great enemy of wrinkles, and cheerfulness helps the complexion. If we could only keep from being annoyed at little things, it would add to the luxury of living. Great sorrows are few, and after all do not affect us as much as the many irritating, almost nothings that attack from every side. The traveler is bothered more with dust than mountains. It is a great thing to have an object in life – something to work for and think for. If a man thinks only about himself, his own comfort, his own importance, he will not grow old gracefully. More and more his spirit, small and mean, will leave its impress on his face, and especially in his eyes. You look at him and feel that there is no jewel in the casket; that a shriveled soul is living in a tumble-down house.

The body gets its grace from the mind. I suppose that we are all more or less responsible for our looks. Perhaps the thinker of great thoughts, the doer of noble deeds, molds his features in harmony with his life.

Probably the best medicine, the greatest beautifier in the world, is to make somebody else happy. I have noticed that good mothers have faces as serene as a cloudless day in June, and the older the serener. It is a great thing to know the relative importance of things, and those who do get the most out of life. Those who take an interest in what they see and keep their minds busy are always young.

The other day I met a blacksmith who has given much attention to geology and fossil remains. He told me how happy he was in his excursions. He was nearly 70 years old, and yet he had the enthusiasm of a boy. He said he had some fine specimens, "but," said he, "nearly every night I dream of finding perfect ones."

That man will keep young as long as he lives. As long as a man lives he should study. Death alone has the right to dismiss the school. No man can get too much knowledge. In that, he can have all the avarice he wants, but he can get too much property. If the businessmen would stop when they get enough, they might have a chance to grow old gracefully. But the most of them go on and on, until, like the old stage horse, stiff and lame, they drop dead in the road. The intelligent, the kind, the reasonably contented, the courageous, the self-poised, grow old gracefully.

Q. Are not the restraints to free religious thought being worn away as the world grows older, and will not the recent attacks of the religious press and pulpit on the unorthodoxy of Dr. Briggs, Rev. R. Heber Newton, and the prospective Episcopal bishop of Massachusetts, Dr. Phillip Brooks, and others have a tendency still further to extend this freedom?

A. Of course, the world is growing somewhat wiser – getting more sense day by day. It is amazing to me that any human being or beings ever wrote the Presbyterian creed. Nothing can be more absurd – more barbaric than that creed. It makes man the sport of an infinite monster, and yet good people, men, and women of ability, who have gained eminence in almost every department of human effort, stand by this creed as if it were filled with wisdom and goodness. They really think that a good God damns his poor ignorant children just for his own glory, and that he sends people to perdition, not for any evil in them, but to the praise of his glorious justice. Dr. Briggs has been wicked enough to doubt this phase of God's goodness, and Dr. Bridgman was heartless enough to drop a tear in hell. Of course, they have no idea of what justice really is.

The Presbyterian general assembly that has just adjourned stood by Calvinism. The "Five Points" are as sharp as ever. The members of that assembly – most of them – find all their happiness in the "creed." They need no other amusement. If they feel blue they read about total depravity – and cheer up. In moments of great sorrow they think of the tale of non-elect infants, and their hearts overflow with a kind of holy joy.

They cannot imagine why people wish to attend the theater when they can read the "confession of faith," or why they should feel like dancing after they do read it.

It is sad to think of the young men and women who have been eternally ruined by witnessing the plays of Shakespeare, and it is also sad to think of the young people, foolish enough to be happy, keeping time to the pulse of music, waltzing to hell in loving pairs – all for the glory of God, and to the praise of this glorious justice. I think, too, of the thousands of men and women who, while listening to the music of Wagner, have absolutely forgotten the Presbyterian creed, and who for a little while have been as happy as if the creed had never been written. Tear down the theater, burn the opera houses, break all musical instruments, and then let us go to church.

I am not at all surprised that the general assembly took up this progressive euchre matter. The word "progressive" is always obnoxious to the ministers. Euchre under another name might go. Of course, progressive euchre is a kind of gambling. I knew a young man, or rather heard of him, who won at progressive euchre a silver spoon. At first this looks like nothing, almost innocent, and yet that spoon, gotten for nothing, sowed the seed of gambling in that young man's brain. He became infatuated with euchre, then with cards in general, then with draw-poker in particular – then into Wall Street. He is now a total wreck, and has the impudence to say that it was all "preordained." Think of the thousands and millions that are being demoralized by games of chance, by marbles – when they play for keeps – by billiards and croquet, by fox and geese, authors, halma, tiddledywinks, and pigs in clover. In all these miserable games is the infamous element of chance – the raw material of gambling. Probably none of these games could be played exclusively for the glory of God. I agree with the Presbyterian general assembly; if the creed is true, why should anyone try to amuse himself? If there is a hell, and all of us are going there, there should never be another smile on the human face. We should spend our days in sighs, our nights in tears. The world should go insane. We find strange combinations – good men with bad creeds, and bad men with good ones – and so the great world stumbles along. — *The Blade,* Toledo, Ohio, June 4, 1891.

CREEDS

There is a natural desire on the part of every intelligent human being to harmonize his information – to make his theories agree – in other words, to make what he knows, or thinks he knows, in one department agree and harmonize with what he knows, or thinks he knows, in every other department of human knowledge.

The human race has not advanced in line, neither has it advanced in all departments with the same rapidity. It is with the race as it is with an individual. A man may turn his entire attention to some one subject – as, for instance, to geology – and neglect other sciences. He may be a good geologist but an exceedingly poor astronomer; or he may know nothing of politics or of political economy. So he may be a successful statesman and know nothing of theology. But if a man, successful in one direction, takes up some other question, he is bound to use the knowledge he has on one subject as a kind of standard to measure what he is told on some other subject. If he is a chemist, it will be natural for him, when studying some other question, to use what he knows in chemistry; that is to say, he will expect to find cause and effect everywhere – succession and resemblance. He will say: It must be in all other sciences as in chemistry – there must be no chance. The elements have no caprice. Iron is always the same. Gold does not change. Prussic acid is always poison – it has no freaks. So he will reason as to all facts in nature. He will be a believer in the atomic integrity of all matter, in the persistence of gravitation. Being so trained, and so convinced, his tendency will be to weigh what is called new information in the same scales that he has been using.

Now, for the application of this. Progress in religion is the slowest, because man is kept back by sentimentality, by the efforts of parents, by old associations. A thousand unseen tendrils are twining about him that he must necessarily break if he advances. In other departments of knowledge inducements are held out and rewards are promised to the one who does succeed – to the one who really does advance – to the man who discovers new facts. But in religion, instead of rewards being promised, threats are

212

made. The man is told that he must not advance; that if he takes a step forward, it is at the peril of his soul; that if he thinks and investigates, he is in danger of exciting the wrath of God. Consequently religion has been of the slowest growth. Now, in most departments of knowledge man has advanced; and coming back to the original statement – a desire to harmonize all that we know – there is a growing desire on the part of intelligent men to have a religion fit to keep company with the other sciences.

Our creeds were made in times of ignorance. They suited well a flat world, and a God who lived in the sky just above us and who used the lightning to destroy his enemies. This God was regarded much as a savage regarded the head of his tribe – as one having the right to reward and punish. And this God, being much greater than a chief of the tribe, could give greater rewards and inflict greater punishments. They knew that the ordinary chief, or the ordinary king, punished the slightest offenses with death. They also knew that these chiefs and kings tortured their victims as long as the victims could bear the torture. So when they described their God, they gave to this God power to keep the tortured victim alive forever – because they knew that the earthly chief, or the earthly king, would prolong the life of the tortured for the sake of increasing the agonies of the victim. In those savage days they regarded punishment as the only means of protecting society. In consequence of this they built heaven and hell on an earthly plan, and they put God – that is to say, the chief, that is to say, the king – on a throne like an earthly king.

Of course, these views were all ignorant and barbaric; but in that blessed day their geology and astronomy were on a par with their theology. There was a harmony in all departments of knowledge, or rather of ignorance. Since that time there has been a great advance made in the idea of government – the old idea being that the right to govern came from God to the king, and from the king to the people. Now intelligent people believe that the source of authority has been changed, and that all just powers of government are derived from the consent of the governed. So there has been a great advance in the philosophy of punishment – in the treatment of criminals. So, too, in all the sciences. The earth is no longer flat; heaven is not immediately above us; the universe has been infinitely enlarged, and we have at last found that our earth is but a grain of sand, a speck on the great shore of the infinite. Consequently there is a discrepancy, a discord, a contradiction between our theology and the other sciences. Men of intelligence feel this. Dr. Briggs concluded that a perfectly good and intelligent God could not have created billions of sentient beings knowing that they were to be eternally miserable. No man could do such a thing, had he the power, without being infinitely malicious. Dr. Briggs began to have a little hope for the human race – began to think that maybe God is better than the creed describes him.

And right here it may be well enough to remark that no one has ever been declared a heretic for thinking God bad. Heresy has consisted in thinking God better than the church said he was. The man who said God will damn nearly everybody was orthodox. The man who said God will save everybody was denounced as a blaspheming wretch, as one who assailed and maligned the character of God. I can remember when the Universalists were denounced as vehemently and maliciously as the Atheists are today.

Now, Dr. Briggs is undoubtedly an intelligent man. He knows that nobody on the earth knows who wrote the five books of Moses. He knows that they were not written until hundreds of years after Moses was dead. He knows that two or more persons were the authors of Isaiah. He knows that David did not write to exceed three or four of the Psalms. He knows that the Book of Job is not a Jewish book. He knows that the Songs of Solomon were not written by Solomon. He knows that the Book of Ecclesiastes was written by a freethinker. He also knows that there is not in existence today – so far as anybody knows – any of the manuscripts of the Old or New Testaments.

So about the New Testament Dr. Briggs knows that nobody lives who has ever seen an original manuscript, or who ever saw anybody that did see one, or that claims to have seen one. He knows that nobody knows who wrote Matthew or Mark or Luke or John. He knows that John did not write John and that the Gospel was not written until long after John was dead. He knows that no one knows who wrote the Hebrews. He also knows that the Book of Revelation is an insane production. Dr. Briggs also knows the way in which these books came to be canonical, and he knows that the way was no more binding than a resolution passed by a political convention. He also knows that many books were left out that had for centuries equal authority with those that were put in. He also knows that many passages – and the very passages on which many churches are founded – are interpolations. He knows that the last chapter of Mark, beginning with the 16th verse to the end, is an interpolation; and he also knows that neither Matthew nor Mark nor Luke ever said one word about the necessity of believing on the Lord Jesus Christ, or of believing anything – not one word about believing the Bible or joining the church, or doing any particular thing in the way of ceremony to insure salvation. He knows that according to Matthew, God agreed to forgive others. Consequently he knows that there is not one particle of what is called modern theology in Matthew, Mark, or Luke. He knows that the trouble commenced in John, and that John was not written until probably 150 years – possibly 200 years – after Christ was dead. So he also knows that the sin against the Holy Ghost is an interpolation; that "I came not to bring peace but a sword," if not an interpolation, is an absolute contradiction. So, too, he knows that the promise to forgive in heaven what the disciples should forgive on earth, and to bind in heaven what they should bind on earth, is an interpolation; and that if it is not an interpolation, it is without the slightest sense in fact.

Knowing these things, and knowing, in addition to what I have stated, that there are 30,000 or 40,000 mistakes in the Old Testament, that there are a great many contradictions and absurdities, that many of the laws are cruel and infamous, and could have been made only by a barbarous people, Dr. Briggs has concluded that, after all, the torch that sheds the serenest and divinest light is the human reason, and that we must investigate the Bible as we do other books. At least, I suppose he has reached some such conclusion. He may imagine that the pure gold of inspiration still runs through the quartz and porphyry of ignorance and mistake and that all we have to do is to extract the shining metal by some process that may be called theological smelting; and if so I have no fault to find. Dr. Briggs has taken a step in advance – that is to say, the tree is growing, and when the tree grows, the bark splits; when the new leaves come, the old leaves are rotting on the ground.

The Presbyterian creed is a bad creed. It has been the stumbling block, not only of the head, but of the heart, for many generations. I do not know that it is, in fact, worse than any other orthodox creed; but the bad features are stated with an explicitness and emphasized with a candor that render the creed absolutely appalling. It is amazing to me that any man ever wrote it or that any set of men ever produced it. It is more amazing to me that any human being ever believed it. It is still more amazing that any human being ever thought it wicked not to believe it. It is more amazing still, than all the others combined, that any human being ever wanted it to be true.

This creed is a relic of the Middle Ages. It has in it the malice, the malicious logic, the total depravity, the utter heartlessness of John Calvin, and it gives me great pleasure to say that no Presbyterian was ever as bad as his creed. And here let me say, as I have said many times, that I do not hate Presbyterians – because among them I count some of my best friends – but I hate Presbyterianism. And I cannot illustrate this any better than by saying I do not hate a man because he has rheumatism, but I hate rheumatism because it has a man.

The Presbyterian church is growing, and is growing because, as I said at first, there is a universal tendency in the mind of man to harmonize all that he knows or thinks he knows. This growth may be delayed. The buds of heresy may be kept back by the north wind of Princeton and by the early frost called Patton. In spite of these souvenirs of the Dark Ages, the church must continue to grow. The theologians who regard theology as something higher than a trade tend toward liberalism. Those who regard preaching as a business, and the inculcation of sentiment as a trade, will stand by the lowest possible views. They will cling to the letter and throw away the spirit. They prefer the dead limb to a new bud or to a new leaf. They want no more sap. They delight in the dead tree, in its unbending nature, and they mistake the stiffness of death for the vigor and resistance of life.

Now, as with Dr. Briggs, so with Dr. Bridgman, although it seems to me that he has simply jumped from the frying pan into the fire; and why he should prefer the Episcopal creed to the Baptist is more than I can imagine. The Episcopal creed is, in fact, just as bad as the Presbyterian. It calmly and with unruffled brow utters the sentence of eternal punishment on the majority of the human race, and the Episcopalian expects to be happy in heaven with his son or his daughter or his mother or wife in hell.

Dr. Bridgman will find himself exactly in the position of the Rev. Mr. Newton, provided he expresses his thought. But I account for the Bridgmans and for the Newtons by the fact that there is still sympathy in the human heart and that there is still intelligence in the human brain. For my part, I am glad to see this growth in the orthodox churches, and the quicker they revise their creeds the better.

I oppose nothing that is good in any creed – I attack only that which is ignorant, cruel and absurd, and I make the attack in the interest of human liberty, and for the sake of human happiness.

Q. What do you think of the action of the Presbyterian general assembly at Detroit, and what effect do you think it will have on religious growth?

A. That general assembly was controlled by the orthodox within the church, by the strict constructionists and by the Calvinists; by gentlemen who not only believe the creed, not only believe that a vast majority of people are going to hell, but are really glad of it; by gentlemen who, when they feel a little blue, read about total depravity to cheer up, and when they think of the mercy of God as exhibited in their salvation, and the justice of God as illustrated by the damnation of others, their hearts burst into a kind of efflorescence of joy.

These gentlemen are opposed to all kinds of amusements except reading the Bible, the confession of faith, and the creed, and listening to Presbyterian sermons and prayers. All these things they regard as the food of cheerfulness. They warn the elect against theaters and operas, dancing and games of chance.

Well, if their doctrine is true, there ought to be no theaters, except exhibitions of hell; there ought to be no operas, except where the music is a succession of walls for the misfortunes of man. If their doctrine is true, I do not see how any human being could ever smile again – I do not see how a mother could welcome her babe; everything in nature would become hateful; flowers and sunshine would simply tell us of our fate.

My doctrine is exactly the opposite of this. Let us enjoy ourselves every moment that we can. The love of the dramatic is universal. The stage has not simply amused, but it has elevated mankind. The greatest genius of our world poured the treasures of his soul into the drama. I do not believe that any girl can be corrupted, or that any man can be injured, by becoming acquainted with Isabella or Miranda or Juliet or Imogen, or any of the great heroines of Shakespeare.

So I regard the opera as one of the great civilizers. No one can listen to the symphonies of Beethoven, or the music of Schubert, without receiving a benefit. And no one can hear the operas of Wagner without feeling that he has ennobled and refined.

Why is it the Presbyterians are so opposed to music in this world and yet expect to have so much in heaven? Is not music just as demoralizing in the sky as on the earth, and does anybody believe that Abraham or Isaac or Jacob ever played any music comparable to Wagner?

Why should we postpone our joy to another world? Thousands of people take great pleasure in dancing, and I say let them dance. Dancing is better than weeping and wailing over a theology born of ignorance and superstition.

And so with games of chance. There is a certain pleasure in playing games, and the pleasure is of the most innocent character. Let all these games be played at home and children will not prefer the saloon to the society of their parents. I believe in cards and billiards and would believe in progressive euchre were it more of a game – the great objection to it is its lack of complexity. My idea is to get what little happiness you can out of this life, and to enjoy all sunshine that breaks through the clouds of misfortune. Life is poor enough at best. No one should fail to pick up every jewel of joy that can be found in his path. Everyone should be as happy as he can, provided he is not happy at the expense of another, and no person rightly constituted can be happy at the expense of another.

So let us get all we can of good between the cradle and the grave; all that we can of the truly dramatic; all that we can of music; all that we can of art; all that we can of enjoyment; and if, when death comes, that is the end, we have at least made the best of this life; and if there be another life, let us make the best of that.

I am doing what little I can to hasten the coming of the day when the human race will enjoy liberty – not simply of body, but liberty of mind. And by liberty of mind I mean freedom from superstition, and added to that, the intelligence to find out the conditions of happiness; and added to that, the wisdom to live in accordance with those conditions. — *The Morning Advertiser*, New York, June 12, 1891.

THE TENDENCY OF MODERN THOUGHT

Q. Do you regard the Briggs trial as any evidence of the growth of liberalism in the church itself?

A. When men get together and make what they call a creed, the supposition is that they then say as nearly as possible what they mean and what they believe. A written creed of necessity remains substantially the same. In a few years this creed ceases to give exactly the new shade of thought. Then begins two processes, one of destruction and the other of preservation. In every church, as in every party, and as you may say in every corporation, there are two wings – one progressive, the other conservative. In the church there will be a few, and they will represent the real intelligence of the church, who become dissatisfied with the creed and who at first satisfy themselves by giving new meanings to old words. On the other hand, the conservative party appeals to emotions, to memories, and to the experiences of their fellow-members, for the purpose of upholding the old dogmas and the old ideas; so that each creed is like a crumbling castle. The conservatives plant ivy and other vines, hoping that their leaves will hide the cracks and erosions of time; but the thoughtful see beyond these leaves and are satisfied that the structure itself is in process of decay, and that no amount of ivy can restore the crumbling stones.

The old Presbyterian creed, when it was first formulated, satisfied a certain religious intellect. At that time people were not merciful. They had no clear conceptions of justice. Their lives were for the most part hard; most of them suffered the pains and pangs of poverty; nearly all lived in tyrannical governments and were the sport of nobles and kings. Their idea of God was born of their surroundings. God, to them, was an infinite king who delighted in exhibitions of power. At any rate, their minds were so constructed that they conceived of an infinite being who, billions of years before the world was, made up his mind as to whom he would save and whom he would damn. He not only made up his mind as to the number he would save, and the number that should be lost, but he saved and damned without the slightest reference to the character of the individual. They believed then, and some pretend to believe still, that God damns a man not because he is bad, and that he saves a man not because he is good, but simply for the purpose of self-glorification as an exhibition of his eternal justice. It would be impossible to conceive of any creed more horrible than that of the Presbyterians. Although I admit – and I not only admit but I assert – that the creeds of all orthodox Christians are substantially the same, the Presbyterian creed says plainly what it means. There is no hesitation, no evasion. The horrible truth, so-called, is stated in the clearest possible language. One would think after reading this creed that the men who made it not only believed it but were really glad it was true.

Ideas of justice, of the use of power, of the use of mercy, have greatly changed in the last century. We are beginning dimly to see that each man is the result of an infinite number of conditions, of an infinite number of facts, most of which existed before he was born. We are beginning dimly to see that while reason is a pilot, each soul navigates the mysterious sea filled with tides and unknown currents set in motion by ancestors long since dust. We are beginning to see that defects of mind are transmitted precisely the same as defects of body, and in my judgment, the time is coming when we shall no more think of punishing a man for larceny than for having consumption. We shall know that the thief is a necessary and natural result of conditions, preparing, you may say, the field of the world for the growth of man. We shall no longer depend upon accident and ignorance and providence. We shall depend upon intelligence and science.

The Presbyterian creed is no longer in harmony with the average sense of man. It shocks the average mind. It seems too monstrous to be true; too horrible to find a lodgment in the mind of the civilized man. The Presbyterian minister who thinks, is giving new meanings to the old words. The Presbyterian minister who feels, also gives new meanings to the old words. Only those who neither think nor feel remain orthodox.

For many years the Christian world has been engaged in examining the religions of other peoples, and the Christian scholars have had but little trouble in demonstrating the origin of Mohammedanism and Buddhism and all other isms except ours. After having examined other religions in the light of science, it occurred to some of our theologians to examine their own doctrine in the same way, and the result has been exactly the same in both cases. Dr. Briggs, as I believe, is a man of education. He is undoubtedly familiar with other religions and has, to some extent at least, made himself familiar with the sacred books of other people. Dr. Briggs knows that no human being knows who wrote a line of the Old Testament. He knows as well as he can know anything, for instance, that Moses never wrote one word of the books attributed to him. He knows also that the Book of Genesis was made by putting two or three stories together. He also knows that it is not the oldest story but was borrowed. He knows that in this Book of Genesis there is not one word adapted to make a human being better, or to shed the slightest light on human conduct. He knows, if he knows anything, that the Mosaic code, so-called, was, and is, exceedingly barbarous and not adapted to do justice between man and man, or between nation and nation. He knows that the Jewish people pursued a course adapted to destroy themselves; that they refused to make friends with their neighbors; that they had not the slightest idea of the rights of other people; that they really supposed that the earth was theirs, and that their God was the greatest God in the heavens. He also knows that there are many thousands of mistakes in the Old Testament as translated. He knows that the Book of Isaiah is made up of several books. He knows the same thing in regard to the New Testament. He also knows that there were many other books that were once considered sacred that have been thrown away, and that nobody knows who wrote a solitary line of the New Testament.

Besides all this, Dr. Briggs knows that the Old and New Testaments are filled with interpolations, and he knows that the passages of Scripture which have been taken as the foundation stones for creeds were written hundreds of years after the death of Christ. He knows well enough that Christ never said: "I came not to bring peace, but a sword." He knows that the same being never said: "Thou art Peter, and on this rock will I build my church." He knows, too, that Christ never said: "Whosoever believes shall be saved, and whosoever believes not shall be damned." He knows that there were interpolations. He knows that the sin against the Holy Ghost is another interpolation. He knows, if he knows anything, that the Gospel according to John was written long after the rest, and that nearly all the poison and superstition of orthodoxy is in that book. He knows also, if he knows anything, that St. Paul never read one of the four Gospels.

Knowing all these things, Dr. Briggs has had the honesty to say that there was some trouble about taking the Bible as

221

absolutely inspired in word and punctuation. I do not think, however, that he can maintain his own position and still remain a Presbyterian or anything like a Presbyterian. He takes the ground, I believe, that there are three sources of knowledge: First, the Bible; second, the church; third, reason. It seems to me that reason should come first, because if you say the Bible is a source of authority, why do you say it? Do you say this because your reason is convinced that it is? If so, then reason is the foundation of that belief. If, again, you say the church is a source of authority, why do you say so? It must be because its history convinces your reason that it is. Consequently, the foundation of that idea is reason. At the bottom of this pyramid must be reason, and no man is under any obligation to believe that which is unreasonable to him. He may believe things that he cannot prove, but he does not believe them because they are unreasonable. He believes them because he thinks they are not unreasonable, not impossible, not improbable. But, after all, reason is the crucible in which every fact must be placed, and the result fixes the belief of the intelligent man.

It seems to me that the whole Presbyterian creed must come down together. It is a scheme based on certain facts, so-called. There is in it the fall of man. There is in it the scheme of the atonement, and there is the idea of hell, eternal punishment, and the idea of heaven, eternal reward; and yet, according to their creed, hell is not a punishment and heaven is not a reward. Now, if we do away with the fall of man we do away with the atonement; then we do away with all supernatural religion. Then we come back to human reason. Personally, I hope that the Presbyterian church will be advanced enough and splendid enough to be honest, and if it is honest, all the gentlemen who amount to anything, who assist in the trial of Dr. Briggs, will in all probability agree with him, and he will be acquitted. But if they throw aside their reason, and remain blindly orthodox, then he will be convicted. To me it is simply miraculous that any man should imagine that the Bible is the source of truth. There was a time when all scientific facts were measured by the Bible. That time is past, and now the believers in the Bible are doing their best to convince us that it is in harmony with science. In other words, I have lived to see a change of standards. When I was a boy, science was measured by the Bible. Now the Bible is measured by science. This is an immense step. So it is impossible for me to conceive what kind of a mind a man has, who finds in the history of the church the fact that it has been a source of truth. How can anyone come to the conclusion that the Catholic church has been a source of intellectual light? How can anyone believe that the church of John Calvin has been a source of truth? If its creed is not true, if its doctrines are mistakes, if its dogmas are monstrous delusions, how can it be said to have been a source of truth?

My opinion is that Dr. Briggs will not be satisfied with the step he has taken. He has turned his face a little toward the light. The farther he walks, the harder it will be for him to turn back. The probability is that the orthodox will turn him out, and the process of driving out men of thought and men of genius will go on until the remnant will be as orthodox as they are stupid.

Q. Do you think mankind is drifting away from the supernatural?

A. My belief is that the supernatural has had its day. The church must either change or abdicate. That is to say, it must keep step with the progress of the world or be trampled under foot. The church as a power has ceased to exist. Today it is a matter of infinite indifference what the pulpit thinks unless there comes the voice of heresy from the sacred place. Every orthodox minister in the United States is listened to just in proportion that he preaches heresy. The real, simon-pure, orthodox clergyman delivers his homilies to empty benches and to a few ancient people who know nothing of the tides and currents of modern thought. The orthodox pulpit today has no thought, and the pews are substantially in the same condition. There was a time when the curse of the church whitened the face of a race, but now its anathema is the food of laughter.

Q. What, in your judgment, is to be the outcome of the present agitation in religious circles?

A. My idea is that people more and more are declining the postponement of happiness to another world. The general tendency is to enjoy the present. All religions have taught men that the pleasures of this world are of no account; that they are nothing but husks and rags and chaff and disappointment; that whoever expects to be happy in this world makes a mistake; that there is nothing on the earth worth striving for; that the principal business of mankind should be to get ready to be happy in another world; that the great occupation is to save your soul, and when you get it saved, when you are satisfied that you are one of the elect, then pack up all your worldly things in a small trunk, take it to the dock of time that runs out into the ocean of eternity, sit down on it and wait for the ship of death. And, of course, each church is the only one that sells a through ticket which can be depended on. In all religions, so far as I know, is an admixture of asceticism, and the greater the quantity, the more beautiful the religion has been considered. The tendency of the world today is to enjoy life while you have it; it is to get something out of the present moment; and we have found that there are things worth living for even in this world. We have found that a man can enjoy himself with wife and children; that he can be happy in the acquisition of knowledge; that he can be happy in assisting others; in helping those he loves; that there is some joy in poetry, in science and in the enlargement and development of the mind; that there is some delight in music and in the drama and in the arts. We are finding, poor as the world is, that it beats a promise the fulfillment of which is not to take place until after death. The world is also finding out another thing, and that is that the gentlemen who preach these various religions, and promise these rewards, and threaten these punishments, know nothing whatever of the subject; that they are as blindly ignorant as the people they pretend to teach, and the people are as blindly ignorant as the animals below them. We have finally concluded that no human being has the slightest conception of origin or of destiny, and that this life, not only in its commencement but in its end, is just as mysterious today as it was to the first man whose eyes greeted the rising sun. We are no nearer the solution of the problem than those who lived thousands of years before us, and we are just as near it as those who will live millions of years after we are dead. So many people having arrived at the conclusion that nobody knows and that nobody can know, like sensible folks they have made up their minds to enjoy this life. I have often said, and I say again, that I feel as if I were on a ship not knowing the port from which it sailed, not knowing the harbor to which it was going, not having a speaking acquaintance with any of the officers, and I have made up my mind to have as good a time with the other passengers as possible under the circumstances. If this ship goes down in midsea I have at least made something, and if it reaches a harbor of perpetual delight, I have lost nothing and I have had a happy voyage. And I think millions and millions are agreeing with me.

Now, understand, I am not finding fault with any of these religions or with any of these ministers. These religions and these ministers are the necessary and natural products of sufficient causes. Mankind has traveled from barbarism to what we now call civilization by many paths, all of which, under the circumstances, were absolutely necessary; and while I think the individual does as he must, I think the same of the church, of the corporation, and of the nation, and not only of the nation, but of the whole human race. Consequently I have no malice and no prejudices. I have likes and dislikes. I do not blame a gourd for not being a cantaloupe, but I like cantaloupes. So I do not blame the old hardshell Presbyterian for not being a philosopher, but I like philosophers. So to wind it all up with regard to the tendency of modern thought, or as to the outcome of what you call religion, my own belief is that what is known as religion will disappear from the human mind. And by "religion" I mean living in this world for another, or living in this world to gratify some supposed being whom we never saw and about whom we know nothing and of whose existence we know nothing. In other words, religion consists of the duties we are supposed to owe to the first cause, and of certain things necessary for us to do here to insure happiness hereafter. These ideas, in my judgment, are destined to perish, and men will become convinced that all their duties are within their reach and that obligations can exist only between them and other sentient beings. Another idea, I think, will force itself on the mind, which is this: That he who lives the best for this world lives the best for another if there be one. In other words, humanity will take the place of what is called "religion." Science will displace superstition, and to do justice will be the ambition of men.

My creed is this: Happiness is the only good. The place to be happy is here. The time to be happy is now. The way to be happy is to make others so.

Q. What is going to take the place of the pulpit?

A. I have for a long time wondered why somebody didn't start a church on a sensible basis. My idea is this: There are, of course, in every community, lawyers, doctors, merchants, and people of all trades and professions who have not the time during the week to pay any particular attention to history, poetry, art or song. Now, it seems to me that it would be a good thing to have a church and for these men to employ a man of ability, of talent, to preach to them Sundays, and let this man say to this congregation: "Now, I am going to preach to you for the first few Sundays — eight or ten or twenty, we will say — on the art, poetry, and intellectual achievements of the Greeks." Let this man study all the week and tell his congregation Sunday what he has ascertained. Let him give to his people the history of such men as Plato and Socrates, what they did; of Aristotle, of his philosophy; of the great Greeks, their statesmen, their dramatists, their poets, actors, and sculptors, and let him show the debt that modern civilization owes to these people. Let him, too, give their religions, their mythology – a mythology that has sown the seed of beauty in every land. Then let him take up Rome. Let him show what a wonderful and practical people they were; let him give an idea of their statesmen, orators, poets, lawyers – because probably the Romans were the greatest lawyers. And so let him go through with nation after nation, biography after biography, and at the same time let there be a Sunday school connected with this church where the children shall be taught something of importance. For instance, teach them botany, and when a Sunday is fair, clear, and beautiful, let them go to the fields and woods with their teachers, and in a little while they will become acquainted with all kinds of trees and shrubs and flowering plants. They could also be taught entomology so that every bug would be interesting, for they would see the facts in science – something of use to them. I believe that such a church and such a Sunday school would at the end of a few years be the most intelligent collection of people in the United States. To teach the children all of these things and to teach their parents, too, the outlines of every science so that every member could tell the manner in which they find the distance of a star – how much better that would be than the old talk about Abraham, Isaac, and Jacob, and quotations from Haggai and Zephaniah, and all this this eternal talk about the fall of man and the Garden of Eden, and the flood, and the atonement, and the wonders of Revelation! Even if the religious scheme be true, it can be told and understood as well in one day as in 100 years. The church says: "He that hath ears to hear let him hear." I say: "He that hath brains to think, let him think." So, too, the pulpit is being displaced by what we call places of amusement, which are really places where men go because they find there is something which satisfies in a greater or less degree the hunger of the brain. Never before was the theater so popular as it is now. Never before was so much money lavished on the stage as now. Few men having their choice would go to hear a sermon, especially of the orthodox kind, when they had a chance to see a great actor.

The man must be a curious combination who would prefer an orthodox sermon, we will say, to a concert given by Theodore

Thomas. And I may say in passing that I have great respect for Theodore Thomas, because it was he who first of all opened to the American people the golden gates of music. He made the American people acquainted with the great masters, and especially with Wagner, and it is a debt that we shall always owe him. In this day the opera – that is to say, music in every form – is tending to displace the pulpit. The pulpits have to go in partnership with music now. Hundreds of people have excused themselves to me for going to church, saying they have splendid music. Long ago the Catholic church was forced to go into partnership not only with music, but with painting and with architecture. The Protestant church for a long time thought it could do without these beggarly elements, and the Protestant church was simply a drygoods box with a small steeple on top of it, its walls as bleak and bare and unpromising as the creed. But even Protestants have been forced to hire a choir of ungodly people who happen to have beautiful voices, and they, too, have appealed to the organ. Music is taking the place of creed, and there is more real devotional feeling summoned from the temple of the mind by great music than by any sermon ever delivered. Music, of all other things, gives wings to thought and allows the soul to rise above all the pains and troubles of this life, and to feel for a moment as if it were absolutely free, above all clouds, destined to enjoy forever. So, too, science is beckoning with countless hands. Men of genius are everywhere beckoning men to discoveries, promising them fortunes compared with which Aladdin's lamp was weak and poor. All these things take men from the church; take men from the pulpit. In other words, prosperity is the enemy of the pulpit. When men enjoy life, when they are prosperous here, they are in love with the arts, with the sciences, with everything that gives joy, with everything that promises plenty, and they care nothing about the prophecies of evil that fall from the solemn faces of the parsons. They look in other directions. They are not thinking about the end of the world. They hate the lugubrious, and they enjoy the sunshine of today. And this, in my judgment, is the highest philosophy: First, do not regret having lost yesterday; second, do not fear that you will lose tomorrow; third, enjoy today.

Astrology was displaced by astronomy. Alchemy and the black art gave way to chemistry. Science is destined to take the place of superstition. In my judgment, the religion of the future will be Reason. — *The Tribune,* Chicago, Illinois, November 1891.

MISSIONARIES

Q. What is your opinion of foreign missions?

A. In the first place, there seems to be pretty good opening in this country for missionary work. We have a good many Indians who are not Methodists. I have never known one to be converted. A good many have been killed by Christians, but their souls have not been saved. Maybe the Methodists had better turn their attention to the heathen of our own country. Then we have a good many Mormons who rely on the truth of the Old Testament and follow the example of Abraham, Isaac, and Jacob. It seems to me that the Methodists better convert the Mormons before attacking the tribes of central Africa. There is plenty of work to be done right here. A few good bishops might be employed for a time in converting Dr. Briggs and Professor Swing, to say nothing of other heretical Presbyterians.

There is no need of going to China to convert the Chinese. There are thousands of them here. In China our missionaries tell the followers of Confucius about the love and forgiveness of Christians, and when the Chinese come here they are robbed, assaulted, and often murdered. Would it not be a good thing for the Methodists to civilize our own Christians to such a degree that they would not murder a man simply because he belongs to another race and worships other gods?

So, too, I think it would be a good thing for the Methodists to go south and persuade their brethren in that country to treat the colored people with kindness. A few efforts might be made to convert the "Whitecaps" in Ohio, Indiana, and some other states.

My advice to the Methodists is to do what little good they can right here and now. It seems cruel to preach to the heathen a gospel that is dying out even here, and fill their poor minds with the absurd dogmas and cruel creeds that intelligent men have outgrown and thrown away.

Honest commerce will do a thousand times more good than all the missionaries on earth. I do not believe that an intelligent Chinese or an intelligent Hindu has ever been or ever will be converted into a Methodist. If Methodism is good, we need it here, and if it is not good, do not fool the heathen with it. — *The Press,* Cleveland, Ohio, Nov. 12, 1891.

MY BELIEF AND UNBELIEF

Q. I have heard people in discussing yourself and your views express the belief that way down in the depths of your mind you are not altogether a "disbeliever." Are they in any sense correct?

A. I am an unbeliever, and I am a believer. I do not believe in the miraculous, the supernatural, or the impossible. I do not believe in the "Mosaic" account of the creation, or in the flood, or the Tower of Babel, or that General Joshua turned back the sun or stopped the earth. I do not believe in the Jonah story, or that God and the Devil troubled poor Job. Neither do I believe in the Mt. Sinai business, and I have my doubts about the broiled quails furnished in the wilderness. Neither do I believe that man is wholly depraved. I have not the least faith in the Eden, snake, and apple story. Neither do I believe that God is an eternal jailer; that he is going to be the warden of an everlasting penitentiary in which the most of men are to be eternally tormented. I do not believe that any man can be justly punished or rewarded on account of his belief.

But I do believe in the nobility of human nature; I believe in love, and home, and kindness, and humanity. I believe in good fellowship and cheerfulness, in making wife and children happy. I believe in good nature, in giving to others all the rights that you claim for yourself. I believe in free thought, in reason, observation, and experience. I believe in self-reliance and in expressing your honest thought. I have hope for the whole human race. What will happen to one, will, I hope, happen to all, and that, I hope, will be good. Above all, I believe in Liberty. — *The Blade,* Toledo, Ohio, Jan. 9, 1892.

MUST RELIGION GO?

Q. What is your idea as to the difference between honest belief, as held by honest religious thinkers, and heterodoxy?

A. Of course, I believe there are thousands of men and women who honestly believe not only in the improbable, not only in the absurd, but in the impossible. Heterodoxy, so-called, occupies the halfway station between superstition and reason. A heretic is one who is still dominated by religion, but in the east of whose mind there is a dawn. He is one who has seen the morning star; he has not entire confidence in the day and imagines in some way that even the light he sees was born of the night. In the mind of the heretic, darkness and light are mingled, the ties of intellectual kindred bind him to the night, and yet he has enough of the spirit of adventure to look toward the east. Of course, I admit that Christians and heretics are both honest; a real Christian must be honest and a real heretic must be the same. All men must be honest in what they think; but all men are not honest in what they say. In the invisible world of the mind every man is honest. The judgment never was bribed. Speech may be false, but conviction is always honest, so that the difference between honest belief, as shared by honest religious thinkers and heretics, is a difference of intelligence. It is the difference between a ship lashed to the dock and one making a voyage; it is the difference between twilight and dawn – that is to say, the coming of the night and the coming of the morning.

Q. Are women becoming freed from the bonds of sectarianism?

A. Women are less calculating than men. As a rule they do not occupy the territory of compromise. They are natural extremists. The woman who is not dominated by superstition is apt to be absolutely free, and when a woman has broken the shackles of superstition, she has no apprehension, no fears. She feels that she is on the open sea, and she cares neither for wind nor wave. An emancipated woman never can be re-enslaved. Her heart goes with her opinions and goes first.

Q. Do you consider that the influence of religion is better than the influence of liberalism on society; that is to say, is society less or more moral, is vice more or less conspicuous?

A. Whenever a chain is broken an obligation takes its place. There is and there can be no responsibility without liberty. The freer a man is, the more responsible, the more accountable he feels; consequently the more liberty there is, the more morality there is. Believers in religion teach us that God will reward men for good actions, but men who are intellectually free know that the reward of a good action cannot be given by any power but that it is the natural result of the good action. The free man, guided by intelligence, knows that his reward is in the nature of things, and not in the caprice even of the infinite. He is not a good and faithful servant, he is an intelligent free man.

The vicious are ignorant; real morality is the child of intelligence; the free and intelligent man knows that every action must be judged by its consequences; he knows that if he does good he reaps a good harvest; he knows that if he does evil he bears a burden, and he knows that these good arid evil consequences are not determined by an infinite master, but that they live in and are produced by the actions themselves. — *Evening Advertiser,* New York, Feb. 6, 1892.

CATHOLICISM AND PROTESTANTISM
THE POPE, THE A. P. A.,
AGNOSTICISM, AND THE CHURCH

Q. Which do you regard as the better, Catholicism or Protestantism?

A. Protestantism is better than Catholicism because there is less of it. Protestantism does not teach that a monk is better than a husband and father, that a nun is holier than a mother. Protestants do not believe in the confessional. Neither do they pretend that priests can forgive sins. Protestantism has fewer ceremonies and less *opéra bouffe*, clothes, caps, tiaras, miters, crooks, and holy toys. Catholics have an infallible man – an old Italian. Protestants have an infallible book, written by Hebrews before they were civilized. The infallible man is generally wrong, and the infallible book is filled with mistakes and contradictions. Catholics and Protestants are both enemies of intellectual freedom – of real education, but both are opposed to education enough to make free men and women.

Between the Catholics and Protestants there has been about as much difference as there is between crocodiles and alligators. Both have done the worst they could, both are as bad as they can be, and the world is getting tired of both. The world is not going to choose either – both are to be rejected.

Q. Are you willing to give your opinion of the Pope?

A. It may be that the Pope thinks he is infallible, but I doubt it. He may think that he is the agent of God, but I guess not. He may know more than other people, but if he does he has kept it to himself. He does not seem satisfied with standing in the place and stead of God in spiritual matters but desires temporal power. He wishes to be Pope and King. He imagines that he has the right to control the belief of all the world; that he is the shepherd of all "sheep" and that the fleeces belong to him. He thinks that in his keeping is the conscience of mankind. So he imagines that his blessing is a great benefit to the faithful and that his prayers can change the course of natural events. He is a strange mixture of the serious and comical. He claims to represent God and admits that

232

he is almost a prisoner. There is something pathetic in the condition of this pontiff. When I think of him, I think of Lear on the heath, old, broken, touched with insanity, and yet, in his own opinion, "every inch a king."

The Pope is a fragment, a remnant, a shred, a patch of ancient power and glory. He is a survival of the unfittest, a souvenir of the theocracy, a relic of the supernatural. Of course, he will have a few successors, and they will become more and more comical, more and more helpless and impotent as the world grows wise and free. I am not blaming the Pope. He was poisoned at the breast of his mother. Superstition was mingled with her milk. He was poisoned at school – taught to distrust his reason and to live by faith. And so it may be that his mind was so twisted and tortured out of shape that he now really believes that he is the infallible agent of an infinite God.

Q.   Are you in favor of the A. P. A.?

A.   In this country I see no need of secret political societies. I think it is better to fight in the open field. I am a believer in religious liberty, in allowing all sects to preach their doctrines and to make as many converts as they can. As long as we have free speech and a free press I think there is no danger of the country being ruled by any church. The Catholics are much better than their creed, and the same can be said of nearly all members of orthodox churches. A majority of American Catholics think a great deal more of this country than they do of their church. When they are in good health they are on our side. It is only when they are sick that they turn their eyes toward Rome. If they were in the majority, of course, they would destroy all other churches and imprison, torture, and kill all Infidels. But they will never be in the majority. They increase now only because Catholics come from other countries. In a few years that supply will cease, and then the Catholic church will grow weaker every day. The free secular school is the enemy of priestcraft and superstition, and the people of this country will never consent to the destruction of that institution. I want no man persecuted on account of his religion.

Q.   If there is no beatitude, or heaven, how do you account for the continual struggle in every natural heart for its own betterment?

A.   Man has many wants, and all his efforts are the children of wants. If he wanted nothing, he would do nothing. We civilize the savage by increasing his wants, by cultivating his fancy, his appetites, his desires. He is then willing to work to satisfy these new wants. Man always tries to do things in the easiest way. His constant effort is to accomplish more with less work. He invents a machine; then he improves it, his idea being to make it perfect. He wishes to produce the best. So in every department of effort and knowledge he seeks the highest success, and he seeks it because it is for his own good here in this world. So he finds that there is a relation between happiness and conduct, and he tries to find out what he must do to produce the greatest enjoyment. This is the basis of morality, of law and ethics. We are so constituted that we love proportion, color, harmony. This is the artistic man. Morality is the harmony and proportion of conduct – the music of life. Man continually seeks to better his condition – not because he is immortal – but because he is capable of grief and pain, because he seeks for happiness. Man wishes to respect himself and to gain the respect of others. The brain wants light, the heart wants love. Growth is natural. The struggle to overcome temptation, to be good and noble, brave and sincere, to reach, if possible, the perfect, is no evidence of the immortality of the soul or of the existence of other worlds. Men live to excel, to become distinguished, to enjoy, and so they strive, each in his own way, to gain the ends desired.

Q. Do you believe that the race is growing moral or immoral?

A. The world is growing better. There is more real liberty, more thought, more intelligence than ever before. The world was never so charitable or generous as now. We do not put honest debtors in prison, we no longer believe in torture. Punishments are less severe. We place a higher value on human life. We are far kinder to animals. To this, however, there is one terrible exception. The vivisectors, those who cut, torture, and mutilate in the name of science, disgrace our age. They excite the horror and indignation of all good people. Leave out the actions of those wretches, and animals are better treated than ever before. So there is less beating of wives and whipping of children. The whip is no longer found in the civilized home. Intelligent parents now govern by kindness, love, and reason. The standard of honor is higher than ever. Contracts are more sacred, and men do nearer as they agree. Man has more confidence in his fellow man and in the goodness of human nature. Yes, the world is getting better, nobler, and grander every day. We are moving along the highway of progress on our way to the Eden of the future.

Q. Are the doctrines of Agnosticism gaining ground, and what, in your opinion, will be the future of the church?

A. The Agnostic is intellectually honest. He knows the limitations of his mind. He is convinced that the questions of origin and destiny cannot be answered by man. He knows that he cannot answer these questions, and he is candid enough to say so. The Agnostic has good mental manners. He does not call belief or hope or wish a demonstration. He knows the difference between hope and belief – between belief and knowledge – and he keeps these distinctions in his mind. He does not say that a certain theory is true because he wishes it to be true. He tries to go according to evidence, in harmony with facts, without regard to his own desires or the wish of the public. He has the courage of his convictions and the modesty of his ignorance. The theologian is his opposite. He is certain and sure of the existence of things and beings and worlds of which there is, and can be, no evidence. He relies on assertion, and in all debate attacks the motive of his opponent instead of answering his arguments. All savages know the origin and destiny of man. About other things they know but little. The theologian is much the same. The Agnostic has given up the hope of ascertaining the nature of the "first cause" – the hope of ascertaining whether or not there was a "first cause." He admits that he does not know whether or not there is an infinite being. He admits that these questions cannot be answered, and so he refuses to answer. he refuses also to pretend. He knows that the theologian does not know, and he has the courage to say so.

He knows that the religious creeds rest on assumption, supposition, assertion – on myth and legend, on ignorance and superstition, and that there is no evidence of their truth. The Agnostic bends his energies in the opposite direction. He occupies himself with this world, with things that can be ascertained and understood. He turns his attention to the sciences, to the solution of questions that touch the well-being of man. He wishes to prevent and to cure diseases; to lengthen life; to provide homes and raiment and food for man; to supply the wants of the body.

He also cultivates the arts. He believes in painting and sculpture, in music and the drama – the needs of the soul. The Agnostic believes in developing the brain, in cultivating the affections, the tastes, the conscience, the judgment, to the end that man may be happy in this world. He seeks to find the relation of things, the condition of happiness. He wishes to enslave the forces of nature to the end that they may perform the work of the world. Back of all progress are the real thinkers; the finders of facts, those who turn their attention to the world in which we live. The theologian has never been a help, always a hindrance. He has always kept his back to the sunrise. With him all wisdom was in the past. He appealed to the dead. He was and is the enemy of reason, of investigation, of thought, and progress. The church has never given "sanctuary" to a persecuted truth.

There can be no doubt that the ideas of the Agnostic are gaining ground. The scientific spirit has taken possession of the intellectual world. Theological methods are unpopular today, even in theological schools. The attention of men everywhere is being directed to the affairs of this world, this life. The gods are growing indistinct, and, like the shapes of clouds, they are changing as they fade. The idea of special providence has been substantially abandoned. People are losing, and intelligent people have lost, confidence in prayer. Today no intelligent person believes in miracles – in a violation of the facts of nature. They may believe that there used to be miracles a good while ago, but not now. The "supernatural" is losing its power, its influence, and the church is growing weaker every day.

The church is supported by the people, and in order to gain the support of the people it must reflect their ideas, their hopes and fears. As the people advance, the creeds will be changed, either by changing the words or giving new meanings to the old words. The church, in order to live, must agree substantially with those who support it, and consequently it will change to any extent that may be necessary. If the church remains true to the old standards then it will lose the support of progressive people, and if the people generally advance the church will die. But my opinion is that it will slowly change, that the minister will preach what the members want to hear, and that the creed will be controlled by the contribution box. One of these days the preachers may become teachers, and when that happens the church will be of use.

Q. What do you regard as the greatest of all themes in poetry and song?

A. Love and death. The same is true of the greatest music. In *Tristan and Isolde* is the greatest music of love and death. In Shakespeare the greatest themes are love and death. In all real poetry, in all real music, the dominant, the triumphant tone, is love, and the minor, the sad refrain, the shadow, the background, the mystery, is death.

Q. What would be your advice to an intelligent young man just starting out in life?

A. I would say to him: "Be true to your ideal. Cultivate your heart and brain. Follow the light of your reason. Get all the happiness out of life that you possibly can. Do not care for power, but strive to be useful. First of all, support yourself so that you may not be a burden to others. If you are successful, if you gain a surplus, use it for the good of others. Own yourself and live and die a free man. Make your home a heaven, love your wife and govern your children by kindness. Be good-natured, cheerful, forgiving, and generous. Find out the conditions of happiness, and then be wise enough to live in accordance with them. Cultivate intellectual hospitality, express your honest thoughts, love your friends, and be just to your enemies." — *New York Herald,* Sept. 16, 1894.

REPLY TO THE CHRISTIAN ENDEAVORERS

Q. How were you affected by the announcement that the united prayers of the Salvationists and Christian Endeavorers were to be offered for your conversion?

A. The announcement did not affect me to any great extent. I take it for granted that the people praying for me are sincere and that they have a real interest in my welfare. Of course, I thank them one and all. At the same time I can hardly account for what they did. Certainly they would not ask God to convert me unless they thought the prayer could be answered. And if their God can convert me, of course he can convert everybody. Then the question arises why does he not do it. Why does he let millions go to hell when he can convert them all. Why did he not convert them all before the flood and take them all to heaven instead of drowning them and sending them all to hell. Of course, these questions can be answered by saying that God's ways are not our ways. I am greatly obliged to these people. Still, I feel about the same, so that it would be impossible to get up a striking picture of "before and after." It was good-natured on their part to pray for me, and that act alone leads me to believe that there is still hope for them. The trouble with the Christian Endeavorers is that they don't give my arguments consideration. If they did, they would agree with me. It seemed curious that they would advise divine wisdom what to do, or that they would ask infinite mercy to treat me with kindness. If there be a God, of course he knows what ought to be done and will do it without any hints from ignorant human beings. Still, the Endeavorers and the salvation people may know more about God than I do. For all I know, this God may need a little urging. He may be powerful but a little slow; intelligent but sometimes a little drowsy, and it may do good now and then to call his attention to the facts. The prayers did not, so far as I know, do me the least injury or the least good. I was glad to see that the Christians are getting civilized. A few years ago they would have burned me. Now they pray for me.

Suppose God should answer the prayers and convert me, how would he bring the conversion about? In the first place, he would

238

have to change my brain and give me more credulity – that is, he would be obliged to lessen my reasoning power. Then I would believe not only without evidence, but in spite of evidence. All the miracles would appear perfectly natural. It would then seem as easy to raise the dead as to waken the sleeping. In addition to this, God would so change my mind that I would hold all reason in contempt and put entire confidence in faith. I would then regard science as the enemy of human happiness, and ignorance as the soil in which virtues grow. Then I would throw away Darwin and Humboldt and rely on the sermons of orthodox preachers. In other words, I would become a little child and amuse myself with a religious rattle and a Gabriel horn. Then I would rely on a man who has been dead for nearly 2,000 years to secure me a seat in paradise.

After conversion, it is not pretended that I will be any better so far as my actions are concerned; no more charitable, no more honest, no more generous. The great difference will be that I will believe more and think less.

After all, the converted people do not seem to be better than the sinners. I never heard of a poor wretch clad in rags, limping into a town and asking for the house of a Christian.

I think that I had better remain as I am. I had better follow the light of my reason, be true to myself, express my honest thoughts, and do the little I can for the destruction of superstition, the little I can for the development of the brain, for the increase of intellectual hospitality and the happiness of my fellow-beings. One world at a time. — *New York Journal,* Dec. 15, 1895.

SPIRITUALISM

There are several good things about the spiritualists. First, they are not bigoted; second, they do not believe in salvation by faith; third, they don't expect to be happy in another world because Christ was good in this; fourth, they do not preach the consolation of hell; fifth, they do not believe in God as an infinite monster; sixth, the spiritualists believe in intellectual hospitality. In these respects they are far superior to the saints.

I think that the spiritualists have done good. They believe in enjoying themselves – in having a little pleasure in this world. They are social, cheerful, and good-natured. They are not the slaves of a book. Their hands and feet are not tied with passages of Scripture. They are not troubling themselves about getting forgiveness and settling their heavenly debts for a cent on the dollar. Their belief does not make them mean or miserable.

They do not persecute their neighbors. They ask no one to have faith or to believe without evidence. They ask all to investigate, and then to make up their minds from the evidence. Hundreds of thousands of well-educated, intelligent people are satisfied with the evidence and firmly believe in the existence of spirits. For all I know, they may be right – but...

Q. The spiritualists have indirectly claimed that you were in many respects almost one of them. Have you given them reason to believe so?

A. I am not a spiritualist, and have never pretended to be. The spiritualists believe in free thought, in freedom of speech, and they are willing to hear the other side – willing to hear me. The best thing about the spiritualists is that they believe in intellectual hospitality.

Q. Is spiritualism a religion or a truth?

A. I think that spiritualism may properly be called a religion. It deals with two worlds – teaches the duty of man to his fellows – the relation that this life bears to the next. It claims to be founded on facts. It insists that the "dead" converse with the living, and that information is received from those who once lived in this world. Of the truth of these claims I have no sufficient evidence.

Q. Are all mediums impostors?

A. I will not say that all mediums are impostors, because I do not know. I do not believe that these mediums get any information or help from "spirits." I know that for thousands of years people have believed in mediums – in spiritualism. A spirit in the form of a man appeared to Samson's mother, and afterward to his father.

Spirits, or angels, called on Abraham. The witch of Endor raised the ghost of Samuel. An angel appeared with three men in the furnace. The handwritings on the wall was done by a spirit. A spirit appeared to Joseph in a dream, to the wise men and to Joseph again.

So a spirit and angel, or a God, spoke to Saul, and the same happened to Mary Magdalene.

The religious literature of the world is filled with such things. Take spiritualism from Christianity and the whole edifice crumbles. All religions, so far as I know, are based on spiritualism – on communications received from angels, from spirits.

I do not say that all the mediums, ancient or modern, were, and are, impostors – but I do think that all the honest ones were, and are, mistaken. I do not believe that man has ever received any communication from angels, spirits, or gods. No whisper, as I believe, has ever come from any other world. The lips of the dead are always closed. From the grave there has come no voice. For thousands of years people have been questioning the dead. They have tried to catch the whisper of a vanished voice. Many say that they have succeeded. I do not know.

Q. What is the explanation of the startling knowledge displayed by some so-called "mediums" of the history and personal affairs of people who consult them? Is there any such thing as mind-reading or thought-transference?

A. In a very general way, I suppose that one person may read the thought of another – not definitely, but by the expression of the face, by the attitude of the body, some idea may be obtained as to what a person thinks, what he intends. So thought may be transferred by look or language, but not simply by will. Everything that is, is natural. Our ignorance is the soil in which mystery grows. I do not believe that thoughts are things that can be seen or touched. Each mind lives in a world of its own, a world that no other mind can enter. Minds, like ships at sea, give signs and signals to each other, but they do not exchange captains.

Q. Is there any such thing as telepathy? What is the explanation of the stories of mental impression received at long distances?

A. There are curious coincidences. People sometimes happen to think of something that is taking place at a great distance. The stories about these happenings are not well authenticated, and seem never to have been of the least use to anybody.

Q. Can these phenomena be considered aside from any connection with, or form of, superstition?

A. I think that mistake, emotion, nervousness, hysteria, dreams, love of the wonderful, dishonesty, ignorance, grief, and the longing for immortality – the desire to meet the loved and lost, the horror of endless death – account for these phenomena. People often mistake their dreams for realities – often think that their thoughts have "happened." They live in a mental mist, a mirage. The boundary between the actual and the imagined becomes faint, wavering, and obscure. They mistake clouds for mountains. The real and the unreal mix and mingle until the impossible becomes common, and the natural absurd.

Q. Do you believe that any sane man ever had a vision?

A. Of course, the sane and insane have visions, dreams. I do not believe that any man, sane or insane, was ever visited by an angel or spirit, or ever received any information from the dead.

Q. Setting aside from consideration the so-called physical manifestation of the mediums, has spiritualism offered any proof of the immortality of the soul?

A. Of course, spiritualism offers what it calls proof of immortality. That is its principal business. Thousands and thousands of good, honest, intelligent people think the proof sufficient. They receive what they believe to be messages from the departed, and now and then the spirits assume their old forms – including garments – and pass through walls and doors as light passes through glass. Do these things really happen? If the spirits of the dead do return, then the fact of another life is established. It all depends on the evidence. Our senses are easily deceived, and some people have more confidence in their reason than in their senses.

Q. Do you not believe that such a man as Robert Dale Owen was sincere? What was the real state of mind of the author of *Footfalls on the Boundaries of Another World*?

A. Without the slightest doubt, Robert Dale Owen was sincere. He was one of the best of men. His father labored all his life for the good of others. Robert Owen, the father, had a debate, in Cincinnati, with the Rev. Alexander Campbell, the founder of the Campbellite church. Campbell was no match for Owen, and yet the audience was almost unanimously against Owen.

Robert Dale Owen was an intelligent, thoughtful, honest man. He was deceived by several mediums, but remained a believer. He wanted spiritualism to be true. He hungered and thirsted for another life. He explained everything that was mysterious or curious by assuming the interference of spirits. He was a good man, but a poor investigator. He thought that people were all honest.

Q. What do you understand the spiritualist means when he claims that the soul goes to the "summerland" and there continues to work and evolute to higher planes?

A. No one pretends to know where "heaven" is. The celestial realm is the blessed somewhere in the unknown nowhere. So far as I know, the "summerland" has no metes and bounds, and no one pretends to know exactly or inexactly where it is. After all, the "summerland" is a hope – a wish. Spiritualists believe that a soul leaving this world passes into another, or into another state, and continues to grow in intelligence and virtue, if it so desires.

Spiritualists claim to prove that there is another life. Christians believe this, but their witnesses have been dead for many centuries. They take the "hearsay" of legend and ancient gossip; but spiritualists claim to have living witnesses; witnesses that can talk, make music; that can take to themselves bodies and shake hands with the people they knew before they passed to the "other shore."

Q. Has spiritualism, through its mediums, ever told the world anything useful, or added to the store of the world's knowledge, or relieved its burdens?

A. I do not know that any medium has added to the useful knowledge of the world, unless mediums have given evidence of another life. Mediums have told us nothing about astronomy, geology, or history, have made no discoveries, no inventions, and have enriched no art. The same may be said of every religion.

All the orthodox churches believe in spiritualism. Every now and then the Virgin appears to some peasant, and in the old days the darkness was filled with evil spirits. Christ was a spiritualist, and his principal business was the casting out of devils. All of his disciples, all of the church fathers, all of the saints were believers in spiritualism of the lowest and most ignorant type. During the

Middle Ages people changed themselves, with the aid of spirits, into animals. They became wolves, dogs, cats, and donkeys. In those days all the witches and wizards were mediums. So animals were sometimes taken possession of by spirits the same as Balaam's donkey and Christ's swine. Nothing was too absurd for the Christians.

Q. Has not spiritualism added to the world's store of hope? And in what way has not spiritualism done good?

A. The mother holding in her arms her dead child, believing that the babe has simply passed to another life, does not weep as bitterly as though she thought that death was the eternal end. A belief in spiritualism must be a consolation. You see, the spiritualists do not believe in eternal pain, and consequently a belief in immortality does not fill their hearts with fear.

Christianity makes eternal life an infinite horror and casts the glare of hell on almost every grave.

The spiritualists appear to be happy in their belief. I have never known a happy orthodox Christian.

It is natural to shun death, natural to desire eternal life. With all my heart I hope for everlasting life and joy – a life without failures, without crimes and tears.

If immortality could be established, the river of life would overflow with happiness. The faces of prisoners, of slaves, of the deserted, of the diseased, and starving would be radiant with smiles, and the dull eyes of despair would glow with light.

If it could be established.

Let us hope. — *The Journal,* New York, July 26, 1896.

A LITTLE OF EVERYTHING

Q. What should be the attitude of the church toward the stage?

A. It should be, what it always has been, against it. If the orthodox churches are right, then the stage is wrong. The stage makes people forget hell; and this puts their souls in peril. There will be forever a conflict between Shakespeare and the Bible.

Q. What do you think of the new woman?

A. I like her.

Q. Where rests the responsibility for the Armenian atrocities?

A. Religion is the cause of the hatred and bloodshed.

Q. What do you think of international marriages, as between titled foreigners and American heiresses?

A. My opinion is the same as is entertained by the American girl after the marriages. It is a great mistake.

Q. What do you think of England's Poet Laureate, Alfred Austin?

A. I have only read a few of his lines and they were not poetic. The office of Poet Laureate should be abolished. Men cannot write poems to order as they could deliver cabbage or beer. By poems I do not mean jingles of words. I mean great thoughts clothed in splendor.

Q. What is your estimate of Susan B. Anthony?

A. Miss Anthony is one of the most remarkable women in the world. She has the enthusiasm of youth and spring, the courage and sincerity of a martyr. She is as reliable as the attraction of gravitation. She is absolutely true to her convictions, intellectually honest, logical, candid, and infinitely persistent. No human being has done more for woman than Miss Anthony. She has won the respect and admiration of the best people on the earth. And so I say: Good luck and long life to Susan B. Anthony.

Q. Which did more for his country, George Washington or Abraham Lincoln?

A. In my judgment, Lincoln was the greatest man ever president. I put him above Washington and Jefferson. He had the genius of goodness; and he was one of the wisest and shrewdest of men. Lincoln towers above them all.

Q. What gave rise to the report that you had been converted – did you go to church somewhere?

A. I visited the "people's church" in Kalamazoo, Michigan. This church has no creed. The object is to make people happy in this world. Miss Bartlett is the pastor. She is a remarkable woman and is devoting her life to a good work. I liked her church and said so. This is all.

Q. Are there not some human natures so morally weak or diseased that they cannot keep from sin without the aid of some sort of religion?

A. I do not believe that orthodox religion helps anybody to be just, generous, or honest. Superstition is not the soil in which goodness grows. Falsehood is poor medicine.

Q. Would you consent to live in any but a Christian community? If you would, please name one.

A. I would not live in a community where all were orthodox Christians. Such a community would be a penitentiary. I would rather dwell in central Africa. If I could have my choice I would rather live among people who were free, who sought for truth and lived according to reason. Sometime there will be such a community.

Q. Is the noun "United States" singular or plural, as you use English?

A. I use it in the singular.

Q, Have you read Nordau's *Degeneracy?* If so, what do you think of it?

A. I think it substantially insane.

Q. What do you think of Bishop Doane's advocacy of free rum as a solution of the liquor problem?

A. I am a believer in liberty. All the temperance legislation, all the temperance societies, all the agitation, all these things have done no good.

Q. Do you agree with Mr. Carnegie that a college education is of little or no practical value to a man?

A. A man must have education. It makes no difference where or how he gets it. To study the dead languages is time wasted so far as success in business is concerned. Most of the colleges in this country are poor because they are controlled by theologians.

Q. What suggestion would you make for the improvement of the newspapers of this country?

A. Every article in a newspaper should be signed by the writer. And all writers should do their best to tell the exact facts.

Q. What do you think of Niagara Falls?

A. It is a dangerous place. Those great rushing waters – there is nothing attractive to me in them. There is so much noise; so much tumult. It is simply a mighty force of nature – one of those tremendous powers that is to be feared for its danger. What I like in nature is a cultivated field, where men can work in the free open air, where there is quiet and repose – no turmoil, no strife, no tumult, no fearful roar or struggle for mastery. I do not like the crowded, stuffy workshop, where life is slavery and drudgery. Give me the calm, cultivated land of waving grain, of flowers, of happiness.

Q. What is worse than death?

A. Oh, a great many things. To be dishonored. To be worthless. To feel that you are a failure. To be insane. To be constantly afraid of the future. To lose the ones you love. — *The Herald,* Rochester, New York, Feb. 25, 1896.

IS LIFE WORTH LIVING – CHRISTIAN SCIENCE

Q. With all your experiences, the trials, the responsibilities, the disappointments, the heartburnings, Colonel, is life worth living?

A. Well, I can only answer for myself. I like to be alive, to breathe the air, to look at the landscape, the clouds, and stars, to repeat old poems, to look at pictures, and statues, to hear music, the voices of the ones I love. I enjoy eating and smoking. I like good cold water. I like to talk with my grandchildren. I like to sleep and to dream. Yes, you can say that life, to me, is worth living.

Q. What is your idea of Christian Science?

A. I think it is superstition, pure and unadulterated. I think that soda will cure a sour stomach better than thinking. In my judgment, quinine is a better tonic than meditation. Of course, cheerfulness is good and depression bad, but if you can absolutely control the body and all its functions by thought, what is the use of buying coal? Let the mercury go down and keep yourself hot by thinking. What is the use of wasting money for food? Fill your stomachs with think. According to these Christian Science people all that really exists is an illusion, and the only realities are the things that do not exist. They are like the old fellow in India who said that all things were illusions. One day he was speaking to a crowd on his favorite hobby. Just as he said "all is illusion" a fellow on an elephant rode toward him. The elephant raised his trunk as though to strike, thereupon the speaker ran away. Then the crowd laughed. In a few moments the speaker returned. The people shouted: "If all is illusion, what made you run away?" The speaker replied: "My poor friends, I said all is illusion. I say so still. There was no elephant. I did not run away. You did not laugh, and I am not explaining now. All is illusion."

That man must have been a Christian Scientist. — *The InterOcean,* Chicago, November 1897.

A REPLY TO THE REV. L. A. BANKS

Q. Have you read the remarks made about you by the Rev. Mr. Banks, and what do you think of what he said?

A. The reverend gentleman pays me a great compliment by comparing me to a circus. Everybody enjoys the circus. They love to see the acrobats, the walkers on the tight rope, the beautiful girls on the horses, and they laugh at the wit of the clown. They are delighted with the jugglers, with the music of the band. They drink the lemonade, eat the colored popcorn and laugh until they nearly roll off their seats. Now the circus has a few animals so that Christians can have an excuse for going. Think of the joy the circus gives to the boys and girls. They look at the show bills, see the men and women flying through the air, bursting through paper hoops, the elephants standing on their heads, and the clowns, in curious clothes, with hands on their knees and open mouths, supposed to be filled with laughter.

All the boys and girls for many miles around know the blessed day. They save their money, obey their parents, and when the circus comes they are on hand. They see the procession and then they see the show. They are all happy. No sermon ever pleased them as much, and in comparison even the Sunday school is tame and dull.

To feel that I give as much joy as the circus fills me with pleasure. What chance would the Rev. Dr. Banks stand against a circus?

The reverend gentleman has done me a great honor, and I tender him my sincere thanks.

Q. Dr. Banks says that you write only one lecture a year, while preachers write a brand new one every week – that if you did that people would tire of you. What have you to say to that?

A. It may be that great artists paint only one picture a year, and it may be that sign painters can do several jobs a day. Still, I would not say that the sign painters were superior to the artists. There is quite a difference between a sculptor and a stone-cutter.

There are thousands of preachers and thousands and thousands of sermons preached every year. Has any orthodox minister in the year 1898 given just one paragraph to literature? Has any

249

orthodox preacher uttered one great thought, clothed in perfect English that thrilled the hearers like music – one great strophe that became one of the treasures of memory?

I will make the question a little broader. Has any orthodox preacher, or any preacher in an orthodox pulpit uttered a paragraph of what may be called sculptured speech since Henry Ward Beecher died? I do not wonder that the sermons are poor. Their doctrines have been discussed for centuries. There is little chance for originality; they not only thresh old straw, but they thresh straw that has been threshed a million times – straw in which there has not been a grain of wheat for hundreds of years. No wonder that they have nervous prostration. No wonder that they need vacations, and no wonder that their congregations enjoy the vacations as keenly as the ministers themselves. Better deliver a real good address 52 times than 52 poor ones – just for the sake of variety.

Q. Dr. Banks says that the tendency at present is not toward Agnosticism, but toward Christianity. What is your opinion?

A. When I was a boy "Infidels" were rare. A man who denied the inspiration of the Bible was regarded as a monster. Now there are in this country millions who regard the Bible as the work of ignorant and superstitious men. A few years ago the Bible was standard. All scientific theories were tested by the Bible. Now science is the standard and the Bible is tested by that.

Dr. Banks did not mention the names of the great scientists who are or were Christians, but he probably thought of Laplace, Humboldt, Haeckel, Huxley, Spencer, Tyndall, Darwin, Helmholtz, and Draper. When he spoke of Christian statesmen he likely thought of Jefferson, Franklin, Washington, Paine, and Lincoln – or he may have thought of Pierce, Filmore, and Buchanan.

But, after all, there is no argument in names. A man is not necessarily great because he holds office or wears a crown or talks in a pulpit. Facts, reasons, are better than names. But it seems to me that nothing can be plainer than that the church is losing ground – that the people are discarding the creeds and that superstition has passed the zenith of its power.

Q. Dr. Banks says that Christ did not mention the Western Hemisphere because God does nothing for men that they can do for themselves. What have you to say?

A. Christ said nothing about the Western Hemisphere because he did not know that it existed. He did not know the

250

shape of the earth. He was not a scientist – never even hinted at any science – never told anybody to investigate – to think. His idea was that this life should be spent in preparing for the next. For all the evils of this life, and the next faith was his remedy.

I see from the report in the paper that Dr. Banks, after making the remarks about me, preached a sermon on "Herod the Villain in the Drama of Christ." Who made Herod? Dr. Banks will answer that God made him. Did God know what Herod would do? Yes. Did he know that he would cause the children to be slaughtered in his vain efforts to kill the infant Christ? Yes. Dr. Banks will say that God is not responsible for Herod because he gave Herod freedom. Did God know how Herod would use his freedom? Did he know that he would become the villain in the drama of Christ? Yes. Who, then, is really responsible for the acts of Herod?

If I could change a stone into a human being, and if I could give this being freedom of will, and if I knew that if I made him he would murder a man, and if with that knowledge I made him, and he did commit a murder, who would be the real murderer?

Will Dr. Banks in his 52 sermons of next year show that his God is not responsible for the crimes of Herod?

No doubt Dr. Banks is a good man, and no doubt he thinks that liberty of thought leads to hell, and honestly believes that all doubt comes from the devil. I do not blame him. He thinks as he must. He is a product of conditions.

He ought to be my friend because I am doing the best I can to civilize his congregation. — *The Plain Dealer,* Cleveland, Ohio, 1898.

ZOLA AND PHILOSOPHY

Q. What about Zola's trial and conviction?

A. It was one of the most infamous trials in the history of the world. Zola is a great man, a genius, the best man in France. His trial was a travesty on justice. The judge acted like a bandit. The proceedings were a disgrace to human nature. The jurors must have been ignorant beasts. The French have disgraced themselves. Long live Zola.

Q. Having expressed yourself less on the subject of theosophy than on other religious beliefs, and as theosophy denies the existence of a God as worshipped by Christianity, what is your idea of the creed?

A. Insanity. I think it is a mild form of delusion and illusion; vague, misty, obscure, half dream, mixed with other mistakes, and fragments of facts – a little philosophy, absurdity – a few impossibilities – some improbabilities – some accounts of events that never happened – some prophecies that will not come to pass – a structure without foundation. But the theosophists are good people; kind and honest. Theosophy is based on the supernatural and is just as absurd as the orthodox creeds. — *The Courier Journal,* Louisville, Kentucky, February 1898.

HOW TO BECOME AN ORATOR

Q. What advice would you give to a young man who was ambitious to become a successful public speaker or orator?

A. In the first place, I would advise him to have something to say – something worth saying – something that people would be glad to hear. This is the important thing. Back of the art of speaking must be the power to think. Without thoughts words are empty purses. Most people imagine that almost any words uttered in a loud voice and accompanied by appropriate gestures constitute an oration. I would advise the young man to study his subject, to find what others had thought, to look at it from all sides. Then I would tell him to write out his thoughts or to arrange them in his mind so that he would know exactly what he was going to say. Waste no time on the how until you are satisfied with the what. After you know what you are to say, then you can think of how it should be said. Then you can think about tone, emphasis, and gesture; but if you really understand what you say, emphasis, tone, and gesture will take care of themselves. All these should come from the inside. They should be in perfect harmony with the feelings. Voice and gesture should be governed by the emotions. They should unconsciously be in perfect agreement with the sentiments. The orator should be true to his subject, should avoid any reference to himself.

The great column of his argument should be unbroken. He can adorn it with vines and flowers, but they should not be in such profusion as to hide the column. He should give variety of episode by illustrations, but they should be used only for the purpose of adding strength to the argument. The man who wishes to become an orator should study language. He should know the deeper meaning of words. He should understand the vigor and velocity of verbs and the color of adjectives. He should know how to sketch a scene, to paint a picture, to give life and action. He should be a poet and a dramatist, a painter and an actor. He should cultivate his imagination. He should become familiar with the great poetry and fiction, with splendid and heroic deeds. He should be a student of Shakespeare. He should read and devour the great plays.

From Shakespeare he could learn the art of expression, of compression, and all the secrets of the head and heart.

The great orator is full of variety – of surprise. Like a juggler, he keeps the colored balls in the air. He expresses himself in pictures. His speech is a panorama. By continued change he holds the attention. The interest does not flag. He does not allow himself to be anticipated. He is always in advance. He does not repeat himself. A picture is shown but once. So, an orator should avoid the commonplace. There should be no stuffing, no filling. He should put no cotton with his silk, no common metals with his gold. He should remember that "gilded dust is not as good as dusted gold." The great orator is honest, sincere. He does not pretend. His brain and heart go together. Every drop of his blood is convinced. Nothing is forced. He knows exactly what he wishes to do – knows when he has finished it, and stops.

Only a great orator knows when and how to close. Most speakers go on after they are through. They are satisfied only with a "lame and impotent conclusion." Most speakers lack variety. They travel a straight and dusty road. The great orator is full of episode. He convinces and charms by indirection. He leaves the road, visits the fields, wanders in the woods, listens to the murmurs of springs, the songs of birds. He gathers flowers, scales the crags, and comes back to the highway refreshed, invigorated. He does not move in a straight line. He wanders and winds like a stream.

Of course, no one can tell a man what to do to become an orator. The great orator has that wonderful thing called presence. He has that strange something known as magnetism. He must have a flexible, musical voice, capable of expressing the pathetic, the humorous, the heroic. His body must move in unison with his thought. He must be a reasoner, a logician. He must have a keen sense of humor – of the laughable. He must have wit, sharp and quick. He must have sympathy. His smiles should be the neighbors of his tears. He must have imagination. He should give eagles to the air, and painted moths should flutter in the sunlight.

While I cannot tell a man what to do to become an orator, I can tell him a few things not to do. There should be no introduction to an oration. The orator should commence with his subject. There should be no prelude, no flourish, no apology, no explanation. He should say nothing about himself. Like a sculptor, he stands by his block of stone. Every stroke is for a purpose. As he works, the form begins to appear. When the statue is finished the workman stops. Nothing is more difficult than a perfect close. Few poems, few pieces of music, few novels end well. A good story, a great speech, a perfect poem should end just at the proper point. The bud, the blossom, the fruit. No delay. A great speech is a crystallization in its logic, an efflorescence in its poetry.

I have not heard many speeches. Most of the great speakers in our country were before my time. I heard Beecher, and he was an orator. He had imagination, humor, and intensity. His brain was as fertile as the valleys of the tropics. He was too broad, too philosophic, too poetic for the pulpit. Now and then he broke the fetters of his creed, escaped from his orthodox prison, and became sublime.

Theodore Parker was an orator. He preached great sermons. His sermons on "Old Age" and "Webster," and his address on "Liberty" were filled with great thoughts, marvelously expressed. When he dealt with human events, with realities, with things he knew, he was superb. When he spoke of freedom, of duty, of living to the ideal, of mental integrity, he seemed inspired.

Webster I never heard. He had great qualities; force, dignity, clearness, grandeur; but, after all, he worshipped the past. He kept his back to the sunrise. There was no dawn in his brain. He was not creative. He had no spirit of prophecy. He lighted no torch. He was not true to his ideal. He talked sometimes as though his head was among the stars, but he stood in the gutter. In the name of religion he tried to break the will of Stephen Girard – to destroy the greatest charity in all the world; and in the name of the same religion he defended the Fugitive Slave Law. His purpose was the same in both cases. He wanted office. Yet he uttered a few great paragraphs, rich with thought, perfectly expressed.

Clay I never heard, but he must have had a commanding presence, chivalric bearing, an heroic voice. He cared little for the past. He was a natural leader, a wonderful talker – forcible, persuasive, convincing. He was not a poet, not a master of metaphor, but he was practical. He kept in view the end to be accomplished. He was the opposite of Webster. Clay was the morning, Webster the evening. Clay had large views, a wide horizon. He was ample, vigorous, and a little tyrannical.

Benton was thoroughly commonplace. He never uttered an inspired word. He was an intense egotist. No subject was great enough to make him forget himself. Calhoun was a political

Calvinist – narrow, logical, dogmatic. He was not an orator. He delivered essays, not orations. I think it was in 1851 that Kossuth visited this country. He was an orator. There was no man, at that time, under our flag, who could speak English as well as he. In the first speech I read of Kossuth's was this line: "Russia is the rock against which the sigh for freedom breaks." In this you see the poet, the painter, the orator.

S. S. Prentiss was an orator, but, with the recklessness of a gamester, he threw his life away. He said profound and beautiful things, but he lacked application. He was uneven, disproportioned – saying ordinary things on great occasions, and now and then, without the slightest provocation, uttering the sublimest and most beautiful thoughts.

In my judgment, Corwin was the greatest orator of them all. He had more arrows in his quiver. He had genius. He was full of humor, pathos, wit, and logic. He was an actor. His body talked. His meaning was in his eyes and lips. Gov. O. P. Morton, of Indiana, had the greatest power of statement of any man I ever heard. All the argument was in his statement. The facts were perfectly grouped. The conclusion was a necessity.

The best political speech I ever heard was made by Gov. Richard J. Oglesby of Illinois. It had every element of greatness – reason, humor, wit, pathos, imagination, and perfect naturalness. That was in the grand years, long ago. Lincoln had reason, wonderful humor, and wit, but his presence was not good. His voice was poor, his gestures awkward – but his thoughts were profound. His speech at Gettysburg is one of the masterpieces of the world. The word "here" is used four or five times too often. Leave the "heres" out, and the speech is perfect.

Of course, I have heard a great many talkers, but orators are few and far between. They are produced by victorious nations – born in the midst of great events, of marvelous achievements. They utter the thoughts, the aspirations of their age. They clothe the children of the people in the gorgeous robes of genius. They interpret the dreams. With the poets, they prophesy. They will the future with heroic forms, with lofty deeds. They keep their faces toward the dawn – toward the ever-coming day. — *New York Sun,* April 1898.

PSYCHICAL RESEARCH AND THE BIBLE

As an incident in the life of one favored with the privilege, a visit to the home of Col. Robert G. Ingersoll is certain to be recalled as a most pleasant and profitable experience. Although not a sympathizer with the great Agnostic's religious views, yet I have long admired his ability, his humor, his intellectual honesty and courage. And it was with gratification that I accepted the good offices of a common friend who recently offered to introduce me to the Ingersoll domestic circle in Gramercy Park. Here I found the genial Colonel, surrounded by his children, his grandchildren, and his amiable wife, whose smiling greeting dispelled formality and breathed "welcome" in every syllable. The family relationship seemed absolutely ideal – the very walls emitting an atmosphere of art and music, of contentment and companionship, of mutual trust, happiness, and generosity.

But my chief desire was to elicit Colonel Ingersoll's personal views on questions related to the New Thought and its attitude on matters on which he is known to have decided opinions. My request for a private chat was cordially granted. During the conversation that ensued – (the substance of which is presented to the readers of Mind *in the following paragraphs, with the Colonel's consent) – I was impressed most deeply, not by the force of his arguments, but by the sincerity of his convictions. Among some of his more violent opponents, who presumably lack other opportunities of becoming known, it is the fashion to accuse Ingersoll of having really no belief in his own opinions. But, if he convinced me of little else, he certainly, without effort, satisfied my mind that this accusation is a slander. Utterly mistaken in his views he may be; but if so, his errors are more honest than many of those he points out in the Kng James Version of the Bible. If his pulpit enemies could talk with this man by his own fireside, they would pay less attention to Ingersoll himself and more to what he says. They would consider his meaning, rather than his motive.*

As the Colonel is the most conspicuous denunciator of intolerance and bigotry in America, he has been inevitably the

257

greatest victim of these obstacles to mental freedom. "To answer Ingersoll" is the pet ambition of many a young clergy-man – the older ones have either acquired prudence or are broad enough to concede the utility of even Agnostics in the economy of evolution. It was with this very subject that we began our talk – the uncharitableness of men, otherwise good, in their treatment of those whose religious views differ from their own.

Q. What is your conception of true intellectual hospitality? As truth can brook no compromises, has it not the same limitations that surround social and domestic hospitality?

A. In the republic of mind we are all equals. Each one is sceptered and crowned. Each one is the monarch of his own realm. By "intellectual hospitality" I mean the right of everyone to think and to express his thought. It makes no difference whether his thought is right or wrong. If you are intellectually hospitable you will admit the right of every human being to see for himself; to hear with his own ears, see with his own eyes, and think with his own brain. You will not try to change his thought by force, by persecution, or by slander. You will not threaten him with punishment – here or hereafter. You will give him your thought, your reasons, your facts; and there you will stop. This is intellectual hospitality. You do not give up what you believe to be the truth; you do not compromise. You simply give him the liberty you claim for yourself. The truth is not affected by your opinion or by his. Both may be wrong. For many years the church has claimed to have the "truth," and has also insisted that it is the duty of every man to believe it, whether it is reasonable to him or not. This is bigotry in its basest form. Every man should be guided by his reason; should be true to himself; should preserve the veracity of his soul. Each human being should judge for himself. The man that believes that all men have this right is intellectually hospitable.

Q. In the sharp distinction between theology and religion that is now recognized by many theologians, and in the liberalizing of the church that has marked the last two decades, are not most of your contentions already granted? Is not the "lake of fire and brimstone" an obsolete issue?

A. There has been in the last few years a great advance. The orthodox creeds have been growing vulgar and cruel. Civilized people are shocked at the dogma of eternal pain, and the belief in

258

hell has mostly faded away. The churches have not changed their creeds. They still pretend to believe as they always have – but they have changed their tone. God is now a father – a friend. He is no longer the monster, the savage described in the Bible. He has become somewhat civilized. He no longer claims the right to damn us because he made us. But in spite of all the errors and contradictions, in spite of the cruelties and absurdities found in the Scriptures, the churches still insist that the Bible is *inspired*. The educated ministers admit that the Pentateuch was not written by Moses; that the Psalms were not written by David; that Isaiah was the work of at least three; that Daniel was not written until after the prophecies mentioned in that book had been fulfilled; that Ecclesiastes was not written until the 2nd century after Christ; that Solomon's Song was not written by Solomon; that the Book of Esther is of no importance; and that no one knows or pretends to know who were the authors of Kings, Samuel, Chronicles, or Job. And yet these same gentlemen still cling to the dogma of inspiration! It is no longer claimed that the Bible is true – but *inspired*.

Q. Yet the sacred volume, no matter who wrote it, is a mine of wealth to the student and the philosopher, is it not? Would you have us discard it altogether?

A. Inspiration must be abandoned, and the Bible must take its place among the books of the world. It contains some good passages, a little poetry, some good sense, and some kindness; but its philosophy is frightful. In fact, if the book had never existed I think it would have been far better for mankind. It is not enough to give up the Bible; that is only the beginning. The *supernatural* must be given up. It must be admitted that nature has no master; that there never has been any interference from without; that man has received no help from heaven; and that all the prayers that have ever been uttered have died unanswered in the heedless air. The religion of the supernatural has been a curse. We want the religion of usefulness.

Q. But have you no use whatever for prayer – even in the sense of aspiration – or for faith, in the sense of confidence in the ultimate triumph of the right?

A. There is a difference between wishing, hoping, believing, and – knowing. We can wish without evidence or probability, and we can wish for the impossible – for what we believe can never be. We cannot hope unless there is in the mind a possibility that the thing hoped for can happen. We can believe only in accordance with evidence, and we know only that which has been demonstrated. I have no use for prayer; but I do a good deal of wishing and hoping. I hope that some time the right will triumph – that truth will gain the victory; but I have no faith in gaining the assistance of any God, or of any supernatural power. I never pray.

Q. However fully materialism as a philosophy may accord with the merely human reason, is it not wholly antagonistic to the instinctive faculties of the mind?

A. Human reason is the final arbiter. Any system that does not commend itself to the reason must fall. I do not know exactly what you mean by materialism. I do not know what matter is. I am satisfied, however, that without matter there can be no force, no life, no thought, no reason. It seems to me that mind is a form of force, and force cannot exist apart from matter. If it is said that God created the universe, then there must have been a time when he commenced to create. If at that time there was nothing in existence but himself, how could he have exerted any force? Force cannot be exerted except in opposition to force. If God was the only existence, force could not have been exerted.

Q. But don't you think, Colonel, that the materialistic philosophy, even in the light of your own interpretation, is essentially pessimistic?

A. I do not consider it so. I believe that the pessimists and the optimists are both right. This is the worst possible world, and this is the best possible world – because it is as it must be. The present is the child, and the necessary child, of all the past.

Q. What have you to say concerning the operations of the society for psychical research? Do not its facts and conclusions prove, if not immortality, at least the continuity of life beyond the grave? Are the millions of spiritualists deluded?

A. Of course, I have heard and read a great deal about the doings of the society; so, I have some knowledge as to what is claimed by spiritualists, by theosophists, and by all other believers in what are called "spiritual manifestations." Thousands of wonderful things have been established by what is called "evidence" – the testimony of good men and women. I have seen things done that I could not explain, both by mediums and magicians. I also know that it is easy to deceive the senses and that the old saying "that seeing is believing" is subjected to many exceptions. I am perfectly satisfied that there is, and can be, no force without matter; that everything that is – all phenomena – all actions and thoughts, all exhibitions of force, have a material basis – that nothing exists – ever did, or ever will exist, apart from matter. So I am satisfied that no matter ever existed, or ever will, apart from force.

We think with the same force with which we walk. For every action and for every thought, we draw on the store of force that we have gained from air and food. We create no force; we borrow it all. As force cannot exist apart from matter, it must be used *with* matter. It travels only on material roads. It is impossible to convey a thought to another without the assistance of matter. No one can conceive of the use of one of our senses without substance. No one can conceive of a thought in the absence of the senses. With these conclusions in my mind – in my brain – I have not the slightest confidence in "spiritual manifestations," and do not believe that any message has ever been received from the dead. The testimony that I have heard – that I have read – coming even from men of science – has not the slightest weight with me. I do not pretend to see beyond the grave. I do not say that man is, or is not, immortal. All I say is that there is no evidence that we live again, and no demonstration that we do not. It is better ignorantly to hope than dishonestly to affirm.

Q. And what do you think of the modern development of metaphysics – as expressed outside of the emotional and semi-ecclesiastical schools? I refer especially to the power of mind in the curing of disease – as demonstrated by scores of drugless healers.

A. I have no doubt that the condition of the mind has some effect on the health. The blood, the heart, the lungs answer – respond to – emotion. There is no mind without body, and the body is affected by thought – by passion, by cheerfulness, by depression. Still, I have not the slightest confidence in what is called "mind cure." I do not believe that thought, or any set of ideas, can cure a cancer, or prevent the hair from falling out, or remove a tumor, or even freckles. At the same time I admit that cheerfulness is good and depression bad. But I have no confidence in what you call "drugless healers." If the stomach is sour, soda is better than thinking. If one is in great pain, opium will beat meditation. I am a believer in what you call "drugs," and when I am sick I send for a physician. I have no confidence in the supernatural. Magic is not medicine.

Q. One great object of this movement is to make religion scientific – an aid to intellectual as well as spiritual progress. Is it not thus to be encouraged, and destined to succeed – even though it prove the reality and supremacy of the spirit and the secondary importance of the flesh?

A. When religion becomes scientific, it ceases to be religion and becomes science. Religion is not intellectual – it is emotional. It does not appeal to the reason. The founder of a religion has always said: "Let him that hath ears to hear, hear!" No founder has said: "Let him that hath brains to think, think!" Besides, we need not trouble ourselves about "spirit" and "flesh." We know that we know of no spirit – without flesh. We have no evidence that spirit ever did or ever will exist apart from flesh. Such existence is absolutely inconceivable. If we are going to construct what you call a "religion," it must be founded on observed and known facts. Theories, to be of value, must be in accord with all the facts that are known; otherwise they are worthless. We need not try to get back of facts or behind the truth. The *why* will forever elude us. You cannot move your hand quickly enough to grasp your image back of the mirror. — *Mind,* New York, March 1899.